The Cuban Missile Crisis
and the
Threat of Nuclear War

The Cuban Missile Crisis and the
Threat of Nuclear War

Lessons from History

LEN SCOTT

continuum

Continuum UK
The Tower Building
11 York Road
London SE1 7NX

Continuum US
80 Maiden Lane
Suite 704
New York, NY 10038

www.continuumbooks.com

First published 2007

British Library Cataloguing-in-Publication Data
A catalogue record for this book is available from the British Library.

ISBN: 1–8470–6026–9

Typeset by Kenneth Burnley, Wirral, Cheshire
Printed and bound in Great Britain by Cromwell Press, Trowbridge, Wilts

This book is dedicated to Peter Hennessy:
an inspiration to British historians,
an unwavering friend,
and a dedicated supporter of
West Ham United Football Club.

Contents

Acknowledgements

It is a pleasure as well as a duty to record my thanks to various people who have helped in the completion of this book. My friends and colleagues in the Department of International Politics and the Centre for Intelligence and International Security Studies at the University of Wales, Aberystwyth, have provided the congenial, supportive and stimulating environment in which my work has developed. To them, and to the many students whom I have taught on issues relevant to this study, I give my thanks. More specifically, I am especially grateful to those who read and commented on various drafts, in particular Jonathan Colman, Gerry Hughes, Simon Rushton, and Stephen Twigge. Writing any book is a challenge to both stamina and morale, and I thank several people who provided discrete but significant support, notably Richard Aldrich and David Welch. I should also record my thanks to Andrew Humphrys for his patience and help. Jonathan Colman provided invaluable research assistance at the outset of the project, when my main preoccupation was in my role as Dean of Social Sciences. His post was facilitated by the Department of International Politics and the University of Wales, Aberystwyth, who also provided me with the sabbatical provision to pursue my endeavours. It was thanks to the Arts and Humanities Research Council Research Leave Scheme that I was then able to complete this book. To these various institutions and to the people who ran them, notably Ken Booth, Noel Lloyd, Colin McInnes and Derek Llwyd Morgan I express my appreciation. I would also like to thank the staff at the

National Archives at Kew and at the JFK Library at Boston. The journey from conception to realization has been an interesting one and I record my thanks to Robin Baird-Smith for his help in bringing the project to fruition. Finally, I want to extend a particular thanks to two friends whose support and encouragement were crucial to the enterprise at crucial moments: Nick Wheeler and Peter Hennessy.

I have remarked in previous introductions to books that it is a custom to thank those who help, but not to berate those who obstruct. And, again, in departing from this tradition, I wish to single out a group of people who have distracted, disrupted and disregarded my efforts to complete this monograph: my family – Frances, James and Lucy. Over the last couple of years I have been bombarded with demands to return home in the evenings and weekends, and fritter away quality research time on Christmas Day and other public holidays. Despite this, I have maintained a cheerful demeanour throughout, and at no point have been obsessive, reclusive or generally bad tempered for months on end. I am sure they would wish to thank me for this.

Len Scott
Aberystwyth
May 2007

Abbreviations

ASW	Anti-Submarine Warfare
BMEWS	Ballistic Missile Early Warning System
CIA	Central Intelligence Agency
CINCSAC	Commander in Chief, Strategic Air Command
CMEWS	Cuban Missile Early Warning System
DEFCON	Defense Condition
EXCOMM	Executive Committee of the National Security Council
GDR	German Democratic Republic
GLCM	Ground-Launched Cruise Missile
GRU	Chief Intelligence Directorate of the Soviet General Staff
ICBM	Intercontinental Ballistic Missile
IRBM	Intermediate-Range Ballistic Missile
JCS	Joint Chiefs of Staff
JIB	Joint Intelligence Bureau
KGB	Soviet Committee for State Security
MAD	Mutual Assured Destruction
MRBM	Medium-Range Ballistic Missile

NAC	North Atlantic Council
NATO	North Atlantic Treaty Organisation
NIE	National Intelligence Estimate
NORAD	North American Air Defence Command
NSC	National Security Council
OAS	Organization of American States
PAL	Permissive Action Links
POL	Petroleum, Oil, Lubricants
QRA	Quick Reaction Alert
RAF	Royal Air Force
SAC	Strategic Air Command
SACEUR	Supreme Allied Commander Europe
SAM	Surface to Air Missile
SIOP	Single Integrated Operational Plan
SIS	Secret Intelligence Service
SLBM	Submarine-Launched Ballistic Missile
SLCM	Submarine-Launched Cruise Missile
SSBN	Nuclear-powered Ballistic Missile Submarine
SSIP	Submarine Surfacing and Identification Procedures
USAF	United States Air Force

CHAPTER 1

Domain of the Scorpions

We may anticipate a state of affairs in which two Great Powers will each be in a position to put an end to the civilisation and life of the other. We may be likened to two scorpions in a bottle each capable of killing the other, but only at the risk of his own life.[1]

Robert Oppenheimer, 1953

The Cuban missile crisis is the term used in the West to describe the events of October 1962. For the Soviets it was the 'Caribbean crisis'. The Cubans refer to the 'October crisis'. Such differences are as semiotic as they are semantic, in that they denote differing perspectives on the nature and origins of the crisis. In Washington, the missile crisis lasted thirteen days. In Havana, where the threat of American attack persisted on a continuing basis after 1961, the time horizon was more like thirteen months.[2] How serious the crisis was, and what risk there was of nuclear war, are also matters of perspective and contention. For Ray Cline, the CIA Deputy Director for Intelligence, the risk of nuclear war was 'no more than one in a thousand'.[3] Paul Nitze, Deputy-Secretary for Defense, concluded that there was greater risk of armed conflict with the Soviet Union over Berlin in October 1961 than over Cuba in October 1962.[4] And, together with fellow 'hawks' in the Kennedy administration, he believed that overwhelming American nuclear superiority, together with conventional superiority in the Caribbean, obviated the risk of Soviet military action. Other American officials viewed the threat of nuclear war differently.

1

Defense Secretary Robert McNamara recalled that on 27 October, 'as I left the White House and walked through the garden to my car to return to the Pentagon on that beautiful fall evening, I feared I might never live to see another Saturday night.'[5] Around the world, not least in Moscow and Havana, senior officials and ordinary citizens experienced similar emotions as the crisis reached its climax.

The events of October 1962 are generally seen as the closest humankind has come to thermo-nuclear war. Robert Kennedy wrote afterwards that the world was brought 'to the abyss of nuclear destruction and the end of mankind'.[6] A recent history of the crisis opens with the statement, 'The Cuban Missile Crisis was the most dangerous event in human history.'[7] The crisis is also commonly seen as a turning point in the Cold War, a catharsis from which emerged Soviet–American détente. One of the foremost American students of the crisis, Raymond Garthoff, describes it as the 'turning point in the Cold War'.[8] A vast amount of historical research into the crisis has been undertaken over many decades. Kennedy's National Security Assistant, McGeorge Bundy, observed in 1988 that 'forests have been felled to print the reflections and conclusions of participants, observers and scholars'.[9] Since then, deforestation has continued apace. Yet debate continues about the risk of nuclear war and what lessons might be learned from the events of 1962 about the role of nuclear weapons in international politics.

Scope and Focus of this Study

The aim of this study is to examine the role of nuclear weapons in the light of this research and to evaluate the risk of inadvertent nuclear war. Over the last few decades, research on the crisis has revealed aspects at the operational level that suggest that the risk of nuclear war was greater than assumed, either by decision-makers or by students of the crisis. Yet much greater insight has also been generated into the attitudes and perceptions of the principal decision-makers, Kennedy and Khrushchev. Evidence has emerged of how the two leaders behaved during the crisis and how they sought to pursue their political objectives without escalation to war. These two general findings point in different directions: one suggests that the risk of nuclear war was greater than thought; the other suggests that decision-makers were increasingly determined to avoid escalation.

These diverging perspectives reflect differing analytical approaches to the study of decision-making and have particular significance for studying the role of nuclear weapons. The decision to use nuclear weapons represents the most awesome responsibility that any human being could have. Cold War mutual deterrence meant that the use of nuclear weapons might not just involve the infliction of genocidal-level carnage, it could also mean national (as well as personal) suicide for those firing first. In theory, the study of nuclear decision-making should encompass all aspects that inform how individual political leaders discharge such responsibility, e.g. ideology, morality, spirituality and psychology. Yet the analytical frameworks within which the prospective decisions of the individual leader are explored are a matter of fundamental disagreement. The assumptions of rationality upon which theories and policies of nuclear deterrence have developed have been challenged on various grounds, including ethical, psychological and organizational.

The concept of rationality has remained at the heart of Western thinking about nuclear deterrence. The American strategist, Herman Kahn, once said that he would give $1,000 to anyone who could provide a plausible scenario of a nuclear war between the United States and the Soviet Union. As Graham Allison explained, plausibility was defined in terms of rationality, and as Kahn was the arbiter of what was rational, he ensured he kept his money.[10] The idea that Soviet aggression would be deterred by the threat of nuclear weapons became the foundation of American and NATO strategy during the Cold War. At root was the belief that the risks and costs were so great that political leaders would draw back from the nuclear devastation of their countries. McGeorge Bundy believed that it was crucial to 'recognise how the prospect of a thermo-nuclear war really looks to a statesman . . . It is not what one can do to the enemy that is decisive when a political leader considers this risk. It is what such a war might do to his own country, his own power, and his place in history.'[11]

'Places in history' echoes the celebrated 1964 black comedy, *Dr Strangelove*, when the Chairman of the Joint Chiefs of Staff, General

Buck Turgidson, advocates a pre-emptive nuclear attack on the Soviet Union.[12] President Merkin Muffley replies: 'I will not go down in history as the biggest mass murderer since Adolf Hitler', to which General Turgidson retorts, 'Hell, Mr President, I think we should be worrying about more than your image in the history books.' Moral aspects of nuclear decision-making are an often hidden dimension, though of potentially crucial importance. Inherent in rationalist accounts is the assumption that decision-makers will kill scores, if not hundreds, of millions of people unless they are deterred from doing so by threats of retaliation in kind (or with interest). The suggestion that they might refrain from genocidal carnage because they recognize that they would be committing crimes against humanity rarely enters the narratives or the equations. Of course, the key assumption during the Cold War for many American observers was that Soviet leaders recognized only power, and were bereft of moral or humanitarian perspectives.

The one occasion when nuclear weapons were used provides insights into moral aspects of what, at first glance, was the exemplar of rational military action: Truman's decision to drop the bomb on Japan. This decision reflected his desire to bring the war to an end without further allied casualties. Using the bomb also had implications for future relations with the Soviets. Yet moral qualms about deliberately targeting enemy cities surfaced at various points. Secretary of War Stimson's refusal to allow Kyoto to be atom-bombed reflected his abhorrence at the idea of attacking centres of population, as well as his personal familiarity with the ancient capital and its significance for the Shinto and Buddhist religions.[13] Truman confided in his diary that he had told Stimson to use the bomb,

> so that military objectives and soldiers and saliors [sic] are the target and not women and children. Even if the Japs are savages, ruthless, merciless and fanatic, we as the leader of the world for the common welfare cannot drop this terrible bomb on the old Capitol [sic] or the new. He & I are in accord. The target will be a purely military one . . .[14]

4

There is also evidence that moral considerations informed the dropping of the third atomic bomb. Having delegated authority to the American military to begin the atomic bombing of Japan, Truman rescinded his instructions after Nagasaki, and made it clear that no further action would occur except on his explicit order. According to Henry Wallace, this was because 'the thought of wiping out another 100,000 people was too horrible. He didn't like the idea of killing . . . "all those kids".'[15] The Japanese surrendered before the third bomb was ready so, in the end, a decision was not required.

If some of Truman's initial remarks about bombing only military targets suggested lack of understanding about atomic weapons in 1945, then no-one in 1962 lacked understanding of what thermo-nuclear weapons would accomplish. Yet distinguishing between the moral/ humanitarian impulses and the strategic/political calculations is far from easy, and the prospect of responsibility for the deaths of millions of one's own citizens weighed heavily upon decision-makers. Moral sentiments may be couched in political rather than moral terms. Dean Rusk, for example, told colleagues on the executive committee of the national security council (ExComm), that any nation using nuclear weapons would bear the mark of Cain for generations. He later reflected that 'moral and ethical considerations play a very important part, even though people don't wear these things on their shirtsleeves or put things in official memoranda . . . People act in reference to their basic moral commitments, and they are likely to come to the fore when situations become critical.'[16] A challenge for the historian is to distinguish between moral concerns in political guise and genuine political concerns. A further problem is that moral considerations are only part of the equation. This is illustrated in the arguments within ExComm over whether to launch a surprise attack on the Soviet missiles in Cuba, in which the historical analogy of Pearl Harbor played an important part. Douglas Dillon recalled that Robert Kennedy's use of the Pearl Harbor analogy changed his mind about the surprise air strike.[17] Separating moral/humanitarian from strategic/rational is far from easy. The Pearl Harbor analogy may have persuaded Dillon. The prospect of Soviet retaliation against West Berlin most likely played the greater part in President Kennedy's thinking.

Ornithological Paradigms

The Cuban missile crisis provided us with the terms 'hawks' and 'doves', denoting those American officials who wanted to use military force and those who did not (or at least not yet). The hawks were exponents of rational thinking about the threat and use of force, who believed that American nuclear superiority effectively precluded military reaction by the Soviet Union. The doves took a different view of the risk of war and had a greater reluctance to use force. In his seminal text on decision-making, Graham Allison drew a distinction between the 'rational actor model' and other paradigms of decision-making ('organisational process' and 'bureaucratic politics').[18] The rational actor model drew upon economics and game theory, and underpinned the field of strategic studies. Decisions on the use (or non-use) of nuclear weapons were taken by unitary rational actors whose behaviour was driven by assessments of costs and risks. In the 1980s, psychological critiques of rational deterrence theory questioned assumptions about how decision-makers behave under severe stress, and how they might behave in situations where the use of nuclear weapons was actively considered.[19] Greater understanding of organizational and bureaucratic processes also facilitated important critiques of rational deterrence. A body of literature emerged in the United States that emphasized the risk of inadvertent nuclear war.[20] If thinking about deterrence was driven by the historical analogies of Munich and Pearl Harbor, the threat of inadvertent conflict was informed by the coming of the Great War in 1914. A new ornithological perspective gained ground. 'Owls' believed that 'a major war would not arise from careful calculations but from organisational routines, malfunctions of machines or of minds, misperceptions, misunderstandings, and mistakes.'[21]

Nuclear Contexts

Since 1945 war has remained endemic in world politics, though the purposes for which it is fought and the manner in which it is waged have varied greatly. War has not been waged with nuclear weapons, and some conceive of a taboo against their use.[22] In Europe – the crucible of the Cold War – there has been peace and prosperity. This has led many to claim that deterrence kept 'the long peace', in John Lewis Gaddis's phrase.[23] Others contend that nuclear weapons have been essentially irrelevant in world politics.[24] And some have gone further, claiming a direct relationship between nuclear weapons, 'the deep structure of the Cold War', and exploitation and suffering in the Third World, where millions have died in conventional and civil wars.[25]

Whether 'nuclear taboos' affected decision-makers, they did not extend to the production and deployment of nuclear weapons, nor to training and planning for their use. By 1961, the United States had developed an integrated nuclear war plan, entitled the 'Single Integrated Operational Plan' (SIOP). Although details of targeting remain sparse, an estimate of casualties in the execution of the first SIOP (SIOP-62) was that, in a pre-emptive attack using 2,258 missiles and bombers with 3,423 nuclear weapons, 285 million Soviet and Chinese people would be killed and a further 40 million seriously injured.[26] The estimates do not appear to include casualties in Warsaw Pact countries or victims from radioactive fallout outside the targeted states. Nor do they include longer-term fatalities from starvation and disease in societies that had been returned to a pre-industrial (and in many areas pre-agricultural) state of existence. Moreover, whether or not American planners believed it was possible to win a nuclear war in the early 1960s, it now seems clear that such thinking was a dangerous chimera. In the 1980s, it was first hypothesized that nuclear attacks on only several hundred cities would create the climatic catastrophe of a 'nuclear winter' that would extinguish human life in the northern hemisphere.[27] If the climatic hypothesis is correct, then unbeknownst to its architects, implementation of SIOP-62 would have entailed national suicide for the United States, regardless of whether the Soviets exploded a single nuclear weapon on American territory.

The Kennedy administration reviewed and revised American war plans, and by October 1962, SIOP-63 contained additional options for sub-Armageddon warfare. The emphasis in declaratory strategy was on control and discrimination. While all-out escalation remained possible, there was also the prospect of restraint and termination. The humanitarian consequences of limited nuclear exchanges would have been on a horrendous scale, and the political, social, ecological and economic consequences might have been devastating. Yet the end of the world would not necessarily have been nigh.

Oppenheimer's Scorpions

In 1953, Robert Oppenheimer likened the Americans and Soviets to 'two scorpions in a bottle each capable of killing the other, but only at the risk of his own life'.[28]

The suggestion that the survival of humanity can be understood in terms of malevolent arachnids may appear absurd reductionism. Yet Oppenheimer's simile conveys the logic of what Winston Churchill told the House of Commons in 1955 when he suggested that by 'a process of sublime irony . . . safety will be the sturdy child of terror, and survival the twin brother of annihilation'.[29] Churchill's metaphor alluded to thermo-nuclear weapons (whereas Oppenheimer was discussing atomic bombs). Later in the 1960s, the concept of assured destruction emerged in the West, which Robert McNamara defined as 'the capacity to absorb the total weight of an enemy's nuclear strike and retain the capability to launch an attack in a response that would inflict unacceptable damage on the aggressor'.[30] Mutual Assured Destruction (MAD) was where each adversary had sufficient invulnerable retaliatory forces to provide this capacity. Whether MAD existed during the Berlin and Cuba crises depends in part on what is meant by 'unacceptable damage'. Whether mutual deterrence existed is another matter.

It is now estimated that there were over 30,000 nuclear weapons in 1962, of which the United States possessed 27,387 and the Soviet Union had 3,322.[31] The United Kingdom had over 200.[32] According to McNamara, the United States possessed some 5,000 deliverable nuclear warheads compared with a figure of 300 for the Soviets: a 17:1 superiority.[33] Using a different methodology, Raymond Garthoff calculated that the Americans possessed some 3,000 warheads that could be used in a first strike, compared with a figure of 250 for the Soviets. The USSR had only 20–30 operational intercontinental ballistic missiles (ICBMs) in October 1962,[34] together with some 180 long-range nuclear bombers,[35] and a limited submarine-based capability.[36] By comparison, the United States had on alert 182 ICBMs, 112 submarine-launched ballistic missiles (SLBMs) and some 1,500 strategic bombers.[37] To these should be added 105 European-based intermediate-range ballistic missiles (IRBMs) and hundreds of tactical strike aircraft in the European and Pacific theatres, and on aircraft carriers. In 1962, the two scorpions were very different in size and shape.

The question of whether nuclear superiority mattered in the crisis has generated robust argument among surviving ExComm members (hereafter termed 'ExCommites') concerning the nature and composition of nuclear deterrence. Beyond the arithmetic of the nuclear balance in 1962 were the central strategic equations. Richard Ned Lebow and Janice Gross Stein suggest that at this time the United States had 'an expanding capability to attack the Soviet Union with nuclear weapons without the prospect of direct retaliation'.[38] Desmond Ball states: 'A counterforce strike by the United States in the early 1960s could perhaps have fully disarmed the Soviet Union.'[39] Richard Betts argues, however, that Soviet retaliatory capabilities were sufficient to deter the United States.[40] In the 1980s, McNamara, Bundy and other ExCommites argued strongly that numerical superiority was meaningless.[41] McNamara and Bundy, in particular, took the view that Kennedy would not have launched a nuclear attack on the USSR in the knowledge that even one American city would be destroyed in retaliation. Other veterans of the Kennedy administration, notably Paul Nitze, argued that superiority was vital in 1962 and vital subsequently.[42]

European Perspectives

Whether or not an American first strike on the USSR would have prevented Soviet attacks on the United States, it would not have removed the nuclear threat to Western Europe, upon which the

Soviets (according to Western estimates) had targeted some 700 medium-range ballistic missiles (MRBMs) and IRBMs[43] and some 1,350 medium-range bombers.[44] Richard Betts suggests that before recognition of mutual deterrence, Moscow was 'relying primarily on its capability to destroy Western Europe'.[45] The European dimension provides an important context to the nuclear history of the missile crisis. It underlines the fact that throughout the Cold War, procurement, production and deployment of nuclear weapons was often only tangentially related to Oppenheimer's scorpions or concepts of mutual destruction. In part this was because in the West, no one concept of deterrence determined policy and strategy. Distinguishing between theories of nuclear deterrence and of nuclear war-fighting became a matter of almost theological disputation. During the 1950s and the 1960s, both NATO and the Soviets developed a panoply of tactical nuclear weapons for use in Europe. The Americans deployed nuclear artillery shells, atomic demolition munitions, cruise missiles, ballistic missiles, free-fall bombs, air-to-air missiles and even nuclear bazookas.[46] Even as the Kennedy administration strove to persuade European allies to improve conventional forces and move away from nuclear first use against Soviet aggression, the stockpile of nuclear weapons in NATO Europe was growing, and by the mid-sixties stood at 7,000 weapons.[47]

Many Europeans were also conscious of the symmetry of missiles in Cuba and missiles in Europe. Over a hundred IRBMs were targeted on the Soviet Union from NATO territory. If Soviet missiles in Cuba were 'offensive', why were American missiles in Turkey so different? NATO had Jupiter IRBMs in Turkey and Italy, Thor IRBMs and Polaris submarines in Britain, Matador ground-launched cruise missiles (GLCMs) in West Germany, as well as hundreds of nuclear-armed aircraft on airfields and aircraft carriers within range of the USSR. Likewise, Western Europeans had learned to live with what Harold Macmillan called the 'shadow of annihilation', and his initial observation when shown the CIA's photographic evidence of missiles in Cuba on 22 October, was that after their initial shock, Americans would make a similar adjustment.[48] 'Life goes on somehow,' he mused.

Intriguingly, the person in Washington, in October 1962, who seemed best to understand the analogy between Caribbean and European missiles was President Kennedy. And, as the crisis reached its climax, he was willing to withdraw the 45 Jupiters from Turkey and Italy to help reach agreement on Cuba. On the other hand, one of the more bizarre moments of the crisis came on 16 October, when he pondered Khrushchev's actions: 'Why does he put these in there though? . . . It's just as if we suddenly began to put a major number of MRBMs in Turkey. Now that'd be goddamn dangerous, I would think.'[49] McGeorge Bundy had to remind him that the United States had indeed deployed Jupiter IRBMs in Turkey. Fifteen Jupiters, capable of firing megaton-yield warheads at targets beyond Moscow, were deployed in Turkey under NATO auspices, along with 30 Jupiters in Italy. A further 60 Thor IRBMs were based in the United Kingdom under a bilateral agreement with the British. As Philip Nash comments, Kennedy's exchange with Bundy bears resemblance to the scene in *Dr Strangelove* when General Turgidson has to remind the President of his previous approval of an emergency plan to delegate nuclear command authority to 'lower echelon' military commanders (one of whom has just despatched his bombers to attack the Soviet Union).[50]

American IRBMs were conceived in the mid-1950s as a stopgap, pending the deployment of ICBMs. The impetus for their deployment in Europe came when the Soviets launched the Sputnik satellite using an ICBM launcher in October 1957. Eisenhower was keen to base the Thor IRBMs in the UK, both to provide a general psychological boost to NATO and more, specifically, to bolster the British–American relationship. However, the Americans produced the Jupiter IRBMs before NATO countries were invited to house them. By the time they were deployed, the IRBMs were already considered obsolete. Liquid-fuelled, fixed-site missiles were seen as vulnerable, threatening and an invitation to pre-emption. Members of NATO disagreed over the wisdom of basing them on their territory, and most refused. Eisenhower came to view the Jupiter IRBMs as a political liability rather than a strategic asset: 'It would have been better to have dumped them in the ocean,' he lamented, 'instead of trying to dump them on our allies.'[51] Yet he persevered with their deployment in Italy and Turkey.

So why did it matter that the Soviets had nuclear weapons in Cuba when their longer-range missiles and bombers could destroy American cities? As Robert McNamara observed in ExComm, the missiles made no difference to the nuclear balance and were 'primarily a domestic political problem'.[52] Why did America risk military confrontation with the Soviet Union? Why did Kennedy impose a naval blockade around Cuba, which he himself had described as 'an act of war' only a month earlier?[53]

These questions are examined in the next chapter. The general conclusion is that Kennedy's determination to secure the removal of the missiles reflected various considerations, but was primarily motivated by foreign policy rather than strictly military or domestic political concerns. From a European perspective, one factor was crucial: Kennedy's refusal to tolerate Soviet missiles in Cuba derived in part from America's commitment to Western Europe, and in particular, Kennedy's commitment to West Berlin. There remains debate over the significance of West Berlin in the missile crisis (as there remains debate over many key issues). Whether or not Berlin was in the mind of the Soviet Premier when he sent the missiles, it was certainly in the mind of the American President when he contemplated how to remove them. Only a year earlier, Kennedy had considered his military options in the event of a Soviet move on West Berlin. In essence, he would have to choose between military defeat and using nuclear weapons. For Kennedy, Soviet missiles in Cuba would strengthen Khrushchev's hand in any renewed attempt to force the Berlin issue.

Nuclear Arsenals and Nuclear Strategy

The Cuban missile crisis occurred at a time of significant military change in the Cold War. Both 'superpowers' had recently begun to deploy ICBMs and SLBMs. In the United States there had been deep concern that the Soviets were moving ahead in intercontinental missiles and Kennedy exploited the 'missile gap' in the presidential election. But with the advent of the Corona satellite programme, augmented by human and electronic intelligence, a more accurate estimate was achieved.[54] Washington realized, that far from lagging behind in the arms race, it was moving well ahead. Despite this, Kennedy and McNamara embarked upon a significant acceleration of the principal strategic weapons programmes (the Minuteman ICBM and Polaris SLBM).[55] This expansion was despite Kennedy's recognition that the missile gap was in America's favour and was clearly designed to perpetuate American superiority. Whatever McNamara and Bundy might say in retrospect about the meaningless of superiority in a crisis, there was bureaucratic and political consensus in Washington that the United States needed nuclear superiority. When, shortly after the missile crisis, Kennedy discussed procurement proposals from the armed services with his senior advisers, McNamara told him: 'My recommendation to you on our strategic forces is to take the requirement and double it and buy it.'[56] The Soviet Union was in a very different position. It first-generation ICBM, the R-7, had proved a failure, and only a handful were deployed. Its first nuclear-powered ballistic missile-carrying submarine (SSBN) experienced near-disastrous technical problems in 1961 and was withdrawn for refitting. Polmar and Gresham state that the Project 658 (NATO designation Hotel-class) submarines were not ready for regular patrols until 1963.[57] In both numbers and technological capabilities, the Soviets were well behind in the arms race.

Fierce debates took place in both countries about nuclear strategy and nuclear procurement. In the West, the late 1950s and early 1960s witnessed growing doubt about the credibility of the strategy of Massive Retaliation, which involved the threat of all-out strategic nuclear attack on the USSR in the event of 'Soviet aggression'. President Eisenhower explained in more prosaic terms to Congressional leaders that the strategy was 'to blow hell out of them in a hurry if they start anything.'[58] In fact, nuclear strategy under Eisenhower envisaged greater flexibility than his remarks, or those of his Secretary of State, John Foster Dulles, were seen to suggest.[59] Work on the first co-ordinated American nuclear war plan, SIOP-62, was developed under the Eisenhower administration.[60] Yet, when McNamara reviewed the plan in 1961 he was deeply concerned at the lack of options for the President: there was provision for only one huge attack. The principal choice was whether it would be pre-emptive or retaliatory.

The Kennedy administration's attempts at greater flexibility in US war-planning generated SIOP-63 (introduced in August 1962).[61] SIOP-63 reflected McNamara's goal of controlled and discriminate use of nuclear weapons. A primary objective was to provide incentives for the Soviets to withhold attacks on American cities even where the United States had attacked the USSR first. This would be done by avoiding Soviet cities in initial attacks, but threatening further destruction to deter attacks on American cities. McNamara articulated this strategy to NATO in May 1962 and then publicly in June 1962, when it became known as the 'no-cities' approach. The ensuing counterforce strategy would nevertheless kill many millions of Soviet people, and made a number of presumptions about Soviet behaviour in a nuclear war that critics challenged. For the Soviets it inevitably raised the prospect of a disarming first strike.

There was also anxiety within NATO at McNamara's agenda for raising the nuclear threshold. American 'extended deterrence' involved the willingness of the United States to strike the Soviet Union with nuclear weapons to deter attack on Western Europe. Once Moscow possessed the capacity to strike the United States, then, in the celebrated phrase, America was risking Chicago for Hamburg. When the Soviets launched Sputnik in 1957, they demonstrated that they were developing missiles of intercontinental range that could destroy American cities. The American commitment to threaten the Soviets involved willingness to use nuclear weapons *first*, to offset Soviet conventional superiority. McNamara was determined to move away from a situation in which the American President was called upon to initiate a nuclear war in the face of non-nuclear attack. Civilian analysts at the Pentagon quickly began reviewing the conventional balance and concluded that existing planning exaggerated Soviet strength and undersold Western capabilities.[62] Improving NATO's conventional defences, however, meant NATO Europe needed to increase defence spending. And in some quarters, there was concern that raising the nuclear threshold would increase the risk that conventional war could be fought without involving American strategic nuclear forces. Reconciling extended deterrence, the perceived NATO–Warsaw Pact military imbalance and the capacity of the Soviets to attack the United States, became an enduring preoccupation for NATO governments. In 1959–63 and 1983–7 it generated deployments of land-based nuclear missiles in Europe.

The 1961 Berlin crisis reinforced Kennedy and McNamara's desire to address the problem that the President could face a choice between 'humiliation and holocaust'. Yet in 1962, Kennedy appeared to embrace the old way of thinking. In his televised address on 22 October, the President warned that 'any nuclear missile launched from Cuba against any nation in the Western hemisphere' would meet with 'a full retaliatory response upon the Soviet Union'.[63] John Foster Dulles would have been proud, though what the word 'full' meant was not specified. Kennedy's words were designed to deter Khrushchev from aggression. But what would Kennedy have done if nuclear missiles had been launched from Cuba? If an MRBM from Cuba had destroyed an American city, would the United States have responded 'in full' against the Soviet Union? And if a nuclear attack had been mounted on the USSR, against what targets and with what weapons?

These questions raise difficult – and recurring – issues concerning how we judge the intentions of nuclear decision-makers, including whether their words (and deeds) provide insights into their intentions. It is now very clear that Nikita Khrushchev's public statements on nuclear weapons were designed to bluff, as well as to intimidate. He issued nuclear threats to the British and French over Suez in 1956 and to the Americans over Cuba in 1960. He took a particular delight in discussing with the British Ambassador, Sir Frank Roberts, how many nuclear weapons it would need to destroy the United Kingdom (six or nine) and how many his generals had allocated to the task ('scores').[64] Even at a time when the Soviet ICBM programme was seriously stalled, Khrushchev saw nuclear missiles as a means to further Soviet ambitions. When, in 1959, he told Ambassador Averill Harriman that, if the Americans used force in Berlin, 'our rockets will fly automatically', the Soviets did not have operational ICBMs (though they did have MRBMs targeted on Western Europe).[65] In retrospect, it is now clear that much of what Khrushchev said was designed to disguise Soviet weakness.

With some access to Soviet archives, and the testimony of former officials and confidants of Khrushchev, including his son Sergei, a picture has emerged of someone on a steep learning curve when it came to nuclear weapons. Zubok and Harrison write of 'The Nuclear Education of Nikita Khrushchev'.[66] A crucial political context was the legacy of Stalin's insistence that war was inevitable between capitalism and socialism, and that the latter would triumph. When, after Stalin's death, Khrushchev's rival, Malenkov, declared that nuclear weapons rendered war unthinkable, Khrushchev was sufficiently, and astutely, uneducated to outmanoeuvre him. When in power, however, he quickly embraced peaceful co-existence, while at the same time pursuing confrontation in Europe and supporting revolutionary struggle in the Third World. The missiles in Cuba were, indeed, a manifestation of his belief that he could combine support for revolutionary goals with a working relationship with the Americans. Ironically, the missile crisis became the means by which the contradictions of this approach were reconciled – at least for the duration of Khrushchev's premiership.

Khrushchev's plans for military reform embraced nuclear weapons, and especially nuclear missiles. He proclaimed that nuclear weapons had created a revolution in military affairs and looked to ballistic missiles to reduce the huge size of the Red Army (just as Eisenhower and Macmillan saw reliance on nuclear weapons as a means of cutting their defence burden). Within the Soviet military, debate paralleled Western attempts to grapple with the problems of nuclear weapons, though within very different doctrinal, bureaucratic and political contexts. There was debate within the Soviet military about the implications of nuclear weapons for all aspects of warfare. Intriguingly, the Americans and British gained access to Soviet thinking as a result of an espionage operation in 1961–2 involving a spy within Soviet Military Intelligence. Colonel Oleg Penkovsky was run in a joint operation by the CIA and the British Secret Intelligence Service (SIS) and supplied secret and top-secret editions of the Special Collection of the Journal of Military Thought (*Voyennaya Mysl*), in which debates about military strategy and nuclear weapons were conducted.[67]

Organization of this Book

In 1962, nuclear weapons played different roles in different contexts. The main themes of this book are the role of nuclear weapons in the conduct of foreign policy, in deterring armed conflict and in risking nuclear war. Chapter 2 examines Khrushchev's decision to deploy nuclear missiles in Cuba, and outlines differing and shifting interpretations of Soviet objectives. Defending Cuba is now seen as a principal Soviet objective, although other military and foreign goals were significant – most importantly, addressing Soviet strategic inferiority. The chapter briefly discusses Soviet–American and Cuban–American relations, which provided context and pretext for Khrushchev's actions. Yet, having decided that nuclear weapons should be deployed in Cuba, the Soviets had various options, including tactical nuclear weapons, shorter-range ballistic missiles and submarine-based missiles. Whether military means could have been more effectively integrated with political goals is closely studied. Furthermore, *what* the Soviets sent to Cuba was one thing. *How* they sent them was another. Khrushchev's emphasis on secrecy, and moreover, deception, were crucial and certainly counter-productive. Had Khrushchev listened to Castro, for example, and made the deployment public, the crisis would surely have been very different.

How might nuclear war have broken out in October 1962? And, had the nuclear weapons' threshold been crossed, how might escalation have occurred? The focus in Chapters 3 and 4 is on how nuclear war might have begun. Chapter 3 examines how Kennedy and Khrushchev sought to reach a diplomatic accommodation without the use of force. It then explores what might have happened had diplomacy not succeeded, and when decisions on using nuclear weapons could have become necessary. Could the first use of nuclear weapons have been a rational act of national policy in October 1962? Kennedy himself was quoted in April 1962, as saying that Khrushchev must never be certain that the United States would never strike first:

'in some circumstances we might have to take the initiative'.[68] Declaratory NATO strategy envisaged first use of nuclear weapons against Soviet aggression in Europe, and Kennedy had reviewed the option of striking first over Berlin in October 1961. Soviet operational doctrine also placed the emphasis on firing first, and discounted any suggestion of limited or protracted nuclear war. Various scenarios are considered, including those where American action in the Caribbean might have provoked a Soviet move against West Berlin. Evidence from British archives is considered that suggests the Americans had resolved to strike first against the Soviet Union in these circumstances.

However calculated or calibrated, the United States enjoyed massive nuclear superiority over the Soviet Union in 1962. Yet consideration is also given to scenarios in which Soviet first use might have been considered. Indeed, there is a case for believing that the risk of Soviet pre-emption was greater than the risk of American pre-emption. Possibly one of the most dangerous moments of the crisis was when a U-2 strayed off course into Soviet air space, exciting concern in Moscow that the aircraft might be on pre-strike reconnaissance, and concern in Washington that, faced with the threat of attack, the Soviets might decide on their own pre-emption.

Chapter 4 explores scenarios, mostly informed by recent research, concerning how the nuclear threshold could have been crossed by unauthorized acts (or accident). Concern that subordinate commanders might usurp or misinterpret their authority exercised both Kennedy and Khrushchev during the crisis. Kennedy, for example, was anxious that Jupiter missiles in Turkey might be fired without his approval, should the bases came under Soviet attack. Concern about unauthorized Soviet (or Cuban) action was brought home to Khrushchev when an American U-2 was shot down by a surface-to-air missile at the height of the crisis. Considerable evidence has emerged of episodes involving nuclear weapons about which decision-makers were unaware. In 1993 Robert McNamara commented:

> The actions of the Soviet Union, Cuba and the United States in October 1962 brought those nations to the verge of military

conflict. What was not known then, and what is not fully recognized today, was how close the world came to the brink of nuclear disaster.[69]

A catalogue of incidents and circumstances has emerged to suggest that the risk that nuclear weapons could have been used was greater than was recognized at the time. These include near-accidents and failures of American command and control; the revelation that the Soviets had deployed tactical nuclear weapons in Cuba unbeknownst to Washington; evidence that American fighters sent to support the straying U-2 were armed with nuclear ordnance; and details of encounters between nuclear-armed Soviet submarines and US navy anti-submarine warfare (ASW) forces.

What would have happened if nuclear weapons had been used? Chapter 5 explores whether retaliation would have occurred. Would nuclear war have escalated or could decision-makers have brought the world back from the brink? Conclusions are necessarily tentative, but draw upon findings in the previous chapters. A central argument is that as the crisis reached its climax both leaders strove to prevent escalation. The use of nuclear weapons would have shocked (and frightened) political leaders. Would this have accelerated their willingness to adjust political goals and draw back, or would the psychological and military 'imperatives' of pre-emption have swiftly led to escalation? Assessments are made of the scenarios outlined in Chapters 3 and 4, and conclusions drawn that the use of nuclear weapons in various circumstances would have accelerated diplomatic accommodation rather than nuclear escalation. Yet at the same time, pressures to escalate would have mounted, and once the first few nuclear weapons began to explode, the technologies of command and control could have broken down more swiftly than individuals could manage and control events.

Chapter 6 provides an overview of the political and military role of nuclear weapons and explores whether lessons can be drawn for contemporary debates. It traces lessons that were learned and argues that, contrary to the received wisdom, the experience of the crisis was of limited importance for nuclear decision-making in the 1960s and

1970s. Although in the short term, the crisis facilitated important arms control agreements, and ushered in a period of détente, basic attitudes to nuclear weapons continued much as before. Within less than twenty years these attitudes had generated a period of international tension of potentially significant nuclear danger. The 1980s nevertheless saw exchanges in which the legacy and lessons of the missile crisis were vigorously debated, in particular by surviving ExCommites. Similarly, renewed Soviet interest in the Caribbean crisis reflected Mikhail Gorbachev's nuclear agenda and his fear that miscalculation could lead to catastrophe.

With the end of the Cold War, nuclear weapons did not go away. The problem of proliferation is now a focus for global concern, though – at least in the United States – there has been serious academic debate over whether nuclear proliferation is a problem or a solution in some areas of regional instability. Evidence from the missile crisis has featured in debates between proliferation optimists and proliferation pessimists.[70] The argument that nuclear weapons provide security (rather than insecurity) is a primary rationale for states to possess them. Writing in the late 1980s Blight, Nye and Welch concluded that 'though the world of 1962 is becoming increasingly remote, some of its lessons seem timeless'.[71] If there are enduring general lessons to be learned from the missile crisis about nuclear deterrence, the British government's announcement that it needs to replace its Trident SSBN fleet is a suitable moment to ponder them. The relevance of both general propositions about deterrence and specific aspects of the missile crisis to emerging debates about global nuclear issues and Britain's nuclear future are identified and explored.

Method

'The missile crisis maintains its special claim on policymakers and citizens alike because no other event so clearly demonstrates the awesome crack between the *unlikelihood* and *impossibility* of nuclear war', Allison and Zelikow conclude.[72] We cannot seek to determine what is impossible and what is unlikely without exploring the question of how things might have been different, whether that question is framed in terms of 'What if . . . ?' or 'What might have been?' Such exploration involves devising alternative historical scenarios or counterfactuals. The value of these questions is that they can illuminate choices facing decision-makers and heighten awareness of human agency (as well as constraints on human agency). They can also illuminate contingency and chance. And, as Barton Bernstein has argued, it is 'chastening to understand the role of unrecognised contingencies' in the crisis, which recent scholarship provides much material for exploring.[73]

Counterfactual approaches have generated fierce debate among historians. Critics see the emphasis on contingency as an aberration. E. H. Carr, for example, bemoaned the role of accident in writing history, claiming it was 'seriously exaggerated by those who are interested to stress its importance'.[74] For Carr, the suggestion that history was a chapter of accidents undermined the principal purpose of the historian to provide a coherent sequence of cause and effect. The focus on contingency is certainly susceptible to underestimation of other causal factors. Yet that should not mean contingency itself may not be important, even though its significance is context-bound. An explicit aim of Chapter 4, for example, is to explore how risks from incidents at the operational level can be assessed within a broader analysis of diplomatic and strategic decision-making.

Moreover, counterfactual thinking is itself essential for exploring causality. As Tetlock and Belkin contend, 'We can avoid counterfactuals only if we eschew all causal inference and limit ourselves to strictly non-causal narratives'.[75] Or, as Allison and Zelikow argue, 'the causal bottom line', the 'painful "but for which" test, demands that one identify major factors, *but for which* the outcome would not have occurred, or would have been materially different.'[76] Various attempts have been made to devise criteria by which the credibility of counterfactuals can be assessed.[77] Any one scenario can be calibrated in a myriad ways. One device frequently used in this context is what Tetlock and Belkin term the 'minimum-rewrite rule', in which only one variable is changed.[78] While this approach is adopted here, various problems with its application are recognized. As Tetlock and Belkin themselves observe, every counterfactual requires compound counterfactuals. In other words, minimum re-writes are less minimal than they seem, and can in turn raise complex questions about causality. To pose the question of whether Soviet tactical nuclear weapons in Cuba would have been used against invading American forces, for example, is to presuppose Kennedy would have ordered an invasion.

Second, the assumption that one antecedent variable can be changed while all others remain the same may be problematic. One reason why much counterfactual history generates both popularity and controversy is the boldness of the claims writers make about causation. Yet changing one variable without changing others may make unwarranted assumptions about the interaction of relevant historical phenomena. Counterfactual histories are often constructed to preclude 'reversionary counterfactuals' that negate the effects of the first-order counterfactual.[79] One important consideration in exploring escalation, for example, is that those incidents that could precipitate escalation could equally have dramatically changed the minds of decision-makers about previously central objectives.

Decision-makers themselves posited counterfactual questions and explored anticipatory scenarios to guide them in their own actions. Some did so more effectively than others. Khrushchev failed to consider the question of what would happen if Kennedy reacted angrily to Soviet deception and decided that missiles in Cuba were intolerable. Kennedy, however, gave much more serious thought to how Khrushchev would react to the various options for removing the missiles (even if he doubted the blockade would succeed and expected Khrushchev to retaliate in Berlin). One of the more articulate exponents of thinking through scenarios was Robert McNamara, who provided a striking illustration when the American U-2 was shot down on 27 October.[80] He outlined four propositions to ExComm. First, as more U-2s would need to be sent the next day and it was 'without question' that they would be fired upon, the United States would have to attack Cuba quickly. Secondly, this would 'almost certainly' lead to an invasion. This would, thirdly, then 'probably' provoke the Soviets into attacking the missiles in Turkey, which fourthly, would mean that the United States 'must' respond. 'We cannot allow a Soviet attack on the Jupiter missiles in Turkey without a military response by NATO,' he argued (a position from which he later retreated). McNamara's logic is an illustration of what Robert Jervis conceptualized as a spiral of escalation.[81] The conclusion the Defense Secretary drew was, however, different from that of the President. For McNamara the idea was to remove the third rung on the ladder of escalation by withdrawing the missiles from Turkey. Kennedy, however, decided not to step on the ladder in the first place, and withheld retaliation against the SAM sites to give Khrushchev time to respond diplomatically.

Exploring counterfactuals is essential in examining how close we may have been to nuclear war. How they are constructed and configured is nevertheless a matter of judgement. Some are readily derived from the discussion of policy options, and are an essential means of assessing the actual outcomes. What if Kennedy had not drawn back from the idea of an attack on the missiles and, instead of a blockade, had launched an air attack, followed by an invasion of Cuba? What if Khrushchev had persevered with his initial response and ordered his ships to run the blockade, precipitating confrontation with the US navy? Both approaches were actively considered and initially endorsed by the two leaders. How each saw the likely consequences helped inform the responses they made.

Other counterfactuals are drawn from recent research into the crisis, some of which recount near-misses in crossing the nuclear threshold. How likely was it that nuclear weapons might have been used in such circumstances? In some cases the answer is close to Allison and Zelikow's *impossibility*. With others it is closer to *unlikelihood*. In some it veers towards *distinctly possible*. Yet a central question in this study is what would have then happened. If nuclear weapons had been used in or around Cuba, for example, would escalation to major or all-out nuclear war have occurred? This question is essential in assessing the nuclear dangers of the Cold War. Yet little attempt is generally made to explore the answer, not least because of the complexities and uncertainties of attempting to do so.

Conclusions in this study are therefore generally circumspect. Potential answers are explored rather than asserted. Much counterfactual history, by contrast, is written as alternative historical narrative, in which changing one event or decision is shown to have enormous consequences for the direction of history. In 1962, once nuclear weapons had been used, decision-makers would have faced choices about retaliation and escalation. Various scholars have identified plausible paths to Armageddon, involving an escalatory spiral of action and reaction.[82] This book explores such spirals and, at each stage, adjudications are attempted on how political (or military) leaders would have acted and reacted. The credibility of these adjudications depends on our understanding and interpretation of decision-makers and their choices, which is in turn based on the interpretation of evidence.

The missile crisis has generated a huge amount of archival record, personal testimony, and memoir. New techniques of historical enquiry have been generated, in the form of critical oral history, which brought together surviving officials, academics and archival sources.[83] Moreover, these surviving officials and archival sources came from both the United States and the Soviet Union, and then Cuba, including most notably Fidel Castro. In the 1990s this generated robust debate in the United States about the credibility of uncorroborated Soviet testimony.[84] Most of the substantive issues appear to have now been resolved, largely through authoritative studies of Soviet decision-making, drawing upon a degree of access to Soviet records.[85] On the American side one source of unprecedented insight into high-level decision-making was the secret recordings made by President Kennedy of his meetings and discussions. Whatever insights have been generated, problems of interpretation and understanding abound. In the nuclear context one reason for this is that the point at which there was serious discussion of nuclear options had not occurred. Some key decisions (and possibly key conversations) took place out of earshot of the microphones. And even where laborious effort has been made to generate 'The Kennedy Tapes', dispute remains over the representation and meaning of ExComm transcripts.[86] It should also, of course, be noted that we do not have the Soviet equivalent of the ExComm transcripts.

The available evidence, nevertheless, enables exploration of key aspects of nuclear decision-making, and in particular, the role of

nuclear weapons in foreign policy. Khrushchev depl[
missiles in Cuba for various reasons, but a key one wa:
United States from attacking Cuba. Likewise, we now
picture of how the crisis ended. And this includes und
the importance (or lack of importance) of the withdrawal of the
Jupiter missiles from Turkey. Evidence of *how* the crisis ended may
not necessarily tell us *why* the crisis ended. In his persuasive psychological analysis of the crisis, James Blight argues that fear of inadvertent war compelled Kennedy and Khrushchev to seek rapid
resolution of a diplomatic solution.[87] Yet finding clear evidence of
such fear is as much a challenge as finding evidence of moral aspects
of decision-making.

Assessments of how decision-makers would have contemplated the
use of nuclear weapons nevertheless need to draw upon what we
know they did and said (and the contexts in which they acted and
spoke). At the same time, there remains the question of whether we
can extrapolate from our understanding of the crisis to what might
have happened in war. When the U-2 was shot down over Cuba on
27 October, Kennedy drew back from retaliation. Does this show how
he would have reacted if a nuclear weapon had been used against
American targets? Or was it merely evidence of how he saw that event
at that time? On what criteria can we make this choice? There are no
simple answers. The nuclear history of the Cold War is inevitably and
appropriately written in terms of policy, strategy and diplomacy. It
encompasses nuclear force structures, deployments, operational
strategies, command and control, targeting and intelligence. It also
entails answers to the question of whether decision-makers would
have used nuclear weapons, and if so, how? And with what consequences? At one level the questions are unanswerable. Yet they are
essential to exploring the risk of nuclear war in 1962 (and beyond).
Decisions about whether to use nuclear weapons that faced political
(and military) leaders forty-five years ago may be the choices facing
future leaders in future crises.

CHAPTER 2

Nature of the Beast: Hedgehog, Porcupine or Cobra?

What about putting one of our hedgehogs down the Americans' trousers?

Nikita Khrushchev[1]

... once [some or all of the missiles become operational] Cuba would become a combination of porcupine and cobra.

Dean Acheson[2]

The missiles in Cuba are in the end not a cobra, even when operable, if we do not accept them as such.

McGeorge Bundy[3]

When Nikita Khrushchev explained his idea of deploying nuclear missiles in Cuba to his Minister of Defence, Marshal Malinovsky, he mused: 'What about putting one of our hedgehogs down the Americans' trousers?'[4] By contrast, Dean Acheson suggested that once the Soviet missiles were operational, the deployment would be 'a combination of porcupine and cobra'.[5] The nature of the beast remains an important question for understanding both the Soviet action and the American response. Why the missiles were deployed in Cuba was certainly a question that exercised President Kennedy and his officials. This chapter examines how the Soviets saw the political and military role of nuclear weapons in Cuba. It discusses the genesis of the crisis, including why the Soviets deployed nuclear missiles in Cuba and why the Americans responded. It explores whether Khrushchev's attempts to extend nuclear deterrence to Cuba could have been achieved without provoking confrontation with Washington.

The historiography of the crisis has examined various explanations for why Khrushchev put nuclear missiles into Cuba.[6] In the version of his memoirs first published in the West in 1970, Khrushchev maintained that:

> The main thing was that the installation of the missiles in Cuba would, I thought, restrain the United States from precipitous military action against Castro's government. In addition to protecting Cuba, our missiles would have equalized what the West likes to call 'the balance of power'.[7]

For many years, American commentators downplayed or dismissed the suggestion that Khrushchev's motive was to protect Cuba, and instead emphasized Soviet–American disparity in strategic nuclear weapons. The testimony of Soviet officials suggested, however, that the defence of Cuba was a personal as well as strategic objective of the Soviet leader. Most of these sources, nevertheless, make clear that the 'nuclear balance' was a central objective, and the most recent authoritative study of Khrushchev's decision-making places the principal emphasis on Soviet strategic objectives.[8]

Defending Cuba?

Until he came to power, Fidel Castro's relationship with communism was tenuous and ambiguous. His links with Moscow were non-existent, although Fursenko and Naftali reveal that both Raul Castro and Che Guevara were secret members of the Moscow-aligned Cuban Communist Party.[9] Within a short time, however, Castro's attitudes changed and he embraced Marxism-Leninism in theory and Nikita Khrushchev in person. Why, and how, that happened have been crucial questions on which there remains disagreement. For critics of American foreign policy, Cuba was driven into the hands of Moscow. And as Tom Paterson contends, 'It may be plausibly argued that, had there been no exile expedition, no destructive covert activities, and no economic and diplomatic boycott – had there been no concerted United States vendetta to quash the Cuban revolution – there would not have been an October missile crisis.'[10] Eisenhower and Kennedy confronted, intimidated and sought to overthrow the Cuban government. Whether Washington could have accommodated itself to Castro remains an intriguing question. Although discrete diplomatic feelers were made by Che Guevara in August 1961, the period from Kennedy's inauguration to the missile crisis was marked by mutual hostility.[11]

Whatever American motives, the consequences of American action were apparent. The landing of CIA-supported émigrés at the Bay of Pigs in April 1961 was a personal and political humiliation for John F. Kennedy. Domestic political pressure on the administration increased. And the personal animosity of the President (and his brother) toward Castro fuelled his determination to engineer regime change in Havana. On the other hand, Kennedy learned some lessons about managing crises, and in particular about the judgement of his military commanders. These lessons were applied in the missile crisis when the Joint Chiefs of Staff were kept at a distance from the White House and their views represented by their Chairman, General Maxwell Taylor, who was appointed by Kennedy and who enjoyed his confidence. In general, Kennedy's experience of the Bay of Pigs for the conduct of the missile crisis bears out Robert Lovett's aphorism that 'Good judgement is usually the result of experience. And experience is frequently the result of bad judgement.'[12]

In November 1961, the Kennedy administration embarked upon a major programme of covert action code-named *Operation Mongoose*. The CIA organized and sponsored sabotage and subversion: burning crops, blowing up factories and destroying Cuban exports. The CIA station in Miami became the largest in the world, and the CIA task force there received an annual budget of $50 million.[13] It is also clear from Congressional investigation in 1975 that various attempts were made to assassinate Fidel Castro. The Church Committee found concrete evidence of at least eight assassination attempts involving the CIA between 1960 and 1965.[14] The CIA even sought the assistance of the American Mafia, who were only too pleased to help, as the Cuban revolution had destroyed the profits from their extensive gambling and prostitution rackets in Havana.[15] There was also a plan for the CIA to introduce thallium into Castro's shoes, so that his beard would fall out. Either the plan did not succeed, or the Cuban leader has been walking around with a false beard for the last forty-five years.

Inevitably, the activities of the CIA and of Cuban émigrés increased the threat to the revolutionary government. The relationship between internal repression (including execution of counter-revolutionaries) and external intervention became an important dynamic in Cuban–American affairs. The issue of Cuba's abuse of human rights was a further irritant in Cuban–American relations. It was also a focus for the large Cuban émigré community, predominantly in Florida, which developed into a vocal political constituency in American politics. At the Havana conference in 1992, McNamara, having previously described *Operation Mongoose* as 'reprehensible' and 'stupid', explained why the Kennedy administration had adopted such policies.[16] Cuba's military relationship with the Soviets was the principal concern. Other factors were Cuban support for armed revolution across Latin America (including against the social democratic government in Venezuela), Havana's hostile rhetoric against the United States, and the concern that 'the Cuban government betrayed its promises of a free election and began to establish a dictatorship that violated the civil and political liberties of the Cuban people.'[17]

The collapse of Cuban–American relations after 1959 raises broad questions about American foreign policy in Central America. The CIA intervened on various occasions to subvert and overthrow governments that threatened American interests. Covert action against Cuba should be viewed in a context that includes the overthrow of the leftist government of Jacobo Arbenz in Guatemala in 1954, when he challenged American economic interests and appeared (at least to American eyes) to be moving towards Moscow.[18] Questions arise as to how far the Cuban–American confrontation should be seen in terms of the Cold War Soviet–American struggle, and how much as a problem of regional hegemony and the protection of American economic interests.

American covert action against Cuba was only one element in attempts to isolate and overthrow Castro. A trade embargo was imposed and the US pressured its allies not to trade with Havana.[19] In January 1962, Washington succeeded in getting Cuba suspended from the Organization of American States. There was also military intimidation. The US conducted large-scale military exercises during the summer and autumn, which were planned to include a Marine amphibious attack (Phibriglex-62) against the island of Viques near Puerto Rico, to overthrow a fictional dictator, Señor Ortsac (Castro spelt backwards).[20] This combination of economic sanctions, diplomatic isolation, and military sabre-rattling provided the context for Cuban and Soviet assessments that direct American military intervention would come. McNamara and Bundy have insisted that Kennedy had no intention of attacking Cuba in 1962.[21] Whatever Kennedy's actual intentions, McNamara told the Joint Chiefs on 1 October to prepare plans for an invasion.[22] The original timetable for *Operation Mongoose* also envisaged liberation of Cuba in October 1962, which is when Phibriglex-62 was planned. Military exercises are a traditional means of disguising surprise attacks. During 1962, Moscow and Havana expected an American invasion. McNamara told delegates at the 1989 Moscow conference that while Kennedy had no intention of invading Cuba, 'If I had been a Cuban leader, I think I might have expected a U.S. invasion.'[23] The American military also believed that Kennedy wanted them to carry out an attack, and misunderstanding of the President's intentions toward Cuba was a factor in the friction between the President and the Joint Chiefs.

Minding the Gap: The Nuclear Balance

For decades after the crisis, the consensus among Western scholars and commentators was that the predominant Soviet motive for the Cuban deployment was to reduce Soviet strategic inferiority. The envisaged deployment of 60 MRBMs and IRBMs would have significantly enhanced Soviet strategic capabilities, which then comprised some 20–30 ICBMs, 180 or so long-range bombers and some submarine-based missiles. Until 1961, the American intelligence community overestimated Soviet ICBM strength and helped generate anxiety over 'the missile gap'. Better sources (and better analysis) enabled a less alarming (and more accurate) assessment to be made. In October 1961, the Deputy Secretary of Defense, Roswell Gilpatric, announced that the Americans possessed 'a second strike capability which is at least as extensive as what the Soviets can deliver by striking first.'[24] Implicit was that Khrushchev's claim of Soviet missile superiority was a bluff. Moreover, if as Gilpatric stated, the Americans could deliver retaliatory devastation surpassing what the Soviets could do striking first, then inevitably he fuelled Soviet concern at the prospect of an American first strike. In addition to inferiority in long-range weapons, the USSR also faced what Khrushchev called encirclement. There were IRBMs in Britain, Italy and Turkey, all within range of Moscow. While the Soviets retained numerical superiority in M/IRBMs over NATO Europe, the strategic balance was stacked heavily against them. Moreover, Kennedy had embarked upon a further build-up of ICBMs and SLBMs, encouraged by Khrushchev's rhetoric but also driven by Washington's desire for superiority. When the Soviet General Staff was instructed to plan for nuclear missiles in Cuba, they were given the opportunity to forward-base nuclear forces in ways comparable to how the Americans had stationed their bombers and missiles in Europe. For the Soviet military it was an opportunity to mitigate their military inferiority.

Detailed assessments of Soviet threat perceptions have yet to emerge. There are indications, however, that understandable military concerns were wedded to distorted and misleading intelligence on American behaviour. Fursenko and Naftali recount how both the KGB and the GRU believed they had discovered Pentagon plans for a nuclear first strike on the Soviet Union in 1960–1.[25] What exactly Soviet intelligence discovered, and how it was interpreted by the Soviet leadership, is yet unclear. The American military was indeed engaged in targeting nuclear weapons on the Soviet Union, and was soon tasked by Kennedy and McNamara to redesign its nuclear war plan to provide more credible options, short of all-out attack killing hundreds of millions. The idea, however, that the American government had decided to launch a preventive nuclear attack on the Soviet

Union in September 1961, and was deterred from doing so by the resumption of Soviet nuclear testing, suggests that understanding of American policy was seriously flawed. Without more evidence, it is difficult to assess the reasons for – and consequences of – these intelligence misperceptions. Yet, the suggestion that Soviet intelligence was unable to distinguish between contingency planning and actual intent indicates serious distortions in Soviet assessments.

There is now a general consensus that the principal Soviet motives for sending missiles to Cuba were mixed, though differences in emphasis remain, including among former Soviet officials.[26] In their 1997 study, Fursenko and Naftali invoke Agatha Christie's *Murder on the Orient Express* where all the suspects take part in the murder.[27] With further access to Soviet records they now point the finger at the initial suspect (Soviet strategic inferiority) much as Hercule Poirot did in *The Mysterious Affair at Styles*. They emphasize that Khrushchev's strategic thinking had been based on the assumption of growing Soviet ICBM strength, but that by February of 1962 he had been told that the R-9 was not ready for deployment and the operational capabilities of the R-16 left it vulnerable to American pre-emption.[28] By April he was searching for a cheaper shortcut to becoming competitive in ICBMs.

Much light has been cast on how and when Soviet decisions were taken, although questions remain about the relative significance of Khrushchev's objectives. It is clear that the Soviet leader was exercised over the deployment of NATO IRBMs in Turkey and was concerned at the People's Republic of China's emergence as critic and competitor within the international socialist camp. Khrushchev was also aware that his economic and agricultural reforms were falling short of needs and expectations. Success in foreign policy would help deflect criticisms from failure at home. William Taubman suggests that Khrushchev saw the deployment as 'a cure-all' for a range of problems.[29]

There is nevertheless agreement that Nikita Khrushchev provided the initiative and driving force behind the deployment. And it was Khrushchev who insisted that the plan would proceed in secrecy and by deception. It seems that he made up his mind to deploy missiles in

Cuba during his visit to Bulgaria in April 1962, though Fursenko and Naftali explain that consideration was being given to the idea before then.[30] On his return he persuaded his close associates (or most of them) of the plan before formally gaining agreement of the Presidium of the Communist Party of the Soviet Union in May.[31] Anastas Mikoyan, the First Deputy Premier, strongly opposed the idea. Foreign Minister Gromyko claims that he privately warned against the course of action.[32] And Khrushchev's trusted foreign policy adviser, Oleg Troyanovksy, recounts he later expressed serious reservations (though by then the die was already cast).[33]

The chronology of Soviet decision-making has become clear. On 24 May, the Presidium approved the plan for *Operation Anadyr*, drawn up by the Soviet General Staff to deploy 36 R-12 MRBMs (NATO designation SS-4) and 24 R-14 IRBMs (NATO designation SS-5) in Cuba.[34] Both carried thermo-nuclear payloads. The R-12s would be within range of Washington as well as many air bases, ICBM complexes, and command and control centres. The R-14s could reach virtually all US territory. In addition, 80 Frontovye Krylatye Rakety (FKR) Meteor land-attack cruise missiles, with a range of 90–100 miles and armed with 5.6 to 12 kiloton-yield warheads, were to be deployed at two sites, near Mariel in western Cuba and overlooking the US naval base at Guantánamo Bay.[35] A further aspect of the plan was the establishment of a Soviet naval base at Mariel that would accommodate surface ships, ballistic missile-armed submarines and diesel-electric torpedo submarines.[36] Seven Project 629 (NATO designation Golf-class) submarines were earmarked, each equipped with three 350-mile-range R-13 missiles (NATO designation SS-N-4) carrying explosive yields comparable to the MRBMs. Four diesel-electric Project 641 submarines (NATO designation Foxtrot-class) were also to be sent.

Handling Hedgehogs

Instead of thrusting his hedgehog into Uncle Sam's pants, what if Khrushchev had had placed it there carefully? Various commentators have suggested that if Khrushchev had made public his intention to deploy missiles in Cuba then the crisis would have been very different. May and Zelikow suggest that 'Conceivably, there might have been no crisis at all.'[37] A public declaration was indeed advocated by Fidel Castro who saw no need for secrecy. In August 1962, when Che Guevara and Emilio Aragones travelled to Moscow to formalize a Soviet–Cuban Defence pact, they conveyed Castro's view that the Soviet commitment to Cuba should be made public.[38] In 1992 Castro described this aspect of Khrushchev's approach as 'a big mistake, a very big mistake'. He believed the secrecy and the deception were each 'very damaging'.[39] Cuba was an independent sovereign state whose avowed purpose in accepting Soviet missiles was to strengthen the socialist camp in the global correlation of forces in the struggle against imperialism. So the Cubans saw no need for secrecy.

Various ExCommites have indicated that if they had faced a public announcement from Khrushchev about deploying missiles in Cuba, the confrontation with the Soviets would have been different.[40] Secrecy and deception clearly fuelled Kennedy's belligerence on 16 October and contributed to his conclusion that day that a military response was necessary. 'We're going to do number one. We're going to take out these missiles,' he said, though he was not yet decided on a general air strike or an invasion.[41] If the Americans had believed a decision to use force was necessary that day, Khrushchev's tactics could have tragically rebounded.[42] In the event, Kennedy and his colleagues were able to give more thought to the potential consequences and reconsider the military option.

Khrushchev made clear to Kennedy that he did not intend to create political problems for the Democrats in the mid-term Congressional elections in November. Announcement of the existence of the missiles would be made when Khrushchev visited the United Nations and Cuba in November, when the MRBMs would be deployed and the IRBMs would be nearly ready. Khrushchev also sought to make clear that the missiles in Cuba were defensive. This was part of the deception, but it also reflected Khrushchev's intentions. He did not intend to fire them, merely to deter an attack on Cuba. Castro summed this up at the Havana conference:

Since he did not have the intention of using the weapons in an offensive operation, he considered them defensive. The intention defined the character of the weapons. But it became clear that Kennedy didn't understand it that way. He did not understand this question of intentions. He was looking at the *kind* of weapons – whether or not they were strategic weapons.[43]

When presenting his proposal for the deployment to the Presidium on 21 May, he nevertheless announced, 'This will be an offensive policy.'[44]

Secrecy and Deception

Soviet assurances went further than emphasizing defensive intent. According to Robert Kennedy, both Ambassador Dobrynin and Khrushchev's emissary, Georgi Bolshakov, stated that no nuclear missiles capable of reaching America were being placed in Cuba.[45] On 11 September, the Soviet News Agency, TASS, stated there was no need to deploy nuclear weapons in other countries because Soviet rockets were so powerful. When Kennedy met Gromyko on 18 October, the Foreign Minister reiterated the general Soviet line that aid for Cuba was not offensive in nature. After their meeting Kennedy complained that he had been told 'more bare-faced lies than I have ever heard in so short a time'.[46] Gromyko later denied he had lied: Kennedy did not specify nuclear missiles (or produce low-level photography of the sites from the drawer of his desk).[47] If Kennedy had raised missiles, Gromyko was under instruction to say that 'a small quantity of missiles of a defensive nature' had been deployed.[48] Dobrynin received no such instructions and only learned of the missiles when confronted by Secretary of State Rusk on 22 October, shortly before Kennedy appeared on television. According to Rusk, Dobrynin seemed to age ten years before his eyes.[49]

Khrushchev and Gromyko clearly sought to deceive the Americans. Yet deception was (and remains) a part of political life. The previous year, the American Ambassador to the United Nations, Adlai Stevenson, initially told the UN Security Council that the United States was not involved in the Bay of Pigs fiasco.[50] Since 1960,

American officials at the UN had regularly and indignantly denied Cuban allegations about American subversion and assassination attempts.[51] In 1956, the British had deceived their American allies over attacking Egypt, and the Foreign Secretary, Selwyn Lloyd, lied to the House of Commons about secret British collusion with Israel.[52] And after the crisis, Kennedy was happy to send his senior officials off to deceive Congress on whether there was any arrangement with Khrushchev over the withdrawal of the Jupiters from Turkey.[53] As Bundy later noted, 'we misled our colleagues, our countrymen, our successors, and our allies.'[54]

Deception, when unmasked, nevertheless, carries a degree of opprobrium and a political cost. The President compared Khrushchev's abuse of a trusted diplomatic back-channel, Georgi Bolshakov, to the behaviour of Japanese negotiators before Pearl Harbor. Yet Kennedy could hardly claim the moral high ground when his administration was investing such huge effort and resources in trying to overthrow Castro. Nevertheless, Soviet secrecy and duplicity rebounded on Moscow by diverting world opinion from the fact that Soviet missiles in Cuba could be readily compared to American missiles in Europe. It was very difficult for the Americans to condemn the Soviets for doing in Cuba what they had done in Europe. Moscow's attempts to deploy the missiles in secret gave the Americans the opportunity to portray the Soviets as aggressively undermining the status quo.

Warnings

The build-up of Soviet forces continued throughout summer and into the autumn of 1962. In August, Soviet S-75 surface-to-air missiles (SAMs) (NATO designation SA-2) were identified by U-2 overflights. These non-nuclear missiles were 35-feet long and could be mistaken for MRBMs by those unfamiliar with missile technology (especially when glimpsed in transit at night). Gathering accurate intelligence on Cuba was difficult. There were many reports from refugees and CIA assets, claiming nuclear missiles in Cuba. A CIA re-analysis of these indicated that only 8 of 3,500 reported sightings of possible missiles were retrospectively deemed to be 'reasonably valid indicators' of the actual deployment – though one of these was responsible for identifying the site at San Cristóbal that was then targeted by the U-2s.[55]

Public warnings of nuclear missiles in Cuba, in particular those of Senator Kenneth Keating, caused concern and irritation in the White House. The provenance of his claims has long been a matter of speculation, though it may well be that his information came from privately sponsored Cuban émigrés via their American backers.[56] By the time the blockade came into force the Soviets had successfully shipped nearly 42,000 troops, 36 MRBMs, a squadron of nuclear bombers with six nuclear bombs, 80 cruise missiles, 12 tactical ballistic missiles, and some 158 nuclear warheads into Cuba.[57] The Soviet General Staff had organized the movement of these forces through the Soviet Union, across the oceans and from their Cuban disembarkation ports to pre-arranged sites. It was an extraordinary logistical venture, which succeeded up to the seemingly inexplicable failure to camouflage the MRBM sites. On 14 October, a USAF U-2 was able to photograph the MRBM site at San Cristóbal in western Cuba, and in the ensuing weeks, U-2 overflights enabled CIA photo-analysts to identify six MRBM bases in various stages of completion, as well as the early stages of three IRBM sites.

The R-12s had arrived by the end of September. What if the missiles had been identified earlier? U-2 coverage of Cuba had been interrupted in September after a U-2 flown by a Nationalist Chinese pilot had been shot down over the People's Republic of China (PRC), and Dean Rusk and McGeorge Bundy had successfully pressed for suspension of direct overflights of Cuba for fear of a diplomatic incident. The CIA, then responsible for the U-2s, was hampered by the absence from Washington of Director McCone, who spent a month honeymooning in France. On his return, the decision was reversed and overflights resumed, once weather permitted, now with USAF pilots. Allison and Zelikow argue that discovery of the missiles two weeks earlier – or two weeks later – could have made a significant difference to the outcome of the crisis.[58] Whether the interruptions to the overflight programme had any great significance, however, is unclear. The key point is that the sites had been identified before they were ready:

Washington had time to consider their options before Moscow knew the missiles were detected.

The failure of the Soviets to properly camouflage the missiles has long been a mystery and even generated ingenious conspiracy theories to suggest Khrushchev intended them to be discovered.[59] If the missiles had been better camouflaged, and the Americans not discovered them before they were ready, then the initial debates in Washington might well have been different. If they had not been discovered before Khrushchev announced the deployment, the R-14s would also have reached Cuba, though they would not have been ready until December. How much did the operational readiness of the MRBMs matter? The issue featured in the first ExComm discussions about an air strike when McNamara suggested that the readiness of the missiles was 'highly critical' for US planning,[60] and that any air strike should take place before the missiles became operational.[61] Yet the air strike option remained under consideration even after the missiles were operational. At the first of the critical oral history conferences at Hawk's Cay in 1987, it emerged that there was confusion and disagreement among ExCommites about the importance of the missiles' readiness, and McNamara stated that the operational readiness of the missiles had no effect on his decisions (to the consternation of various colleagues).[62] In retrospect, it seems clear that the circumstances in which the timing of their discovery would have been significant were if they had been caught when their operational readiness was judged imminent and a decision whether to attack them deemed necessary.

In August and September 1962, the Kennedy administration had characterized Soviet weapons in Cuba as defensive in nature. Public and private assurances were received from Moscow that 'offensive' weapons would not be deployed. Nevertheless domestic American pressure remained a problem for Kennedy, and within the administration both John McCone and Robert Kennedy remained exercised about the possibility of nuclear missiles. On 4 September the President authorized a statement to the press, warning that the 'gravest issues would arise' if the Soviets undertook specific actions in Cuba, including the deployment of Soviet combat forces, offensive ground-to-ground missiles or other significant offensive ability.[63] On 13 September, Kennedy went further stating that

> if at any time the Communist build-up in Cuba were to endanger or interfere with our security in any way, including our base at Guantánamo, our passage to the Panama Canal, our missile and space activities at Cape Canaveral, or the lives of American citizens in this country, or if Cuba should ever attempt to export its aggressive purposes by force or the threat of force against any nation in this hemisphere, or become an offensive military base of significant capacity for the Soviet Union, then this country will do whatever must be done to protect its own security and that of its allies.[64]

According to McGeorge Bundy, the public warnings were issued 'because of the requirements of domestic politics, not because we seriously believed that the Soviets would do anything as crazy from our standpoint as placement of Soviet nuclear weapons in Cuba.'[65] Robert Kennedy, however, was clear in his mind of the risk of such a deployment and was the driving force within the administration to issue the September 4 warning to deter the Soviets.[66]

By making his position public, the President strengthened the investment of his credibility in the issue. In the view of McGeorge Bundy, having done so, any suggestion that the United States could tolerate Soviet missiles in Cuba '. . . neglects a reality that could not possibly be neglected by the American administration in the five days after 15 October – that the United States government had publically pledged itself, in a manner wholly unambiguous to itself and its countrymen, not to accept any such deployment.'[67] Whether Soviet nuclear missiles in Cuba, per se, inevitably entailed a crisis has been questioned. One of Kennedy's reactions on 16 October was to say, 'I should have said that we don't care.'[68] According to Theodore Sorensen, the President 'drew the line' over missiles in Cuba because he believed that no missiles would be sent. 'If we had known that the Soviets were putting forty missiles in Cuba, we might under this hypothesis have drawn the line at one hundred, and said with great fanfare that we would absolutely not tolerate the presence of more than one hundred missiles in Cuba.'[69] Other ExCommites have dismissed this suggestion.

When Kennedy issued his warning to Khrushchev the missiles were at sea. It has been suggested that if Kennedy had issued his warning before Khrushchev had taken his decision this could have better deterred the Soviet leader. However, as Lebow and Stein argue, Kennedy had no reason to suspect that Khrushchev would act in this manner, and no incentive to issue a warning.[70] Furthermore, there is no reason to believe that the timing of the American threat would have altered Khrushchev's central calculation that Kennedy would live with a fait accompli, as he had to live with American nuclear weapons in Europe.

Khrushchev's response to Kennedy's September warnings was to press on with *Operation Anadyr* but make changes to the nuclear forces. The original plan included tactical weapons, in the form of 80 cruise missiles. To these were now added 12 Luna battlefield nuclear missiles (NATO designation Free Rocket Over Ground, FROG), each armed with a 2-kiloton payload; and six 8- to 12-kiloton yield gravity bombs for a squadron of Soviet navy Ilyushin-28 jet bombers.[71] Khrushchev rejected the R-11m (NATO designation SCUD-B) which the General Staff proffered as an option, though why is unclear. Initially, Khrushchev wanted the Lunas flown to Cuba, but was persuaded by the military to send them by sea. On the recommendation of the Soviet military, Khrushchev also decided not to send the surface ships, on the grounds that they would attract undue attention.[72] The deployment of the nuclear-armed Project 629s was also shelved. However, the Project 641 submarines would proceed, and a decision was taken to equip each of them with a nuclear-armed torpedo.

Khrushchev was at Pitsunda, at his Black Sea *dacha*, when he contemplated Kennedy's September warnings. Communications with the Soviet military were conducted by means of messengers from the General Staff bearing handwritten drafts.[73] There appears to have been no discussion about the implications of sending the additional tactical nuclear weapons. In retrospect, it appears that Khrushchev accepted the distinction between weapons whose purpose was to deter and those intended to start and fight a nuclear war in Cuba. Throughout the Cold War, Western analysts drew a distinction between Soviet and Western conceptions of nuclear strategy. The West believed in deterrence. The Soviets believed in nuclear war-fighting. Yet accounts of Soviet decision-making draw a distinction between the MRBMs in Cuba whose purpose was to deter, and the tactical weapons intended for use.[74] No evidence has emerged of any consideration in Moscow of how the Americans would react to the use of tactical nuclear weapons against American forces. It remains a matter of astonishment that no thought was given to this, and in particular to whether crossing the nuclear threshold would lead to nuclear escalation. It was only when the crisis began that Khrushchev became concerned at the implications of his planning.

On hedgehogs

What if the hedgehog was genuinely a hedgehog? Were there options available to the Soviets that could have put nuclear weapons in Cuba without provoking a major confrontation with the Americans? What if the Soviets had deployed tactical nuclear weapons alone? What if they had deployed missile-armed submarines from Cuban bases instead of land-based missiles? Or sent weapons that could reach American territory but not strike Washington or vital military targets? Such questions raise complex issues about American and Soviet objectives, and in particular about how the Americans and Soviets viewed nuclear weapons.

Whether alternative force structures could have achieved Soviet objectives depends on how Khrushchev's aims are assessed. If Khrushchev's primary goal was to defend the Cuban revolution, then deploying missiles that could strike America was less crucial than if the primary purpose was to redress Soviet strategic inferiority. If however, the strategic balance was a central objective, tactical nuclear weapons alone would not have met Soviet requirements. Allison and Zelikow indeed suggest that the fact that Khrushchev did not send a tactical nuclear force instead of a strategic force could be used as evidence that the defence of Cuba was not his aim.[75] This argument only holds, however, if it is necessary to choose between Khrushchev's various objectives (rather than adjudicate their relative significance).

Cuban fingers on Soviet buttons?

Even if Khrushchev had decided to send only a tactical force, there is no certainty that the Cubans would have agreed to take them. Castro maintained that Cuba had accepted MRBMs and IRBMs to help the international socialist cause, though some senior officials were aware of the potential deterrent value of the missiles, and there may well have been other factors at work in Cuban decision-making. If, however, Castro's statements are taken at face value, how would weapons whose only purpose was to defend Cuba be seen as a contri-bution to the global balance of forces? One means to overcome Cuban reluctance to host only tactical weapons would have been for the Soviets to hand over the nuclear weapons to the Cuban army. Khrushchev, apparently, did give consideration to providing Castro with direct command of Soviet forces in Cuba (excluding the MRBMs and IRBMs).[76] And in November, the Cubans began to be trained to fire the Meteors and Lunas.[77] The Soviets had previously deployed nuclear weapons on East German, and possibly Polish, territory, though they had never relinquished control of the nuclear warheads. There are no indications of how far Khrushchev thought through these issues.

In Western thinking about deterrence, a distinction was sometimes drawn between deterrence by punishment and deterrence by denial.[78] The capacity to inflict military defeat or unacceptable damage on invading US forces was a potential means of deterring attack. In an invasion, the American beachheads would have been priority targets for the Meteors, Lunas and Ilyushin-28 bombers. The Meteors were also deployed for use against the US naval base at Guantánamo. What might have happened if the US had invaded Cuba, and tactical nuclear weapons been used against American troops on Cuban territory and adjacent waters is explored in Chapter 5. The issue here is whether tactical nuclear weapons alone would have deterred an

American attack without provoking an American response. Castro himself reflected on this in 1992, when he observed that

> if it was a matter of defending Cuba without creating an international problem, the presence of tactical nuclear weapons in Cuba would not have created the same problem that the strategic weapons did. It couldn't have been said that tactical nuclear weapons represented a threat to the United States.[79]

To be deterred by tactical nuclear weapons, the Americans needed to know (or at least suspect) they were there. General Gribkov explained that there was no specific plan to announce their presence.[80] There is an echo here of the scene in *Dr Strangelove* where Dr Strangelove himself berates the Soviet ambassador for creating a Doomsday device that will automatically destroy the world in the event of American attack, which will therefore deter attack on the USSR, but about which the Americans know nothing until it is too late. Soviet military doctrine viewed low-yield weapons as a means of fighting a war. As General Gribkov asserted: 'Arcane theories of nuclear deterrence mattered less to us than the practical questions of assuring our exposed troops the strongest possible armor against attack.'[81] Castro, however, who was keen to retain the tactical nuclear forces after the MRBMs had left, wanted their presence to be made known to the Americans.[82]

How the Americans would have reacted to a tactical nuclear force depends, among other things, on which weapons the Soviet deployed. Various tactical systems were considered at various stages of *Operation Anadyr*. Some had the range to reach the United States. The Ilyushin-28 bombers, for example, could strike American territory. Gribkov states that the nuclear-armed Il-28 had an effective combat range of 200 miles, which enabled them to reach Florida.[83] The Americans believed that their combat radius was 750 miles (which on a one-way mission would place them within range of Washington as well as key military targets).[84] On the other hand, the aircraft were seen as near obsolete. When the bombers were first identified in September, they were not labelled 'offensive'. Indeed, Kennedy's initial concern was only to prevent news of their discovery from leaking, while Bundy publically indicated that aircraft with 'a certain marginal capability of moving against the United States' would be tolerated.[85] They were then, however, included in Kennedy's speech of 22 October and thereafter the Americans insisted on their withdrawal. The squadron of nine aircraft configured to carry the nuclear payloads remained in their crates throughout the crisis.[86] The other bombers, along with the MIG-21 fighters, were to be handed over to the Cuban air force (which created a problem for Moscow when Khrushchev agreed their withdrawal without consulting Castro).

Submarines

What if Khrushchev had sent nuclear submarines rather than land-based missiles? When, in September, the American intelligence community concluded that the Soviets were unlikely to deploy 'offensive' nuclear weapons in Cuba, they nevertheless recognized that the USSR could derive considerable military advantage from M/IRBMs or a Soviet submarine base and that 'as between these two, the establishment of a submarine base would be the more likely'.[87] As we have seen, the original plan for *Operation Anadyr* envisaged a force of seven Project 641 submarines, each with three 350-mile range SLBMs. The aim was, of course, for these to augment the land-based missiles. Would a submarine-based force alone have better achieved Soviet aims? The R-14s operated from fixed-site bases that were vulnerable to pre-emption. Although the R-12s could be dismantled and moved, they too were vulnerable once identified. In crisis, or in war, vulnerability to pre-emption breeds anxiety about the need to 'use them or lose them'. A Cuban submarine base would have presented similar incentives for pre-emption as land-based missiles. Once at sea, however, the submarines were less vulnerable, although the Project 641 submarines were diesel-powered and had to surface to charge their batteries, and unlike American Polaris SSBNs, they were unable to fire their missiles when submerged. Had the Soviets, never-theless, been able and willing to send SSBNs instead, a more credible submarine force could have been deployed. One further option was the deployment of nuclear-armed cruise missile-carrying submarines. Although these were not part of the planning for *Operation Anadyr*, there are indications that during the crisis, several submarines armed with P-5 and P-7 (NATO designation SS-N-3) sea-launched cruise missiles (SLCMs) were deployed into the northern Atlantic.[88]

At the political level, the Soviets tacitly distinguished between NATO IRBMs capable of striking their homeland and American submarines based in European waters. This was true of Soviet responses to Jupiter IRBMs in Turkey as it was later with Pershing-2 MRBMs and GLCMs in Western Europe in the 1980s. In the 1960s, the US forward-based Polaris, and later Poseidon, SSBNs. And to provide reassurance to NATO allies about decoupling, 400 Poseidon warheads were assigned for targeting by NATO's Supreme Allied Commander Europe (SACEUR). While Soviet propaganda was directed at all NATO bases, it was land-based missiles that caused the greatest concern. The idea that SLBMs were preferable to IRBMs was indeed recognized by NATO in 1963 when the Jupiters were withdrawn from Italy and Turkey and a Polaris submarine was deployed in the Eastern Mediterranean to cover targets (Soviet I/MRBM bases) that the Jupiters had covered.

Shorter or Fewer

The Soviets had other ballistic missiles that could strike American territory from Cuba, but were not within range of Washington or key military targets. When the first photographs of the MRBMs appeared, CIA photo-analysts wondered whether they were looking at R-12s or R-5Ms (NATO designation SS-3). Western intelligence estimated the range of the R-12 at 1,100 miles.[89] What targets the R-12s and R-14s were to be assigned is unknown. According to Sergei Khrushchev, the accuracy of the MRBMs precluded counterforce targeting and meant that they were aimed at US cities.[90] Indeed, according to Steven Zaloga, 'During the Khrushchev years no Soviet nuclear weapon system had counterforce capability.'[91] The missiles lacked accuracy, and it was also doubtful that Soviet reconnaissance capabilities could provide necessary target intelligence. President Kennedy was told that 92 million American people, including 58 cities of at least 100,000 population, were within the estimated 1,100-mile range of the R-12s.[92] The R-5M had a range of 750 miles.[93] Contrary to assertions that the Soviets had never deployed nuclear weapons outside their territory, the R-5M was one of several systems they had stationed in East Germany. In 1959, MRBMs were deployed in the German Democratic Republic (GDR) within range of London and Paris, key USAF bases in France, and Thor sites being established in East Anglia. The precise reason for the deployment remains unclear as does the cause of their hasty withdrawal later in 1959.[94] Western intelligence was apparently fully aware of their deployment.[95]

Acceptable Threat?

So, how would the Americans have assessed these different nuclear forces? To explore the question, it is first necessary to evaluate Kennedy's actual response to the MRBMs. A central question in the missile crisis remains why the United States was willing to risk military escalation in response to the Soviet nuclear deployment. The answer reflects long-standing American attitudes to Cuba, concerns about Fidel Castro and his relationship with Moscow, and the military and political implications of the missiles themselves. Many Americans saw it as axiomatic that Soviet 'intrusion' into 'America's backyard' was aggressive in nature and therefore unacceptable. On 26 September, a joint resolution of Congress expressed determination to 'prevent in Cuba the creation or use of an externally supported military capability endangering the security of the United States'. The strength of feeling was evidenced by the size of the majorities: 386 to 7 in the House of Representatives and 86 to 1 in the Senate (the one opposed to the resolution favoured stronger action).[96] Certainly, when Kennedy met Congressional leaders shortly before his televised speech on 22 October, he was made uncomfortably aware of the strength of their feeling. Led by Southern Democrats, Richard Russell and William Fulbright, they were dismissive of the blockade, and wanted military action.[97] There are differing assessments of the importance of domestic factors in Kennedy's policy-making. Paterson and Brophy conclude that 'Kennedy did not engage Cuba and the

Soviet Union in the missile crisis in October in order to silence his noisy Republican critics or to attract votes for Democrats in November.[98] Richard Ned Lebow, however, provides a sympathetic reassessment of the arguments of Kennedy's critics who emphasized the domestic motivations for his behaviour.[99]

For many Americans, missiles in Cuba posed the threat of nuclear devastation and were 'an action aimed at inflicting an almost mortal wound on us'.[100] As one of the 'hawks' within the Kennedy administration, Treasury Secretary Douglas Dillon said later, 'The crisis was unique in the sense that it was the first time that there was a real, imminent, potential threat to the physical safety and well-being of American citizens.'[101] Setting aside whether an 'imminent potential threat' is an oxymoron (and setting aside the existence of Soviet strategic bombers, ICBMs and SLBMs), Dillon's view illustrates the psychology of many American citizens (and some American officials). These same citizens had experienced the debates over bomber gaps and missile gaps and taught their schoolchildren to 'duck and cover' to survive in a nuclear war. Yet confronted with nuclear weapons in close proximity, many saw the threat from Cuba not just as an immediate challenge but as an imminent threat.

The nature of that threat was discussed on the day of the first ExComm meetings. Bundy asked McNamara how gravely the missiles changed the strategic balance. 'Mac, I asked the Chiefs that this afternoon. In effect they said "substantially." My own personal view, Mr President, is not at all.'[102] The Defense Secretary did not question the need to remove the missiles but, as he stated (after Kennedy had left the room): 'I don't believe it's primarily a military problem. It's primarily a domestic political problem.'[103] Kennedy himself observed that it did not matter whether a missile was fired from Cuba or the USSR: 'What difference does it make? They've got enough to blow us up now anyway.'[104] The assessment of the Joint Chiefs was different. Missiles in Cuba enabled the Soviets to circumvent American warning radars, including the new Ballistic Missile Early Warning System (BMEWS), which was oriented against a Soviet attack from over the North Pole. Ballistic missiles launched from Cuba would increase the risk of surprise attack, and threaten destruction of key command posts, ICBM fields and air bases. Concern about the circumvention of the US early warning network was shared by Whitehall.[105]

Curiously, the military aspect of the deployment did not receive close attention among civilian officials. As Raymond Garthoff explains, the issue of how the deployment would affect the military balance 'was not even fully analyzed in the hectic week of initial decisions'.[106] Garthoff, then a State Department analyst, noted in an assessment of 27 October 1962, that the missiles were 'a significant accretion to Soviet strategic capabilities for striking continental United States', which could destroy an appreciably larger proportion of the US strategic force.[107] Yet, as Bundy observed, most members of ExComm agreed with McNamara's assessment that the Soviet missiles in Cuba did not change the strategic balance.[108]

While military issues did not detain ExComm, foreign policy concerns most certainly did. Kennedy had publically warned that offensive Soviet forces would not be tolerated. To do so now would damage his credibility within NATO, the OAS and generally. Bundy later reflected that, 'If the missiles did not come out, no-one would be able to conduct a sensible American foreign policy for years to come.'[109] As Lebow and Stein explain, Kennedy attached considerable importance to the issue of resolve in the conduct of his foreign policy.[110] After the Bay of Pigs he was exercised that Khrushchev would see him as weak for not having intervened directly with American forces. He was plagued by doubts about the impression he had made on Khrushchev at Vienna in June 1961, though there remains debate about how the Soviet leader assessed the young President at the summit.[111] A key concern for Kennedy was West Berlin. American officials anticipated a renewed effort by Khrushchev to resolve the Berlin issue after November. Whether this was, indeed, in Khrushchev's mind is still contested.[112] Key Soviet officials – notably Gromyko and Troyanovsky – have denied this was Khrushchev's goal.[113] Fursenko and Naftali, however, present new evidence about Khrushchev's thinking on Berlin.[114] Having decided in the winter of 1961/2 to avoid further confrontation with Kennedy, in July 1962 he decided that when *Operation Anadyr* was sufficiently advanced, he would push again on Berlin.

American Reactions

In the light of these military and foreign policy concerns, how might Washington have reacted if Khrushchev had sent a different nuclear force to Cuba, as outlined above? What if he had only despatched battlefield nuclear missiles that could not reach the United States? It would have been difficult to characterize them as 'offensive'. And if, as McNamara and Bundy insist, Kennedy had no intention of invading Cuba (before the MRBMs were discovered), then tactical nuclear weapons posed no direct threat to the United States (though Meteor missiles were targeted on the United States naval base at Guantánamo Bay).

A tactical nuclear force could have been deployed with much less visible logistical effort, increasing the likelihood that Khrushchev could have secured his fait accompli. Whether this would have violated the conditions laid down in Kennedy's 13 September warning is a matter of interpretation. It is impossible to be certain about how debates would have taken shape in Washington. Yet, whatever the distinction in military logic to be made between strategic and tactical nuclear forces, the discovery of any Soviet nuclear weapons in Cuba would have entailed a serious political challenge. Without intrusive on-site inspection, verification that only short-range weapons were present would have been problematic. A further question concerns how the Americans would have reacted to the possibility that a tactical nuclear force would have been operated by the Cubans. The prospect of nuclear weapons in Cuban hands would have excited concern and agitation in American opinion. If Congress believed an invasion was warranted by the establishment of Soviet bases in Cuba, the existence of nuclear weapons of any kind would have still presented a domestic political problem, though not a significant military one. If, however, foreign policy considerations were the driving force behind Kennedy's response to the missiles, while tactical nuclear weapons in Cuba would have been seen as an affront to Washington, the implications for any future crisis over Berlin would have been very different.

Was there a level of nuclear force in Cuba that the Soviets could expect the Amercians to tolerate and which could provide a credible deterrent to protect Cuba? Certainly in some minds, the nature of the missile configurations informed the response to them. Initially, Maxwell Taylor was deeply concerned at the invasion option and the prospect of 'that deep mud in Cuba'.[115] However, when he learned that the Soviets were constructing IRBM sites, he supported invasion. Would the Americans, conversely, have accepted a situation where the Soviets could destroy a small number of targets, or targets only within a certain range? A smaller force of R-12s (and without the IRBMs) would have reduced the scale of the threat, though the potential for surprise attack would have remained. A force of R-5Ms could have targeted cities in Florida but not Washington. Would this have been tolerable for the Americans? Possibly, but unlikely. What seems clear is that American action was guided more by political psychology than military logic. As Bundy argues: 'What was decisive for the President was not the number of missiles in prospect, or their strategic value, but the political damage that the United States and its government would suffer if any nuclear missiles *at all* that could reach the United States from Cuba were tolerated.'[116]

Did this apply to submarines operating from a Cuban base? Interestingly, Bundy quotes President Reagan who, in 1984, was asked about the threat of Soviet nuclear submarines deployed in the western Atlantic (in response to GLCM and Pershing-2 missiles in Europe). Reagan's reply was: 'If I thought there was some reason to be concerned about them, I wouldn't be sleeping in this house tonight [laughter] . . . no I don't think they pose any particular threat at all.'[117] The remark reflects a significant change in American nuclear threat perceptions from twenty years earlier. Just as Europeans learned to live with Soviet missiles targeted at them, American attitudes to mutual deterrence had altered. Whether Reagan would have joked about a Soviet SSBN base in Cuba is another matter. A Soviet naval base in 1962 may not have posed the same kind of military threat to land-based missiles. It would nevertheless have caused what Bundy later described as, 'more an intolerable affront than an unacceptable attempt to change the nuclear balance of power'.[118]

Conclusion

If Khrushchev's principal aim was to protect Cuba by means of nuclear deterrence there were probably better choices than MRBMs and IRBMs. Tactical nuclear weapons offered deterrence by denial rather than threat of punishment, and would have presented a difficult political challenge to Washington. They did not, however, add value to Soviet strategic capabilities. Shorter-range MRBMs or submarine-based missiles did help address Soviet strategic inferiority, and could be seen as less militarily threatening than the R-12s and R-14s. The Soviets would have been better able to present them as a defensive deployment, especially if Khrushchev had foresworn deception. Yet they would still have presented the Kennedy administration with a political challenge that it most probably would have felt necessary to confront. While American officials had cogent reasons to be concerned about nuclear weapons in Cuba, the sense of 'nuclear affront' would not have been dispelled by a different MRBM/SLBM force structure.

There was, of course, one further military option available to Khrushchev. This was not to deploy nuclear weapons in Cuba but instead to rely on conventional forces (either the 50,000 troops envisaged under *Operation Anadyr* or some other force structure). From a Soviet perspective, the defence of Cuba was as legitimate as the American threat was imperialist aggression. Both Moscow and Havana concluded in 1962 that Kennedy intended invasion. If Bundy and McNamara are correct that he did not, nuclear deterrence brought vulnerability rather than security. The term 'intelligence failure' is frequently invoked with the clarity of hindsight. Yet it is difficult not to share McNamara's empathy with how his adversaries would have seen the American threat. The origins of the crisis lay in a series of misperceptions and misjudgements. The Soviets and Cubans believed that the Americans intended to invade. Kennedy thought that Khrushchev would not deploy missiles in Cuba, and so warned that such action would provoke a response. Khrushchev believed that he could present Kennedy with a fait accompli and that Washington would live with missiles in Cuba as he had lived with missiles in Turkey. Hedgehogs may be defensive in nature, but inserting them into other people's trousers can cause dangerous complications.

CHAPTER 3

Retreat of the Moles

If people do not show wisdom, then in the final analysis they will come to a clash, like blind moles, and then reciprocal extermination will begin.

Nikita Khrushchev to John F. Kennedy, 26 October 1962[1]

How close we came to nuclear war in 1962 remains a matter of conjecture. John F. Kennedy apparently put the odds at war with the Soviets at 'somewhere between one out of three and even'.[2] His advisers remained divided. The hawks, then, as later, believed that American nuclear superiority, together with conventional superiority in the Caribbean, meant that the risk of a Soviet military response was negligible. The doves were more concerned about the *possibility* of a Soviet reaction, and were exercised over human and procedural fallibility. They were dismissive of the importance of nuclear superiority, though they too recognized the importance of the conventional balance in the Caribbean. Several decades of scholarship have provided much evidence, reflection and debate with which to re-examine these attitudes, review the role of nuclear weapons in the crisis and assess the risk of nuclear war.

What is now clear is how Kennedy and Khrushchev manoeuvred in pursuit of diplomatic accommodation and compromised on their political objectives.[3] At the same time we have also learned of moments on both sides when they reacted belligerently – Kennedy upon discovering the missiles on 16 October – Khrushchev on hearing of imminent actions by Kennedy on 22 October. Initial impulses could have precipitated the use of force. The two most seemingly obvious ways in which the Soviets and Americans could have come to blows were if the Americans had launched a surgical strike on the missiles as soon as they were discovered, and if the Soviet ships had attempted to run the blockade and been intercepted and/or attacked by the American navy. Each leader reacted belligerently and initially favoured confrontation.

Nevertheless, there is now evidence of how the two men acted to resolve the crisis. This chapter begins with a brief account of how the crisis ended. Fear of escalation exercised both leaders.[4] Each recognized the devastating consequences of nuclear war, though both had suggested – by word and deed – that they would use nuclear weapons in specific circumstances. Discussion then focuses on whether there were circumstances in which political leaders could have considered the use of nuclear weapons as a rational instrument of national policy. The general conclusion is that the threat of retaliation rendered the first use of nuclear weapons implausible, though not entirely unthinkable. Preventive and pre-emptive scenarios are considered, as well as the question of whether the United States (and the United Kingdom) would have initiated nuclear attacks in Europe if Khrushchev had moved against West Berlin. Finally, while the general conclusion supports the view that nuclear weapons encouraged caution in political leaders during the crisis, consideration is also given to Fidel Castro's attitude. The views of the Cuban leader suggest that differing political beliefs may inform a very different view of fighting nuclear war.

Climax and Resolution

Understanding of events in Washington and Moscow (as well as in Havana) has been significantly revised by historical research over the last two decades. It is clear that by the climax of the crisis, Kennedy secretly undertook to remove the Jupiter IRBMs from Turkey and Italy. In Washington, the first indications that Moscow might be willing to withdraw the missiles from Cuba came on Friday 26 October after Khrushchev gained the agreement of the Presi▨ the following evening to the idea of withdrawing the m▨ Washington agreed not to invade Cuba.[5] Kennedy received a message from Khrushchev that appeared to resonate with an approach made by a KGB officer from the Soviet embassy, suggesting that in return for an American pledge not to invade Cuba, the missiles would be taken out. However, on 27 October, Khrushchev publically sought the withdrawal of 'analogous weapons' from Turkey as part of a deal to remove their missiles from Cuba.[6] Saturday 27 October became known as 'Black Saturday' in Washington. As Kennedy and his advisers wrestled with a diplomatic response to the two messages, they learned that a U-2 had strayed into Soviet air space, and, later, that another U-2 had been shot down over Cuba and the pilot killed. Events were moving quickly, and possibly out of control.

Original accounts of how Soviet demands on the Turkish missiles were handled were drawn from Washington insiders.[7] Most significant was Robert Kennedy's *13 Days*, published in 1969 after his death. This suggested that he had told the Soviet ambassador that, while a deal over the Jupiters was not possible, the President anticipated they would be gone from Turkey within four or five months.[8] The first account to suggest that Robert Kennedy had provided a 'pledge' to withdraw the Jupiters came with Arthur Schlesinger's biography of Robert Kennedy.[9] In 1989, Theodore Sorensen made a 'confession' that he deliberately altered the *13 Days* manuscript to protect a secret assurance to remove the missiles from Turkey.[10] This approach had been worked out by the President with a group of six close advisers. A letter was drafted to Khrushchev which replied to the personal letter of 26 October rather than the public letter of 27 October (with its inclusion of Turkey).[11] The key point was that Kennedy agreed to lift the blockade and provide assurances against an invasion, in return for removal of 'weapons systems from Cuba under appropriate United Nations observation and supervision'.[12] Robert Kennedy was tasked with conveying both the letter and the assurance to Ambassador Dobrynin. Testimony from surviving ExCommites corroborated Sorensen's revelation that Robert Kennedy told the ambassador that the missiles would be removed from Turkey providing knowledge of the undertaking was kept secret.[13] Evidence from Soviet records now includes the telegram Dobrynin sent back to Moscow explaining what Robert Kennedy had said to him.[14] Dobrynin's recollections also accord with the Soviet archival record.[15]

The precise language used by Robert Kennedy, and the exact meaning of the messages passed to Moscow by Dobrynin, have attracted great interest. ExCommites involved in preparing the secret approach believed that it helped persuade Khrushchev to back down. Bundy believed that while the assurance on the Turkish withdrawal was useful, it was 'far less important than the stick that Robert Kennedy carried to Dobrynin: a threat of further action within days'.[16] Dobrynin reported that the Attorney-General had indeed said that the US government was determined to get rid of the bases even 'up to, in the extreme case, of bombing them'.[17] Having outlined the Turkish assurance, Robert Kennedy 'requested' a reply by the following day, while emphasizing that, 'it is just that – a request, and not an ultimatum'.[18] Dobrynin was careful to convey back to Moscow that the Americans were not presenting an ultimatum. In the record of the conversation the Attorney-General provided for Dean Rusk, the exchange is rather different: 'I said those missile bases had to go and they had to go right away. We had to have a commitment by at least tomorrow that those bases would be removed. This was not an ultimatum, I said, but just a statement of fact.'[19] Interpretation of this raises interesting questions about what an ultimatum is.[20] Certainly, one conclusion is that an effective way of delivering an ultimatum is to explain that it is not an ultimatum. Equally, an effective way of dealing with an ultimatum is not to accept it as one.

However, by the time word reached Khrushchev of Dobrynin's encounter, events had moved on. On the morning of Sunday 28 October, Khrushchev received Kennedy's letter. He was also told that a White House proposal to resolve the crisis had been received by the KGB *Resident* in Washington, Aleksandr Feklisov, from an American journalist, John Scali.[21] Much more worrying was the news that a U-2 had been shot down over Cuba. And, in addition, a message had also arrived from Castro (discussed below) which appeared to advocate pre-emptive nuclear attack on the United States. Fursenko and Naftali record that, at noon, Khrushchev assembled the Presidium at a government *dacha* outside Moscow. Invoking Lenin's signing of the Brest-Litovsk Pact with Germany in 1918, he told them that they faced

> the danger of war and of nuclear catastrophe, with the possible result of destroying the human race. In order to save the world, we must retreat. I called you together to consult and debate whether you are in agreement with this kind of decision.[22]

There are no indications of dissent from Khrushchev's proposal. Then, as the Presidium discussed terms to end the crisis, a telephone call relayed Dobrynin's report of his meeting with Robert Kennedy. It is clear that Khrushchev had decided to retreat because of his concern that events might spiral out of control, and on the basis of assurances as regards Cuba's security in Kennedy's letter. One counterfactual therefore seems clear: if Kennedy had not undertaken to withdraw the missiles from Turkey, Khrushchev would still have withdrawn the missiles from Cuba.

While Kennedy's assurance on the Jupiters may not be as significant for the outcome of the crisis as first thought, it nevertheless indicates Kennedy's determination to resolve the crisis by diplomatic means. The missiles in Turkey and Italy had been deployed under NATO auspices, and yet Kennedy was anxious that NATO did not learn of what had happened. Robert Kennedy told Dobrynin that a public announcement of a withdrawal from Turkey would 'tear apart NATO'.[23] Keeping the secret from his European allies squared the circle of diplomatic accommodation and alliance cohesion, though in many European eyes it would have been seen to sacrifice European security in pursuit of American regional interests. Interestingly, Khrushchev kept his part of the bargain and did not disclose the Turkish assurance, even though to do so would have created problems within NATO for the American President (assuming European governments accepted the Soviet version of events). This obviously reflected the changed Soviet–American relationship after the crisis.

Curiously, Khrushchev did not disclose the Turkish offer when he published his memoirs in 1970, though an account of Kennedy's assurance was provided in the unexpurgated posthumous edition (by which time the ExCommites had revealed what had occurred).[24] He commented that the missiles in Turkey were in any case obsolete and that the matter was 'primarily of moral significance and had no practical consequences'.[25] In October–November 1962 there was no attempt by the Soviets to pursue greater reciprocity between Turkey and Cuba with a broader interpretation of Khrushchev's phrase 'analogous means'. Originally, McNamara envisaged this would include American nuclear strike aircraft in Turkey. However, neither in the negotiation to remove the Ilyushin-28 bombers from Cuba, nor when the Soviets decided to withdraw all their tactical nuclear weapons, did Moscow attempt to barter.[26]

One important question is what would have happened if Khrushchev had not 'retreated' on 28 October. Would Kennedy have attacked Cuba, as his brother warned Dobrynin? In *13 Days*, Robert Kennedy recounted that on the Saturday, 'The expectation was a military confrontation by Tuesday and possibly tomorrow . . .'[27] David Ormsby-Gore, the British ambassador, and close friend of the President, told the Foreign Office in November that the Americans were preparing to attack on Monday (29 October), though he felt that they would have waited until the Tuesday.[28] Taylor, Nitze and Dillon are clear that an invasion would have taken place. Sorensen, Bundy and McNamara, however, have doubted an attack would have come then, and believed that the President would have tried strengthening the blockade instead, by including petroleum, oil and lubricants (POL).[29] There were also other options. On 26 October, Harold Macmillan offered to link immobilizing the missiles in Cuba with the Thors in the UK (which met with a lukewarm response from the White House).[30]

Kennedy's more probable diplomatic path would have involved the missiles in Turkey. In 1987, Dean Rusk disclosed that the President had instructed him to contact former Deputy UN Secretary-General, Andrew Cordier, to lay the foundations for a public trade on the Jupiters.[31] Rusk dictated a statement to Cordier to be made by the Acting Secretary-General, U Thant, proposing removal of missiles

from both Cuba and Turkey. The statement was to be given to U
Thant after a further signal from the Secretary of State. Rusk recalled
that he contacted Cordier on 27 October, though the timing and
content of 'the Cordier ploy' have been queried.[32] British diplomats at
the UN learned of an approach to Cordier from the Americans by
25 October.[33] So, either there was more than one contact or Rusk's rec-
ollection of the timing was in error. This either calls into doubt the
potential significance of the approach, or suggests that Kennedy
decided to prepare the ground *before* Khrushchev raised it publically.
The latter accords with the fact that Kennedy had made clear his
anxiety over the missiles in Turkey within ExComm in the week
before Black Saturday, and had not discounted a trade that some
of his advisers considered anathema. He told Ormsby-Gore on
21 October, for example, that the missiles in Turkey were 'more or less
worthless', though he did not know whether it was possible 'to do a
deal on the reciprocal closing of bases'.[34]

U Thant was not called upon to propose a trade, though many have
interpreted Kennedy's action as willingness to 'go the extra mile for
peace'. Rusk himself downplayed the significance of his revelation and
believed that it was no more than an option.[35] Contingency plans in
themselves are not proof of intent. By comparison, military preparations for the invasion were at an advanced state of readiness, with a
potential D-Day only a matter of days away. Preparation of a diplomatic option was not conclusive proof that Kennedy would have
embarked on a public trade, which he knew would have damaged the
cohesion and unity of NATO and undermined various US objectives,
including changing NATO nuclear strategy and promoting the US
non-proliferation agenda. Nevertheless, the trajectory of Kennedy's
thinking is clear from the ExComm transcripts: within ExComm on
Saturday, 27 October, Kennedy's attraction to some kind of deal over
the missiles in Turkey is now evident.

All manner of scenarios can be constructed in which diplomacy
fails to resolve the crisis and decisions on the use of force become
necessary. What if Khrushchev had indeed decided to call Kennedy's
bluff and run the blockade, or if mishandling of naval interceptions
had led to armed conflict between Americans and Soviets at sea? What

if Khrushchev had not retreated on 28 October and instead sought protracted diplomatic exchanges? This was indeed the initial fear within ExComm at Adlai Stevenson's suggestion that negotiation on US bases (including Guantánamo) was preferable to risking nuclear war.[36] In hindsight, there seems little reason to believe that Khrushchev would have abandoned *Operation Anadyr* without some form of confrontation. The question of whether Kennedy would have invaded Cuba had a settlement not been reached by 28 October nevertheless remains in dispute. There is certainly the possibility that he would have sanctioned the military action that the United States had prepared for on a very large scale. We do not know whether Kennedy would have gone to war over Cuba. We certainly cannot discount the possibility that he might have done so.

Whence the Threat to Peace?

So how might nuclear war have begun? Discussion here focuses on circumstances in which political leaders might have used nuclear weapons *first*. Consideration is given to both an American *first strike* and to what is here termed Soviet *pre-emptive retaliation*. McNamara subsequently defined a first strike as 'a large nuclear attack intended to destroy the retaliatory forces of the opponent, leaving forces insufficient to inflict substantial damage on the attacker'.[37] Such an attack could be preventive or pre-emptive in nature. Pre-emptive retaliation refers to a Soviet launch in the face of imminent American attack but directed at American cities. The central distinction between first strike and pre-emptive retaliation is that the former aims to reduce or eliminate retaliatory damage. The latter seeks to ensure that retaliation takes place in circumstances where societal annihilation is inevitable and unavoidable. It is an anticipatory 'blow from the grave' delivered en route to the graveyard.

When Kennedy established the blockade he had low expectations that it would succeed in getting the missiles out. Moreover, he believed that there was a strong possibility that it would provoke a Soviet response against Berlin. The hawks were confident that it would not. In his meeting with the Joint Chiefs on 19 October the

President was told by the USAF Chief of Staff, General Le May, that an attack on Cuba would not provoke a reprisal against Berlin, providing it was made clear that the United States would fight over Berlin.[38] Reflecting later, Paul Nitze believed that it would have been 'totally irrational' for the Soviets to move against Berlin, although taking out the Jupiters and Thors would have been 'the most reasonable response for Khrushchev to consider'.[39]

Khrushchev issued his first ultimatum over West Berlin in 1958. In 1961, he again threatened to sign a separate peace treaty with East Germany.[40] At their Vienna Summit in June 1961, impasse on the subject provoked belligerent rhetoric and talk of war.[41] Kennedy reacted by announcing that an additional six divisions would be sent to West Germany which, though it strengthened conventional defences, was not seen within NATO to offset Soviet superiority. Although the construction of the Berlin Wall in August 1961 defused the immediate crisis, Soviet–American tensions remained, and confrontation in October almost led to fighting between Soviet and American troops. In October 1962 the problem of how to respond to a Soviet move on Berlin was, at least, familiar for Kennedy.

Debate remains over whether resolution of the status of West Berlin was a specific objective of Khrushchev in putting the missiles into Cuba. During 1962, Khrushchev made clear his intention to resolve the Berlin issue after the mid-term Congressional elections (by which time the MRBMs would be ready). Certainly Kennedy and Macmillan believed Berlin could well be Khrushchev's aim, and both leaders were concerned that Khrushchev would respond there in the event of American action in the Caribbean. After Kennedy's broadcast on 22 October, the American strategist Bernard Brodie was told by a senior British Foreign Office official that his colleagues 'expected to a man, that the Russians would be in West Berlin the following day'.[42] In the event, the Soviets took no action. There were some in the Soviet Foreign Ministry, including Anatoli Dobrynin and Vasili Kuznetsov, First Deputy Foreign Minister, who argued for action against West Berlin in retaliation for the blockade. Khrushchev peremptorily dismissed the idea when Kuznetsov suggested it.[43] In October 1962, to paraphrase Sherlock Holmes in *The Hound of the Baskervilles*, Berlin was the dog that did not bark in the night.

Nevertheless, the question of what action the Soviet leader might take against Berlin if the Americans attacked the missiles or invaded Cuba exercised the President and divided his advisers. Although Kennedy expected a Soviet response against Berlin to the Cuban blockade, he made no attempt to consult European allies before announcing his decision. Emissaries were despatched to London, Paris, Ottawa and Bonn, and the North Atlantic Council was briefed on 22 October, but there was no consultation on how to react to a Soviet challenge. After the Vienna summit in 1961, Kennedy had given increasing attention to Berlin, and Washington pressed for military contingency planning within NATO. Although Kennedy sought diplomatic options and diplomatic solutions, he allowed the hard-line Dean Acheson a key role in developing military plans.[44] By October 1961, American contingency planning over Berlin envisaged four phases. The first three entailed a graduated Western response from diplomatic and economic measures to mobilization and then military action, including a ground probe down the autobahn. The fourth phase involved the use of tactical nuclear weapons.[45]

The choice between accepting military defeat and using nuclear weapons was apparent. According to Bundy, Acheson told Kennedy 'that he believed the President should himself give that question the most careful and private consideration, well before the time when the choice might present itself, and that he should reach his own clear conclusion in advance as to what he would do, and that he should tell no one at all what that conclusion was.'[46] Bundy also concluded that '. . . I believe nobody ever knew, just what Kennedy himself believed about the decision he would make if conventional battle were ever joined over access to Berlin in such a way that he was required to choose between defeat and the release of nuclear weapons.'[47] Acheson himself had concluded in 1959 that accepting defeat was preferable to starting a nuclear war.[48] He nevertheless emphasized the need for credible tactical nuclear options, and advocated conventional military action if necessary.

Kennedy took a close interest in his nuclear options, and in

October 1961, plans for a nuclear first strike on the Soviet Union were reviewed.[49] The President told Congressional leaders on 22 October 1962 that if the Soviets moved on West Berlin in response to the blockade, existing American planning envisaged the use of nuclear weapons.[50] Yet one of the curious aspects of the Cuban missile crisis was how little discussion there was about using nuclear weapons. Consideration was given in ExComm to civil defence measures, when Kennedy raised the idea of evacuating cities in the south-east (only to be told by his Assistant Secretary of Defense for Civil Defense, Stuart Pittman, that cities provided the only protection from nuclear fallout).[51] Yet McNamara recalls that he did not discuss with Kennedy what to do if there was a nuclear attack from Cuba: '. . . we never discussed it. We should have, but we didn't.'[52]

So would Kennedy have used nuclear weapons over the security of West Berlin, when to do so risked escalation to all-out nuclear war? Recent evidence from British archives seems to provide clues about Kennedy's thinking. In November, Macmillan and his Foreign Secretary, Lord Home, received an answer to the question of whether the Kennedy administration intended to use nuclear weapons over Berlin (whether it was the right answer is considered below). When the missiles were discovered in Cuba, senior British intelligence officials were, coincidentally, visiting Washington, and the CIA provided a confidential briefing on 19 October (several days before Kennedy saw Ormsby-Gore).[53] On 19 November, Macmillan and Home were briefed by one of these officials, Major-General Sir Kenneth Strong, the Director-General of the Joint Intelligence Bureau (JIB). Strong had been Eisenhower's chief intelligence officer for the Normandy landings and had extensive contacts in Washington. The meeting with the Prime Minister took place weeks after the crisis had abated, though before Soviet–American agreement was finalized and the blockade lifted.

Strong reported that Kennedy had concluded that if he invaded or blockaded Cuba the Soviets were likely to react in Berlin. According to the Director-General of the JIB, the Americans 'were prepared to go it alone either without consulting their allies or irrespective of what their allies said *had the Russians reacted* against any action in Cuba by moving against Berlin'.[54] Strong told Macmillan that he thought that Washington was prepared for action in Cuba to 'escalate into the nuclear'. Strong believed that this reflected the fact 'that they had pinpointed the position of all the main sites of intercontinental ballistic missiles in the Soviet Union, and they hoped they would be able to take these out with a pre-emptive attack by their bombers'. For Macmillan and Home, American over-confidence in their ability to strike the Soviet Union was of the 'utmost importance'. Macmillan said he would raise this with the President at their next meeting when he

> . . . would warn him of the dangers that would flow from over-confidence on this score. In the first place they could not know for certain where the ICBM sites were; and if they did it was extremely rash to suppose that with bombers they would be able to get through in sufficient numbers to take out the ICBMs. The situation would of course be different with Polaris and Minuteman.[55]

Whether Strong's account is an accurate representation of Kennedy's thinking is far from clear. There is, for example, evidence that American officials misled Strong about when the MRBMs in Cuba were identified. The US intelligence community was certain that MRBMs were present by 15 October and Kennedy was briefed by the CIA the following morning. Strong was told, however, that it was not until 20 October that Kennedy 'was presented with a great deal more material which was then generally accepted as demonstrating that there were offensive missiles in Cuba'.[56] Strong was briefed by the CIA's Deputy-Director, Ray Cline, on the MRBM deployment, though the provenance of his sources on American nuclear intentions is unclear.

Interestingly, when Kennedy met Ormsby-Gore on 21 October, the President said something to the British ambassador that was so startling that Ormsby-Gore felt he could not report it back to Macmillan by diplomatic telegram. At this most dramatic moment in the Cold War, Ormsby-Gore offered to fly back to London and tell the

Prime Minister in person. The context suggests it could well have involved Kennedy's intentions toward West Berlin, although if Kennedy had confided to Ormsby-Gore on 21 October that he would use nuclear weapons over Berlin, it is by no means certain that this would have reflected his intentions by the following weekend. Could Kennedy have made it clear that he would use nuclear weapons over Berlin? Alternatively – and perhaps more plausibly – would the President have made clear he would *not* use nuclear weapons over Berlin?

Telling the British that America was prepared to commit its nuclear forces to the defence of Berlin may have been intended to reassure them about US resolve. Whether they would have been reassured about the fact that nuclear war would break out in Europe regardless of what America's allies felt, is more open to doubt. Strong's information came weeks before the Skybolt debacle and the ensuing British–American summit at Nassau. The suggestion that America would have fought a nuclear war over Europe without heeding the views of its allies could only have fuelled Macmillan's determination to secure an American nuclear delivery system for the British deterrent, and ensure that British views would be taken into account when nuclear decisions affecting vital British interests were considered.

How would Kennedy have responded to Soviet military action against West Berlin in October 1962? Would he have ordered conventional armed forces down the autobahn knowing they were doomed to fail? At what point would Kennedy have considered using nuclear weapons? And in what form and at what targets? If Kennedy had not responded with force to Soviet military action against West Berlin the political consequences for NATO would have been severe. Article Five of the NATO treaty stated that 'an armed attack against one or more of [the signatories] in Europe or North America shall be considered an attack against them all.'[57] This did not automatically commit the United States to the use of force against the Soviet Union in such circumstances. Yet failure to react would fundamentally weaken the credibility of the American guarantees on which the alliance rested. In 1961, Kennedy had emphasized to de Gaulle that America must strike first with nuclear weapons and that an attack on Europe 'would be physically and automatically an attack on us'.[58] Even as he made these assurances he sought to shift NATO strategy towards more effective conventional defence and away from a strategy that could leave him with the choice between suicide and surrender. Robert McNamara recounts that he had recommended 'without qualification' to President Kennedy (and later to President Johnson) that they would 'never initiate, under any circumstances, the use of nuclear weapons'. [59] McNamara believed that both men accepted his recommendation. The potential implications of this claim, both for the Berlin question, and for NATO strategy as a whole, were enormous.

One further scenario that exercised ExComm was Soviet retaliation against Turkey in the event of American action against missiles in Cuba. As noted, Paul Nitze believed that an attack on European IRBMs was 'the most reasonable response' for Khrushchev,[60] and within ExComm there was discussion about a Soviet attack on Turkey. On 22 October, Kennedy insisted on measures to prevent the launch of the Jupiters in the event of a Soviet attack, and on 27 October, there was discussion on how to deal with the threat of a Soviet attack, when McNamara implied that the use of Soviet nuclear weapons in an attack on Turkey might be ridden out, without American retaliation. This is discussed further in Chapters 4 and 5.

The Third Scorpion

If the Soviets had moved on West Berlin, conflict had ensued, and the United States *not* used nuclear weapons, what would the British have done? While many Europeans expressed doubts about the American nuclear commitment, there were also some who saw a British deterrent as a means of engaging the Americans in nuclear hostilities. In his famous speech of June 1962 McNamara had inveighed against 'small' nuclear forces as 'dangerous, expensive, prone to obsolescence and lacking in credibility as a deterrent'.[61] Although he later denied he was referring to RAF Bomber Command,[62] the suggestion that national deterrents were dangerous reflected his desire to develop a strategy based on counter-force targeting and controlled escalation. Yet McNamara's concerns had good foundations. Indeed, Harold

Macmillan himself once remarked, 'The h-bomb is not important in the defense of Britain. We would never use it first. It is important that in case of a Russian attack we can trigger the American nuclear deterrent in our own defense.'[63]

With the exception of Scott Sagan, American scholars have shown little interest in British nuclear forces.[64] Nor have those working on the Soviet side explored how Moscow viewed British nuclear capabilities. Yet, by 1962, the RAF could probably target as many nuclear weapons on the USSR as the Soviets could target on the USA. The circumstances in which British nuclear forces might have been used in October 1962 is of potential interest not only to students of British nuclear history and in debates about the British national deterrent, but also to what might have happened had the nuclear threshold been crossed (explored in Chapter 5).

In his authoritative account of Macmillan and Kennedy's relationship, Nigel Ashton argues that Macmillan advocated invasion of Cuba to prevent Khrushchev trading Cuba for West Berlin.[65] Yet the Prime Minister's initial responses to Kennedy were more ambiguous, and reflected his vexation at not having been consulted on the blockade, whose value he doubted (and which the British government's legal officers later told him was illegal in international law).[66] If Macmillan's immediate response was hawkish, then, like Kennedy, his subsequent flight path was that of a dove. As the Cuban crisis reached its climax Kennedy specifically consulted Macmillan over the telephone on whether he should invade Cuba. Macmillan described this as the $64,000 question and counselled diplomacy.[67] Ornithologically, he was also, at times, a magpie, keen to steal for himself a potentially historic role at the world summit he advocated. Yet beyond his undoubted political calculations lay genuine concern. As his grandson later recalled, 'as an old man he only had nightmares about two things: the trenches in the Great War and what would have happened if the Cuban missile crisis had gone wrong'.[68] Macmillan understood what thermo-nuclear attacks on Britain would mean. He was Minister of Defence in 1955 when Whitehall studied the effects of thermo-nuclear attacks on Britain. The Strath Report estimated that ten ground-bursting H-bombs would kill twelve million people, seriously injure a further four million others and leave thirteen million trapped in their homes.[69] By the time he was Prime Minister in 1960, civil defence planners were working on estimates based on attacks from 159 three-megaton weapons on 87 targets leaving $21^1/_2$ million dead and four million seriously injured.[70]

If an American attack on Cuba had triggered Soviet military action against West Berlin, and if Kennedy had decided against nuclear escalation, what would the British have done? Was the security of West Berlin a greater national interest for the UK than for the US? Would the British government have risked national annihilation for a city that seventeen years earlier the RAF had sought to pound into rubble? Assuming that the British did not see a move on West Berlin as a step towards a Soviet conventional assault on Western Europe, it is difficult to see a British nuclear response as more credible than an American one. On the contrary. The British Chiefs of Staff were much less inclined to use force than the American Joint Chiefs. Fundamental differences persisted over contingency planning for the defence of West Berlin, and the British Chiefs of Staff were strongly opposed to the suggestion that NATO should respond over Berlin with a ground probe in the face of Soviet conventional superiority. They described the idea as 'useless',[71] and during the Cuban crisis wanted the Prime Minister to intervene with the President to restrain General Norstad, the SACEUR. On Sunday 28th October, the Chiefs of Staff made clear to the Defence Secretary, Peter Thorneycroft, and the Chief of Defence Staff, Earl Mountbatten, that such action would be 'foolish'.[72] Mountbatten himself was clearly convinced that there were no circumstances in which nuclear weapons should be used first, and he made this clear to McNamara.[73] Like McNamara, he later became a prominent critic of NATO nuclear strategy, as well as an opponent of an independent British deterrent.

Firing First

No evidence has emerged to suggest that the United States government gave active consideration to initiating a nuclear attack on the Soviet Union in October 1962. Nor is there any evidence that the

Soviets did likewise. US contingency plans for both disarming and all-out first strikes existed in SIOP-63. American nuclear forces were placed on higher states of alert: strategic bombers were dispersed, SAC's B-52 fleet mounted an airborne alert, ICBMs were readied, and Polaris submarines were flushed from their ports on both sides of the Atlantic. Yet none of these activities demonstrated that the President of the United States seriously considered launching a nuclear attack. Nevertheless, the question arises as to whether there were circumstances in which he might have done so. In exploring these scenarios it is helpful to distinguish between preventive and pre-emptive attack. The Pentagon defines pre-emption as 'an attack initiated on the basis of incontrovertible evidence that an enemy attack is imminent'.[74] Preventive war is 'initiated in the belief that military conflict, while not imminent, is inevitable, and that to delay would involve greater risk'.[75]

The doctrine of pre-emption was first articulated by US Secretary of State Webster in 1842 in a formulation that has become the accepted definition in international law. According to Webster, pre-emption involved 'a necessity of self-defense . . . instant, overwhelming, leaving no choice of means, and no moment for deliberation'.[76] If an adversary was about to attack there was justification in striking first. Pre-emption has long been an integral element in warfare. It could also be seen as legally and morally justifiable as a form of 'anticipatory self-defence'. Whereas there is a basis in international law to justify pre-emptive action as 'anticipatory self-defence', preventive war is different. Certainly, from the victim's point of view, preventive war is synonymous with aggression. Japan's attack on Pearl Harbor, for example, could be conceived as a preventive attack (to prevent economic disaster caused by US sanctions), though for Americans it was the most infamous act of aggression in their history.

In the 1950s, there were those in Washington who were attracted to the idea of preventive war against the Soviet Union, although this was explicitly rejected in NSC-68 and by Eisenhower personally. Several prominent air force officers, including the first two commanders of SAC, Curtis Le May and Thomas Power, nevertheless expressed sympathy with the idea.[77] Senior British officials were indeed concerned at the prospect of American preventive war, not least because attacks on the Soviet Union from British bases could lead to Soviet attacks on the UK.[78] There is no suggestion that the Kennedy administration gave any consideration to preventive war against the Soviet Union, although Robert Kennedy records that one of the Joint Chiefs – most probably Le May – expressed support for 'preventive war' against the Soviet Union.[79] In October 1962, the Commander-in-Chief of SAC (CINCSAC), General Thomas Power, was reportedly furious at the cowardice of President Kennedy in missing the opportunity to wage nuclear war on the Soviet Union.[80]

There is evidence, though, that Kennedy himself gave serious thought to preventive attacks on China's nuclear weapons facilities in the early 1960s.[81] Both the CIA and the Pentagon explored covert action and paramilitary options, and the Joint Chiefs examined a range of direct options, including the idea of using tactical nuclear weapons.[82] Kennedy was concerned at the prospect of Beijing acquiring nuclear weapons and believed that China would emerge as the main threat to US interests by the end of the decade. The Kennedy administration sounded out the Soviets about possible joint action, but they were unreceptive. Ironically, when the Soviets sounded out the Nixon administration on preventive war against China in 1969 it was the Americans who showed no interest.[83]

The United States government did give active consideration to an attack on the Soviet missiles in Cuba (when the analogy of Pearl Harbor exercised a powerful influence). As we have seen, Kennedy's initial reaction on 16 October favoured a military response. Whether American officials saw an attack on the missiles as preventive or pre-emptive is less clear. In some ExComm discussions, officials behaved as though they were considering pre-emptive rather preventive measures, although McNamara believed that the prospect of retaliation meant that an attack could only come before the missiles were operational. For the Soviets and Cubans (and much of world opinion) an American air strike would, of course, have been an act of aggression. Nevertheless, it is worth noting that all the discussions concerned conventional air attacks (including both high explosives and napalm). There was no consideration that nuclear weapons would be used.

Pre-emption

Was there a possibility that either side in 1962 would consider nuclear pre-emption? The most plausible scenarios for this were in circumstances in which the Soviets believed the United States intended to destroy their strategic arsenal and where they might consider using, rather than losing, their strategic forces. And at one point in the crisis this possibility became a matter of active concern. The Soviet General Staff was inevitably anxious about an American first strike, given the size and vulnerability of their strategic forces.[84] From what can be understood of Soviet military doctrine in the 1950s and 1960s there was an explicit emphasis on the need for pre-emption or *uprezhdaiushchyi* (forestalling).[85] The assumption was that strategic- and intermediate-range forces would be used in the first hours of nuclear combat.[86]

One incident in the crisis did indeed raise the prospect of nuclear pre-emption in the minds of decision-makers. On the night of 26/27 October, a SAC U-2, on a scheduled high-altitude air-sampling mission, strayed off course and over the Chukotski Peninsula, inside Soviet airspace. The planned route of the aircraft precluded compass navigation, and the aurora borealis prevented the pilot, Major Maultsby, from using celestial navigation to plot his course.[87] The straying U-2 has been known about for many years. Roger Hilsman described it in his 1964 book as 'the "Strangelove" incident'.[88] When news that the plane had flown into Soviet airspace reached the Pentagon there was immediate concern that the Soviets might misinterpret events and assume the aircraft was on pre-strike reconnaissance. There is indeed evidence that the Soviet General Staff advised Khrushchev that the U-2 might be on such a mission.[89] According to Oleg Troyanovsky, the incident was the tensest moment of the crisis for the Soviet leader.[90] Khrushchev was greatly agitated by the incident and afterwards, in his letter of 28 October to Kennedy (when he announced the withdrawal of the missiles from Cuba), he complained that the intruding aircraft could have been mistaken for a nuclear bomber which 'could push us toward a fatal step'.[91]

There was concern in Washington that the Soviets might believe the U-2 was on a mission to identify mobile Soviet targets ahead of an American nuclear strike. Scott Sagan explains that there was indeed provision within the SIOP for such missions *once the decision to launch* the ICBMs had been taken (though there was no reason to believe Soviet intelligence would have known this sequence).[92] Under circumstances in which the Soviets believed their small force of ICBMs was coming under attack, the Soviet General Staff might have perceived a 'use them or lose them' dilemma, in the face of what they believed was an American attempt to disarm the Soviet Union. There is no evidence that the Soviet military advocated such action, nor what options Khrushchev considered. American intelligence believed that the Soviets did not alert their nuclear forces during the crisis. However, according to Steven Zaloga:

> While the crisis was brewing in Cuba, the Soviet Union's nascent strategic forces were placed on high alert for the first time in their history. The strategic bomber divisions began to move from their bases to their forward-staging bases, and they were armed with free-fall bombs. The R7A launchers at Plesetsk were readied and their flight control systems wired for strikes against New York, Washington, Chicago and other major cities. At the time of the Cuban missile crisis, two R-9 missiles were made operational at the Tyuratom proving ground. Several of the R-16 launch sites were also readied for launch.[93]

There is evidence that R-16 ICBMs were at one point made combat ready (with warheads mated to missiles), though there is insufficient evidence to link this with the U-2 episode.[94]

When news of the U-2's flight into Soviet airspace reached McNamara, it is claimed that he, 'turned absolutely white, and yelled hysterically, "This means war with the Soviet Union. The President must get on the hot line [sic] to Moscow,"' before running out of the meeting 'in a frenzy' (though it should be noted that accounts of McNamara's behaviour emanating from American military sources often depict him in derogatory terms).[95] Perhaps equally significantly, if the Americans believed the Soviets were about to attack, they themselves would surely have considered their own pre-emptive action. In these circumstances, Soviet misperception of an American first strike could have become a self-fulfilling prophecy. The United States possessed massive strategic superiority, and air force generals were confident that they could achieve a decisive outcome, although no evidence has emerged that this option was considered at the political or the military level.

In the National Security Council in July 1961, Kennedy had recognized that 'the critical point is to be able to use nuclear weapons at a critical moment before they use them'.[96] It was crucial to take this decision 'without letting the enemy know that we are about to do it'. When he had asked the Joint Chiefs whether it would be possible to eliminate the Soviet ability to retaliate, they had made it clear that the Soviets would be able to strike back hard.[97] By September 1961, the United States intelligence community downwardly revised its estimate of Soviet ICBM strength. Assessments of a first-strike option were reviewed during the Berlin crisis, and in 1962 Kennedy wanted to know the mechanics by which he would order a first strike. The question of whether Kennedy would have considered pre-emption in circumstances in which he was convinced a Soviet attack was imminent is an important one. In September 1961, General Power, had advised the President that, 'if a general atomic war is inevitable, the United States should strike first.'[98]

Crucial to any such calculation was how certain the Americans could be that the Soviets were preparing for war. At this stage in the Cold War, the ability of Western intelligence to provide real-time warning was minimal. Almost certainly, the first warning intelligence would have come when Soviet bombers and/or missiles began appearing on Western radar screens. If the bombers were launched at the same time as the ICBMs, warning would have come too late to do anything about the missiles, though American and NATO air defences would have mobilized against the Soviet air force.

On the Blink[99]

The work of Scott Sagan has generated understanding of other command and control failures that raised 'pre-emptive scenarios', in particular those involving the improvised early warning systems put in place to detect an attack by the MRBMs in Cuba. The ad hoc arrangements became known as the Cuban Missile Early Warning System (CMEWS), code-named Operation Falling Leaves.[100] This consisted of training radars, space-tracking stations and modified air defence radars. Several incidents involving CMEWS briefly raised the prospect that the United States was coming under nuclear attack. On the afternoon of 26 October a Titan II ICBM was test-fired into the South Atlantic. The radar crews at Moorestown base in New Jersey knew nothing of this event until they monitored a ballistic missile moving across their radar screens.[101] It was soon clear that the missile was heading away from the United States.

A more alarming incident occurred two days later. On the morning of Sunday, 28 October, the Moorestown base detected a ballistic missile launched from Cuba at the United States.[102] The headquarters of the North American Air Defence (NORAD) were immediately told that a missile was flying over Florida and would impact shortly after 9 a.m., near the city of Tampa. President Kennedy was not informed of the imminent missile attack, and shortly afterwards, the NORAD command centre was told that a nuclear detonation had not occurred on American territory. A few minutes later, they learned what had actually happened: a test tape of a simulated missile launch had inadvertently been inserted into the equipment at Moorestown and interpreted as a real attack. In his speech of 22 October, Kennedy had warned that 'any missile launched from Cuba' would meet with 'a full retaliatory response'. Was there a risk that inserting the wrong tape in a machine could have triggered Armageddon? The answer is almost certainly no. The United States did not have a 'launch on warning' policy, and McNamara was clear that before any retaliation was ordered, he and the President needed to be certain of what had happened. One report of one incoming missile attack on Florida would not have caused Kennedy to launch a nuclear attack on the

Soviet Union, although it might have contributed to tension in Washington as the President awaited Khrushchev's response to his latest messages.

A different kind of problem was generated at Vandenberg Air Force Base where nine Atlas ICBMs were loaded with their warheads, but where the missile testing programme continued.[103] At 4 p.m. on 26 October an Atlas ICBM was tested. Sagan speculates that if the Soviets were aware that the other ICBMs had been armed they might have assumed the launch was for real. Again nothing is known of Soviet base-watching capabilities and whether the Soviets could have detected the preparations. Would they have considered launching their own forces on warning of a single attack? Whether they could even consider launching their ICBMs on warning would have depended on whether their missiles were already combat-ready. No indications have emerged that the Soviets were aware of the circumstances Sagan describes. As with the false warning of the MRBM attack on Florida on 28 October, if the Soviets had become aware of the false attack warning, it would have heightened tension. Coming as it did on 26 October, it would more likely have fuelled the Soviet leadership's search for an urgent diplomatic settlement than have started a war.

Nuclear Martyrs?

The Cuban missile crisis did not reach the stage where active consideration was given to fighting a nuclear war. Any conclusions about how nuclear weapons inform crisis decision-making must therefore be tempered with circumspection. Bundy's argument that nuclear weapons induced caution in Kennedy and Khrushchev is nevertheless supported by the evidence that has emerged about the denouement of the crisis. Yet the missile crisis provides grounds to challenge the assumption that when political leaders understand the consequences of nuclear war, they will always draw back from the brink. There is evidence that some were willing to wage nuclear war in 1962, regardless of the consequences for themselves, their country and humanity as a whole. Specifically, as the crisis was reaching its climax on

26 October, Fidel Castro appeared in the early hours of the morning at the Soviet embassy in Havana. After consuming an unspecified number of beers and sausages, Castro set about composing a message to Khrushchev, with the help of the Soviet ambassador, Aleksandr Alekseev, who quickly warned Moscow of Castro's message, but explained that he was unclear about his precise meaning and whether Castro was advocating a pre-emptive nuclear attack on the United States.[104] This lack of clarity was fuelled by the absence of an interpreter. Castro's message to Khrushchev declared that:

> If . . . the imperialists invade Cuba with the goal of occupying it, the danger that the aggressive policy poses for humanity is so great that following that event the Soviet Union must never allow the circumstances in which the imperialists could launch the first nuclear strike against it.
>
> I tell you this because I believe that the imperialists' aggressiveness is extremely dangerous and if they carry out the brutal act of invading Cuba in violation of international law and morality, that would be the moment to eliminate such danger forever through an act of clear legitimate defense, however harsh and terrible the solution would be, for there is no other.[105]

Castro's message to Khrushchev reflected his assessment that Cuba was about to be attacked and the Cuban revolution destroyed. The Cubans had prepared for an American attack on a continuing basis after April 1961. So when the party daily, *Revolución*, declared on 23 October that 'The Cuban People Are Prepared to Die for their Independence', the indications are that this demonstrated the national mood and popular will.[106]

Khrushchev interpreted Castro's message as a call for a pre-emptive nuclear attack on the United States. He later described Castro as 'a very hot tempered person [who] failed to think through the obvious consequences of a proposal that placed the planet on the brink of extinction'.[107] Khrushchev's reply to Castro on 30 October 1962 described the proposal as 'incorrect', adding that 'we are not struggling against imperialism in order to die'.[108] Whether Castro advocated nuclear pre-emption depends on what is meant by nuclear pre-emption. In a terse exchange of letters after the crisis, Castro stated that Khrushchev had misinterpreted his message, and he described the idea that the USSR should be the aggressor as 'immoral and contemptible'.[109] Thirty years later, at the Havana conference with McNamara and other veterans of the crisis, Castro clarified his remarks. Saying that his message was intended to bolster Khrushchev, he explained that in circumstances in which nuclear weapons were already being used in and from Cuba, he was concerned that the Soviets should not allow their strategic forces to be destroyed, and what he called at the time, the 'perfidy of the imperialists', allowed to prevail.[110]

Moreover, Castro said, if he had had control of the Soviet tactical nuclear weapons he would have used them against an American invasion, even if this brought nuclear retaliation on Cuba:

> Before having the country occupied – totally occupied – we were ready to die in the defence of our country. I would have agreed, in the event of the invasion that you are talking about, with the use of tactical nuclear weapons . . . I wish we had had the tactical nuclear weapons. It would have been wonderful. We wouldn't have rushed to use them, you can be sure of that. The closer to Cuba the decision of using a weapon effective against a landing, the better. Of course, after we had used ours, they would have replied with, say, 400 tactical weapons – we don't know how many would have been fired at us. In any case we were resigned to our fate.[111]

How should we interpret this posture? Blight, Allyn and Welch argue that the Cubans in the 'moment of deepest peril, were fully prepared to martyr themselves for socialism'.[112] Faced with the choice between 'annihilation with dignity', and 'annihilation with ignominy', Castro would choose the former.[113] In October 1986, the British Labour leader, Neil Kinnock, told his party conference: 'I would fight and die for my country. But . . . I would never let my country die for me.'[114] Castro was also prepared to fight and die, but was willing to allow his country to die for him, or at least for his revolution. The implications of Castro's attitude for notions of rational deterrence are, nevertheless, potentially very significant. Deterrence may simply not work for those who hold fundamentally different conceptions of death, honour, and the glory of their cause. Concepts of martyrdom are now more readily understood in the West after September 11. The realization that we may face enemies who actively seek their own death, as well as inflict casualties on a colossal scale, undermines key tenets of deterrence thinking. The suggestion that in the era of post-modernity we need to comprehend the values of pre-modernity poses radical challenges for the application of reason to the use and threatened use of force.

Nevertheless, the suggestion that Castro's attitudes represent a radical departure from 'rational' Western conceptions of deterrence needs closer scrutiny. During the Cold War, military organizations in all nuclear weapons states looked to nuclear weapons as they looked to other munitions. Nuclear weapons may have been integrated into sophisticated conceptual frameworks at the policy level, but those who operated, trained and prepared to fire them, saw them as weapons to use in war. For the American armed forces, a primary purpose of tactical nuclear forces was to help defeat the armies of the Warsaw Pact and protect the 250,000 troops deployed in Western Europe. For most soldiers, sailors and aircrews, using nuclear weapons would have simply meant obeying orders, and for many, it would have accorded with concepts of military duty and honour.

Had, for whatever reason, the Warsaw Pact launched an offensive across the central German plains at this time, the headline in *Der Spiegel* might not have read, 'The West German People Are Prepared to Die for their Independence', and Konrad Adenauer might not have turned up in the early hours for beer and sausages with General Norstad, but NATO leaders would have faced comparable situations to that which Castro contemplated. European leaders had differing perspectives on when, and how, the United States should attack the Soviet Union with nuclear weapons.[115] There were certainly those who were anxious for 'early first use' of US strategic nuclear forces as the best guarantor of Western European security. Yet NATO looked to tactical nuclear weapons in similar fashion to how Castro saw them. Field-Marshal Viscount Montgomery publicly declared in 1954:

> I want to make it absolutely clear that we at SHAPE [Supreme Headquarters Allied Powers Europe] are basing all our operational planning on using atomic and thermonuclear weapons in our defence. With us it is no longer 'they may be possibly be used,' it is very definitely 'they will be used, if we are attacked.'[116]

In 1957, Adenauer himself had publicly spoken of tactical nuclear weapons as 'basically nothing but the further development of artillery . . . It goes without saying that . . . we cannot forgo these weapons for our troops . . . they are after all practically normal weapons.'[117] A NATO exercise, Carte Blanche, conducted in 1955, was successful in defeating a Soviet attack without recourse to American strategic nuclear weapons, but the 355 nuclear weapons 'used' in the exercise were estimated to have killed 1.7 million Germans and wounded a further 3.5 million (figures which did not include casualties from fallout).[118] The view that tactical nuclear weapons could offset Soviet conventional superiority without recourse to strategic nuclear attacks was viewed by some as a solution to NATO's central security problem.[119] Thus Castro's views on the efficacy of tactical nuclear weapons accorded with thinking and opinion in both NATO and the Soviet Union. There were, of course, important differences between Cuba and NATO Europe. There were also differences between developing strategies and executing them. But before condemning the Cubans for irrational or suicidal beliefs, it is important to acknowledge the parallels with Western European security in the nuclear age, and the reliance placed on using nuclear weapons in the event of conventional war.

Conclusion

The prospect of nuclear war in October 1962 arose when the Soviets sent nuclear missiles to Cuba and the Americans acted to remove them. It receded as the missiles were withdrawn. Scrutiny of how the crisis was resolved suggests that fear of inadvertent escalation to nuclear war increasingly exercised Kennedy and Khrushchev and informed their willingness to reach an accommodation. Contrary to the new received wisdom, however, while the withdrawal of Jupiter IRBMs from Turkey may have contributed to the general mood of Soviet–American relations, it was not crucial to the outcome. Khrushchev had already decided to retreat. The Jupiter 'pledge' was nevertheless an indicator of Kennedy's determination to avoid conflict if he could. What if he could not? Were there circumstances in which he – or Khrushchev – would have initiated nuclear war? Circumstances in which it would have been in any sense rational for political leaders to authorize the use of nuclear weapons are hard to discern (though not impossible). Both leaders understood the reality of nuclear war and both understood that the risk of retaliation was too great to contemplate.

The strategic contexts nevertheless differed for the two main protagonists. There remains dispute about the extent to which the United States could deliver a first strike. Yet for American decision-makers the risk of retaliation from the USSR could not be removed (and the risk of Soviet retaliation against Europe was assured). For the Soviets, striking first was only 'rational' as an anticipatory 'blow from the grave', where the destruction of the Soviet Union was already assured. Yet as we have seen there were episodes, in particular the flight of Major Maultsby's U-2, which generated such possibilities in the minds of political leaders. Kennedy's quip, 'There's always some son of a bitch who doesn't get the message', belied his concern that Khrushchev might 'speculate that we were surveying targets for a pre-emptive nuclear strike'.[120]

Writing in 1988, McGeorge Bundy reflected that, 'On balance, the prudence of both Kennedy and Khrushchev after the issue was publicly joined on October 22 is more impressive than the danger of unpredicted or uncontrolled episodes.'[121] In Bundy's view, prudence was generated by fear of escalation, and realization that any nuclear exchange would entail unacceptable devastation. One specific theme in Bundy's reflections was that Kennedy was deterred from nuclear attack on the USSR by the potential loss of only one or two American cities. Kennedy himself remarked to his advisers shortly after the crisis that 'even what they had in Cuba alone would have been a substantial deterrent to me'.[122] The idea that Kennedy would have initiated nuclear attacks on the Soviet Union (or initiate a nuclear war that would have escalated to attacks on the Soviet Union) seems inherently unlikely. Yet there were circumstances in which the 'rational' use of nuclear weapons was not quite so unthinkable. Moreover, Bundy's survey of nuclear history, *Danger and Survival*, was published as research into the operational aspects of the crisis was gathering momentum. While Bundy alluded to the straying U-2, his reflections took little account of the emerging work on the operational level that led like-minded ExCommites, notably McNamara, to suggest that the risk of inadvertent nuclear war was greater than assumed. It is to that risk that we now turn.

CHAPTER 4

Hawks, Doves and Owls:
Bickering Inhabitants of the
Nuclear Aviary

Hawks see the proximate cause of war as one-sided weakness –
weakness that tempts an aggressive adversary to exploit
advantage . . . For Doves the primary cause of war lies in arms
races that become provocative and undermine deterrence . . .
Beyond the frame of reference shared by Hawks and Doves lies a
different set of concerns, one focused primarily on loss of
control and nonrational factors in history. In this view, a major
war would not arise from careful calculations but from organisational routines, malfunctions of machines or of minds,
misperceptions, misunderstandings, and mistakes. Those who
see the problem this way we call Owls.

Graham Allison, Albert Carnesale and Joseph Nye.[1]

For a generation of Western leaders, the lessons of Munich were
ingrained. Appeasement encouraged aggression. Strength and resolve
prevented aggression. John F. Kennedy had published his undergrad-
uate thesis on Munich under the title, *Why England* [sic] *Slept.*[2] For
Americans, the experience of surprise attack at Pearl Harbor fuelled
concern about surprise attack in the nuclear age. Another historical
analogy, however, pointed to a different path to war. As Robert
Kennedy explains, his brother read Barbara Tuchman's account of the
coming of the Great War in 1914 not long before the missile crisis,

and was determined to avoid stumbling into war in the way European leaders had done.[3] In the 1980s, academic attention focused on the risk of inadvertent nuclear war, and considerable evidence began to emerge about the operational level of the crisis, in particular concerning the command and control of nuclear weapons. It should be emphasized that nuclear command and control remains one of the more secret aspects of Cold War history, and understanding of procedures and technologies remains constrained. Nevertheless, previously unknown events and unrecognized circumstances have strengthened the case for believing the risk of inadvertent nuclear war was greater than assumed. This chapter examines how the nuclear threshold might have been crossed as a result of actions or events beyond the control of political leaders in scenarios involving subordinate actors as well as accidents and third parties.

Before exploring specific scenarios, it is necessary to acknowledge a temptation to exaggerate the risk of inadvertence. In *Dr Strangelove*, President Muffley describes the base commander who has just despatched his nuclear bombers to attack the Soviet Union as 'a psychotic'. General Turgidson responds, 'I'd hold off on a judgement like that until all the facts are in.' The risk of rushing to judgement is compounded where information is restricted by the demands of secrecy. In some cases, initial interpretations suggested that the risk of inadvertence was greater than later research demonstrated. Some assessments may have exaggerated or misinterpreted the risks. In 1985, for example, it became known that when SAC moved to DEFCON-2, the CINCSAC, General Power, decided to issue the change in DEFCON alert state *en clair*.[4] It was suggested that the aim was to intimidate the Soviets, in what Raymond Garthoff described as a 'remarkable display of American power'.[5] However, subsequent research indicated that changes to the DEFCON alert states were transmitted *en clair* as a matter of routine. Furthermore, General Power broadcast a message to his bomber crews, including those flying toward their 'Fail Safe' points, advising that if in doubt about what to do, they should phone home: 'If you are not sure what you should do in any situation, and if time permits, get in touch with us here.'[6] As Sagan observes, the aim appears to have been to 'encourage subordinate commanders to place priority on "calm judgement" and the prevention of mistakes in the crisis'. Whether the Soviets would have found reassurance in a message sent to bombers flying toward the Soviet Union with their multi-megaton bomb loads, advising consultation 'if time permits' is another matter. According to Fursenko and Naftali, the GRU in the Washington embassy intercepted SAC's change in DEFCON alert state on 24 October.[7] The move to DEFCON-2 was unprecedented (and unrepeated), and therefore something the GRU and the Soviet General Staff had never encountered before. Nevertheless, initial interpretations of SAC's communications appear to have been exaggerated.

A more significant illustration of where initial interpretations exaggerated the risk of inadvertence concerns revelations at the 1992 Havana conference. General Anatoli Gribkov, a former Soviet General Staff officer intimately involved in planning *Operation Anadyr*, and who represented the General Staff in Cuba during October 1962, revealed that the Soviets had deployed tactical nuclear weapons in Cuba.[8] These were intended for use against an American invasion. Although the Ilyushin-28 bombers, and Meteor and Luna missiles were spotted by US photoreconnaissance, the US intelligence community was unaware that nuclear warheads for these weapons had been delivered to Cuba. Furthermore, Gribkov explained, the commander of the Group of Soviet Forces in Cuba, General Pliyev, had been given authority by Khrushchev to use the tactical weapons in the event of an American invasion.[9] The potential implications of these revelations were dramatic. In the event of an invasion it was assumed that Pliyev would have used nuclear weapons, and that the Americans would have retaliated with their nuclear forces. The risk of nuclear war during the crisis, Robert McNamara argued, was 'far greater than any of us imagined at the time' because 'we would never have suspected' that 'Soviet commanders in Cuba had the authority to use their short-range nuclear weapons'.[10] The revelations sparked robust debate, in particular about reliance on uncorroborated testimony from former Soviet officials.[11] Subsequently, archival research clarified what happened, and Gribkov himself published an account that revised some of his earlier claims.[12]

Gribkov's statements that nuclear warheads for the tactical weapons had arrived in Cuba have been corroborated.[13] Some of the figures he gave were inaccurate and he incorrectly stated that there were no nuclear bombs for the Ilyushin-28s.[14] Most importantly, however, Gribkov's declarations about the delegation of nuclear release authority were misleading. Subsequently, in his co-authored book with General William Smith, Gribkov explained that Khrushchev personally told General Pliyev that he would have authority to use the tactical weapons in the event of an invasion, if communication with Moscow had broken down.[15] A draft order to this effect was prepared, though Defence Minister Malinovsky decided not to issue it.[16] On 22 October, shortly before Kennedy's televised address, the Presidium also considered whether Pliyev should have authority to use his tactical weapons against an invasion that might be imminent.[17] Khrushchev supported using the tactical nuclear weapons against an American invasion and suggested letting the Cubans announce they would be used. Anastas Mikoyan opposed both the use of nuclear weapons and the idea of handing them over to the Cubans.[18] The Presidium decided against delegation of release authority and on 22 and 27 October Marshal Malinovsky cabled Pliyev to make clear no nuclear weapons *of any kind* were to be used, except on the orders of Khrushchev.[19] So during the crisis, contrary to what was said at the 1992 Havana Conference, authority to use the tactical nuclear weapons resided in Moscow. Gribkov's statements were misleading on the issue of predelegation, though the question of whether missiles might have been fired had the Americans invaded in these circumstances, nevertheless, remains.

Unauthorized Action

The possibility that the actions of subordinates might lead to military escalation or, indeed, to the use of nuclear weapons, was a serious concern for policy-makers in Washington and Moscow in October 1962. Yet, not all unauthorized action was intended to escalate matters. Some subordinates tried to help the cause of stability. The missile crisis provides examples of occasions on which junior figures acted on their own initiative to reduce the risk of conflict. When, for example, the Americans sought to apply the blockade to Soviet submarines (see below), they provided details of special surfacing procedures to the Soviet government. According to Peter Hucht-hausen, the Soviet Naval Commander-in-Chief, Admiral Gorshkov, refused to allow transmission of these procedures to the submarines to avoid compromising communications security. However, the message telling the submarines what the American navy intended was transmitted on the orders of the squadron commander, Rear-Admiral Rybalko, in direct disobedience of his superior.[20]

Another, more intriguing, example of subordinate initiative concerns the actions of the KGB *Resident* in Washington, Aleksandr Feklisov (known officially as Aleksandr Fomin, a counsellor at the Washington embassy). On 26 October, at a hastily arranged lunch with the ABC White House correspondent, John Scali, Feklisov outlined a deal wherein the US would guarantee not to invade Cuba in return for the withdrawal of the missiles under UN verification.[21] Or at least that is Scali's account of what Feklisov said, which he quickly reported to the State Department.[22] With diplomacy stale-mated, the American government believed that the proposal had come from Khrushchev, and that a back-channel had been opened to the Kremlin. However, Fursenko and Naftali, following the archival paper trail, show how communications in Moscow worked – or rather failed to work. The White House's response to Feklisov's approach remained on the desk of the Chairman of the KGB while events passed by.

The provenance of the proposal remains disputed as Feklisov maintains that it was Scali who made the offer.[23] The consensus has been that the outline proposal emerged from this meeting rather than as an initiative from Khrushchev, and it was not, as ExComm members believed, part of a co-ordinated approach from Moscow laying the ground for Khrushchev's personal letter that arrived later on 26 October. Most recently, Fursenko and Naftali have raised the question of whether the timing and wording of the deal indicates Feklisov may have been acting on Khrushchev's instructions (though they themselves note that the Chairman of the KGB, Vladimir

Semichastny, denied receiving such a request from Khrushchev).[24] Though aspects of the incident are unclear, and differing accounts exist, it seems most probable that it was the KGB officer who took the initiative, which he then disguised by suggesting the idea had come from the American journalist.

Crisis Management

Both Kennedy and Khrushchev were concerned about unauthorized action and suspicious of their military commanders. For Kennedy, this dated back to his own service in the navy, and was reinforced by the Bay of Pigs fiasco.[25] His handling of the missile crisis came to be seen as the exemplar of crisis management. He absorbed himself in military detail, insisting that aircraft on Florida airfields should not be parked in vulnerable rows,[26] and that US Navy ships on the blockade should each have a Russian speaker on board.[27] Maxwell Taylor recounted that the President's insistence on knowing the position of each American ship and the instructions it had been given was seen by some naval colleagues as an 'unpardonable intervention in the execution of purely military movements' (though Taylor himself endorsed Kennedy's approach).[28]

An important example of Kennedy's control over military action concerned the response to the shooting down of a U-2 over Cuba on 27 October. On 23 October McNamara explained to ExComm that U-2 overflights were carefully monitored by SAC who would have information on any incident within fifteen minutes.[29] Eight aircraft would then be available to destroy the responsible SAM site within two hours. As a decision to respond was seen as necessary within a short time, Kennedy delegated authority to McNamara if he himself was not available.[30] Authority was not delegated to military commanders to attack the SAM sites, although one account claims that when the U-2 was shot down (see below) General Le May was preparing a military response when the White House intervened to stop him.[31] Kennedy's decision not to retaliate on 27 October created potentially significant risks for other U-2 pilots. Yet, with a diplomatic settlement at least now possible, Kennedy stayed his hand. Joseph

Bouchard describes the President's decision 'as probably one of the most important of the entire crisis'.[32]

What would have happened if the US had retaliated and bombed Soviet SAM sites? One scenario is portrayed in Brendon DuBois' gripping counterfactual novel, *Resurrection Day*. When the U-2 is shot down, the commander of SAC, General Ramsey Curtis, disobeys the President's orders and launches retaliatory attacks on the SAM sites.[33] This, in turn, leads swiftly to military escalation and the use of nuclear weapons, first in Cuba and then globally. If Kennedy had ordered retaliation against the SAM sites, could this have set in motion escalation to nuclear use? It would be unwise to completely rule out escalation. However, it would have needed a dramatic change in Khrushchev's outlook. By 27 October, the Soviet leader was increasingly concerned at an imminent American invasion, and increasingly anxious to avoid war. Although an attack on the SAM sites would have caused Soviet casualties, it would also have brought home the fact that events were moving beyond control. From what we know of Khrushchev's actions that weekend, it is clear that he was increasingly determined to find a peaceful solution. American attacks on the SAM sites would have been a further signal that an invasion was imminent, and most probably a further spur to Khrushchev's diplomacy rather than to military escalation.

Unwelcome Subordinate Initiatives

While the actions of some subordinate actors assisted stability, others did not. Some, indeed, were intended to escalate the crisis. One dramatic example concerns Oleg Penkovsky, the Western agent run from within the GRU by the Secret Intelligence Service (SIS) and the CIA, who may have attempted to provoke an attack on the Soviet Union. In 1961, Penkovsky was given details of an emergency warning procedure, code-named DISTANT, that would be used 'only if he had learned for a fact that the Soviet Union had decided to attack, or that the Soviets had decided to attack should the West take specific action, or that the Soviet Union had decided to attack should the West fail to undertake specific action.'[34] The DISTANT procedure involved a telephone call to one of two numbers in the American embassy in Moscow. Penkovsky was required to blow into the mouthpiece three times, wait one minute and repeat the procedure. The Americans would then empty a 'dead drop' where Penkovsky would leave a detailed message. If that were not possible, it was understood that the telephone signal alone would be sufficient to provide the warning.[35] According to the KGB, Oleg Penkovsky was arrested on 22 October. When an account of the telephone warning first appeared, it was suggested that the DISTANT procedure was activated on 22 October but that CIA officers decided not to pass on the warning, on the basis of their assessment of their agent's psychology.[36] Another account suggests that the SIS Head of Station in Moscow, Gervase Cowell, took a similar decision not to warn London.[37]

Selective declassification of CIA records has clarified aspects of the episode. The emergency procedure was indeed activated by the KGB when two voiceless telephone calls were received in the US embassy.[38] However, this was on 2 November. By then, the immediate crisis was over, although United States (and British) nuclear forces were still at higher than normal states of alert. SAC was still at DEFCON-2, and with a portion of its B-52 force on airborne alert. Contrary to the original account, when the coded warning was sent, news was immediately passed to the Director of the CIA, who in turn briefed the President, on 3 November.[39] McCone explained that the CIA believed their agent had probably been compromised.

Why the KGB activated the DISTANT warning procedure remains a matter for speculation. Raymond Garthoff suggested that Penkovsky could have deliberately tried to provoke a nuclear attack on the Soviet Union: 'when he was about to go down, he evidently decided to play Sampson and bring the temple down on everyone else as well.'[40] This seems eminently plausible. In his first meetings with his case officers he asked to be provided with atomic demolition charges that he would hide at strategic points around Moscow, ready to decapitate the Soviet system at the necessary moment.[41]

No indications have emerged of when authorities in London were informed of Penkovsky's warning, or how it was interpreted. British officials were concerned that such a warning system could lead to miscalculation and war, so any warning was to be evaluated by the Joint Intelligence Committee before military or political commands were informed. As SIS's Maurice Oldfield explained to the CIA: 'a DISTANT report will not be treated by the U.K. as an indicator [of Soviet intent to attack] unless the JIC accept it as such.'[42] There was also concern that Penkovsky might be used to provide disinformation at a crucial moment. The head of the CIA's Soviet Division, Jack Maury, had observed: 'at some critical juncture [Penkovsky] might tell us that the Soviets were now ready to strike unless we made significant concessions. Even though, in fact, the entire Soviet effort was bluff.'[43]

The more alarming possibility was that Penkovsky might seek to provoke a nuclear attack on the Soviet Union as a calculated act. The fact that the message was sent on 2 November meant that the risks were clearly less than if it had been received at the height of the crisis. Yet various scholars have explored how such a false warning could have triggered a military response, if the incident had been one element in a concatenation of misperceptions and mistakes, or if military commanders had interpreted the warning as unambiguous.[44] It, nevertheless, seems unlikely that the President would have counte-nanced pre-emptive nuclear war solely on the basis of heavy breathing on a Moscow telephone.

The Death of Major Anderson

The most significant unauthorized action during the crisis was on 27 October when a USAF U-2 was shot down by a Soviet SAM, and its pilot, Major Rudolf Anderson, killed. It is now clear that the order to fire was given by a subordinate Soviet commander in Cuba, un-beknownst to Moscow, where Khrushchev was urgently struggling to find a diplomatic resolution of the crisis.[45] Details of what happened began to appear at the Moscow conference in 1989, and various misperceptions and conspiracies have been dispelled, in particular the erroneous suggestion that the aircraft had been shot down by Cubans (or indeed by Castro personally). The decision to fire the SAMs was taken by Lieutenant General Grechko, the air defence commander, in consultation with the deputy-chief of Soviet forces, Lieutenant

General Garbuz. The previous day, Fidel Castro had told General Pliyev that his anti-aircraft batteries would open fire at low-level naval reconnaissance aircraft on Saturday morning. Both Cuban and Soviet commanders believed that an American attack was imminent, and with Cuban anti-aircraft batteries by now firing on low-level photo-reconnaissance aircraft, when the U-2 was detected Grechko and Garbuz were unable to contact Pliyev, and it was decided to order the use of the SAMs.

Launch Under Attack?

The shooting down of the U-2 inevitably raises the question of whether Soviet commanders in Cuba in charge of nuclear weapons could likewise have taken the initiative and used either MRBMs or any of the tactical weapons. Command and control arrangements were, of course, designed to prevent unauthorized use of nuclear weapons. While our knowledge of them is incomplete, it is evident that, in 1962, the safeguards were procedural rather than mechanical/electronic for the vast majority of nuclear weapons.[46] The experience of the crisis indeed encouraged Soviet development of technical safeguards.[47] In 1962, Soviet warheads were stored away from the launch platforms until authorization was given to move them. Gribkov states that General Pliyev ordered warheads for tactical nuclear weapons to be deployed closer to launchers as invasion appeared imminent.[48] However, according to the Soviet officer in command of the Soviet warheads in Cuba, General Beloborodov:

> nuclear warheads could have been used only if the missile officers had received orders via their own chain-of-command from the General Staff, and only if we, the officers responsible for storing and operating warheads, had received our own special codes. At no point did I receive any signals to issue warheads for either the medium-range missiles or the tactical weapons.[49]

One scenario that inescapably occupied American policy-makers was whether, in the event of an American attack on the Soviet missiles, a decision would be taken by local commanders to fire the MRBMs, regardless of Moscow's instructions. Robert McNamara later spoke of 'some damn Soviet second lieutenant' launching a missile at the United States in such circumstances.[50] Oleg Penkovsky had indicated to Western intelligence that 'considerable autonomy' lay in the hands of field commanders, which John McCone believed was much more than with the US.[51] As noted, McNamara was initially adamant that any air strike on the missiles needed to be done before the weapons were operational. Some members of ExComm were also concerned at the prospect of the second lieutenant being of Cuban extraction. 'There's always the risk of their falling into Cuban hands,' General Maxwell Taylor, warned the President.[52] From what is known of Soviet command and control procedures in the crisis, however, there was no question whatever of Cuban troops gaining control of nuclear missiles, or for that matter knowing how to arm and fire them at the United States. Cuban troops were to be trained how to use the Meteors and Lunas, though at no point was there any suggestion that they would have (or did have) any role with the MRBMs or IRBMs.

Scenarios of nuclear war involving Soviet MRBMs fired from Cuba at the United States can be readily constructed. In Robert O'Connell's fascinating counterfactual essay, for example, the nuclear threshold is crossed by a Soviet submarine destroying an American aircraft carrier with its nuclear torpedo.[53] This provokes an American attack on the MRBM and SAM sites as a prelude to invasion. Soviet commanders in Cuba then order the use of Luna missiles against Guantánamo Bay, and Meteors at American ships. Two MRBMS survive the initial American air strike, and their crews are able to mate the missiles with their warheads and fire them. One of the two missiles destroys Washington which then provokes a 'full retaliatory response' against the USSR. The result is 'a second holocaust' in which two-thirds of a Soviet population of 233 millions are dead within a month (and a quarter of a million Americans killed).

Aspects of this scenario are considered in other chapters. Here, the focus is on whether 'launch under attack' by the MRBMs was feasible. Blight and Welch provide a systematic and persuasive answer to this question. 'We can say with a high degree of confidence, if not absolute certainty, that it would not have happened.'[54] Less convincingly, they also argue that the information on which their assessment is made was available to ExComm, who failed to draw appropriate conclusions. Given their sources of intelligence, there was no way that the Americans could be completely certain that they had identified all the MRBMs.

From the outset, the Chairman of the Joint Chiefs was cautious in his estimate of what air strikes could achieve. On 16 October he told the President that an air strike could never be 100% effective.[55] This assessment was reiterated in the ensuing days. The mobility of the R-12s increased concern about their survivability. On 20 October McNamara stated that, at best, an air strike could destroy two-thirds of the MRBMs.[56] It seems clear that Kennedy had made up his mind in favour of the blockade by the time he met the commander of the US Tactical Air Command, General Walter Sweeney, on the morning of Sunday, 21 October. Sweeney was confident that the attack would be successful, although he explained that the identified missiles were 'probably no more than 60% of the total missiles on the island'.[57] Of these, he could offer to destroy 90% of known missiles, and on that basis, Sweeney favoured an air strike on the Monday morning.

US intelligence had identified all 24 MRBM launch sites, though only 33 of 42 missiles were detected.[58] By 21 October, the CIA estimated that 8–12 missiles were operational and could hold a firing capability indefinitely for $2^{1}/_{2}$ to 4 hours.[59] It was calculated that the first incoming wave of strike aircraft would give the defenders only ten minutes' warning, and the second wave, 40 minutes'. Blight and Welch argue that:

> Fueling, arming, targeting, and firing an SS-4 are all processes that require coordinated action by a large number of skilled people. Even if warheads were present for the missiles in Cuba, if the crews manning the sites had not panicked and run for cover, if they had not waited for orders from superiors, and if they had escaped death or bodily injury in the attack (all major assumptions), it would still have been virtually impossible to accomplish this extraordinarily complex coordinated activity safely and

effectively while American high-explosive and incendiary bombs were falling in the area.[60]

What is now known about the disposition of Soviet warheads strengthens the argument of Blight and Welch. In 1962, the CIA did not confirm the presence of nuclear warheads on the island, though they had identified nuclear storage facilities at the missile sites. In the Soviet Union, warheads were kept close to the missiles. Fursenko and Naftali explain that at Smolensk, for example, the warheads were stored less than 300 yards from the launchers.[61] In Cuba, however, the warheads for the MRBMs were kept at the central storage depot at Bejucal, some fifty miles from the nearest R-12 regiment.[62] Soviet command and control procedures in Cuba would, therefore, have effectively precluded the inadvertent war scenario. Indeed, it seems very likely that if an American attack was under way, General Pliyev would not have been able to retaliate even if he had received authorization to launch the MRBMs.

As Blight and Welch explain, Sweeney failed to communicate how unlikely 'launch under attack' would be. Kennedy had already made up his mind in favour of the blockade at this stage, before the meeting with Sweeney. American plans for an air attack (OPLAN 312-62) and invasion (OPLAN 316-62), nevertheless, remained under active consideration, and assessments of the likely effectiveness of air attacks continued. Of note is that John McCone told the President on 26 October that further analysis within the CIA had revised the assessment of the likely effectiveness of an attack. McCone said that the CIA believed 'there's a *higher* probability of immobilizing these missiles, *all of them*, with a strike' than had been previously thought.[63]

Luna(tic)s

If an American attack on Cuba would not have led to subordinate commanders firing MRBMs, what about the tactical nuclear weapons? Pondering an American invasion of Cuba, General Gribkov posed an important counterfactual:

would the attackers have found and neutralized the bunkers where the nuclear charges for the 'Lunas' and the cruise missiles were stored? Or would a desperate group of Soviet defenders, with or without orders from above, have been able to arm and fire even one 'Luna' warhead – with a yield one-tenth the power of the bomb dropped on Hiroshima – or one of the powerful FKR charges? If such a rocket had hit U.S. troops or ships, if thousands of Americans had died in the atomic blast, would it have been the last shot of the Cuban crisis or the first of global nuclear war?[64]

Gribkov himself was cautious in assessing the likelihood of this, 'strongly doubt[ing]' that tactical nuclear weapons would have been used. 'The probability of even one such explosion occurring on purpose was very low, and the chance of an unauthorised firing was only a little higher.'[65] When he wrote these words, the Soviet Union had only recently ceased to exist. Even then, it was unusual for a senior general and former head of the Warsaw Pact to publicly question the discipline of elite Soviet troops.

In his discussion of the U-2 shoot down, McGeorge Bundy wrote that, 'The tradition of arms demanded not only that Anderson's death be avenged but also that the men who would follow him be protected.'[66] An American invasion of Cuba would have encountered over 40,000 Soviet troops and some 270,000 Cuban men and women in regular and militias units.[67] Many would have been killed or wounded. Would the 'tradition of arms' have led Soviet troops to desperate measures and violation of orders? Who can say? The circumstances of the tactical nuclear systems were different from that of the MRBMs. As noted previously, the nuclear-capable Ilyushin-28s, at Holguin airfield, had not left their crates. US intelligence had spotted cruise and short-range ballistic missiles, though the Meteors were mistaken for Sopka coastal-defence cruise missiles, which were also deployed but which were not nuclear-capable. It is impossible to know how many of the tactical missiles would have been targeted and destroyed, though it is possible that a higher proportion of them might have survived the initial American air attacks than the MRBMs.

Nevertheless, if General Beloborodov is correct that no warheads were dispersed from the central storage depot, the prospect of unauthorized use can almost certainly be discounted.

Third Parties

During the crisis, the Americans and Soviets had differing experiences with their allies. To the surprise of many, on 23 October, the Organization of American States voted 19–0 in support of the American naval blockade, and provided Washington with what it considered a legal basis for its actions.[68] Had they not done so, the blockade would nevertheless have proceeded. As Kennedy candidly told Congressional leaders on 22 October, the United States would either take action that was 'illegal' in international law or declare war.[69] America's NATO allies also provided diplomatic support, though there was unhappiness in some quarters at the lack of consultation before the blockade was announced. Afterwards, Macmillan, in his inimicably patronizing style, summed up European responses in his diary: the French 'were anyway contemptuous; the Germans *very* frightened, though pretending to want firmness; the Italians windy; the Scandinavians rather sour. But they *said* and did nothing to spoil the American playing of the hand.'[70] His explanation for this was that, 'Our [the UK's] complete calm kept the Europeans calm.'

The Soviets, on the other hand, had Fidel to deal with. And, of course, Fidel had Nikita to deal with. One of the ways in which the historiography of the missile crisis has developed is the way in which Cuba has moved from a location of a superpower struggle to an active participant.[71] Admittedly, this transition eluded the producers of *Thirteen Days*, for whom Cuba was nothing more than a shoot (in the cinematographic sense).[72] Ironically, the moment in the crisis when Cuba, or at least Castro, played the most significant part was the opposite of what Castro intended. Fidel's message to Nikita on 26 October (discussed in the previous chapter) was designed to bolster the Soviet leader. Yet, as Blight, Allyn and Welch succinctly observe:

Castro crafted the letter to address what he feared most at that moment: Khrushchev's weakness and irresolution. Khrushchev saw in Castro's letter what *he* feared most: warning of an imminent attack, and confirmation of Castro's recklessness. The letter intended to buttress Khrushchev's resolve helped to push Khrushchev in the other direction.[73]

Contrary to John McCone's belief that Soviet procedures entailed less control over nuclear weapons than in the West, Western IRBMs were normally at a much higher state of readiness. Nuclear warheads in the Soviet Union were stored apart from the missiles. In Cuba they were fifty miles away, in the mountains. By contrast, during the crisis, 59 of the 60 Thors and 37 of the 45 Jupiters stood with warheads mounted.[74] Once the order to fire was received, the British IRBMs could be launched within thirteen or fourteen minutes.[75] Indeed the Thors (and presumably the Jupiters) could be kept at even higher states of readiness at 'T minus 8' and even at 'T minus 2'.[76] How far the cocked pistol had a hair trigger depended on the effectiveness of command and control. Thor and Jupiter were dual-key weapons that involved USAF and host-nation officers simultaneously turning keys to fire the missiles. Contrary to assurances originally given to Congress about US custody of the warheads, the only thing to prevent host-country launch was an American launch authentification officer. And, while launch keys were meant to be stored in safes, there is evidence that during the crisis some USAF officers copied the practice of the RAF in wearing them around their necks.[77]

In 1992, McNamara told the Havana conference that he had advised Presidents Kennedy and Johnson that 'no nuclear weapon could ever be fired without your personal authority.'[78] Evidence from the early 1960s indicates that during the missile crisis no such assurance could be given. In December 1960, the Joint Committee on Atomic Energy had undertaken an inspection of US custodial arrangements in Europe and produced a disquieting report. NATO Quick Reaction Aircraft (QRA) sat at cockpit-alert with host-country pilots in Germany and Turkey unhampered by any control arrangements save for the presence of American sentries.[79] This meant that for a time, the West German *Luftwaffe* possessed a de facto nuclear capability.

The Kennedy administration responded in June 1962 when it decided that all short-range nuclear weapons in Europe would be fitted with mechanical or electronic devices, known as Permissive Action Links (PALs). This was accomplished within six months and was therefore in place for some, though not all, European-based US nuclear weapons in October 1962. The Jupiters had not yet been given PALs. As the Thors were scheduled for withdrawal they were not intended to receive them. There was concern within ExComm about the possibility that the missiles in Turkey could be attacked in response to American action in the Caribbean. On 20 October, Kennedy suggested informing the Turks and Italians that they should not fire the missiles even if attacked, and said that the warheads could be 'dismantled'.[80] He wanted the Joint Chiefs to issue specific instructions to ensure that, in the event of a Soviet attack, the missiles would not be fired. There was some friction with the Pentagon over this, as the Joint Chiefs were clear that standing orders precluded retaliation without presidential authorization. Kennedy's insistence on issuing further orders reflected his concern about unauthorized use (as well as tensions between himself and the Joint Chiefs).[81]

As a result, on 22 October, Maxwell Taylor cabled the Supreme Allied Commander Europe, General Lauris Norstad, instructing him to make certain that the Jupiters in Italy and Turkey were not fired without express authorization from the President: 'In the event of attack, nuclear or non-nuclear . . . US custodians are to destroy or make inoperable the weapons if any attempt is made to fire them.'[82] Norstad was told not to inform the host nations of these precautions. These instructions, however, do not appear to have resulted in changes to the operational readiness of the missiles during the crisis. There were no expressions of concern about the Thors and no indication of any comparable message sent to commanders in Britain. Kennedy's concern with ensuring the Jupiters were not fired without his authorization demonstrated his determination to retain control over the decision to use nuclear weapons, although as John Gaddis points out, no additional measures were undertaken to prevent

Turkish-based nuclear-armed F-100 aircraft from scrambling in response to an attack.[83]

As shown in Chapter 3, the malign effects of the aurora borealis on Major Maultsby's U-2 created circumstances in which Khrushchev (and Kennedy) could have believed they were about to come under nuclear attack, and considered nuclear pre-emption. There was also the possibility that more junior commanders, including the pilots themselves, could have decided to cross the nuclear threshold. This was because when the aircraft took off, the prevailing DEFCON alert state meant that they were carrying nuclear-armed GAR-11 Falcon air-to-air missiles.[84] There were no electronic locking devices on the aircraft. Polmar and Gresham state that, 'if the F102s and MiG-19s engaged, nuclear weapons would likely have been used by the U.S. fighters'.[85] Certainly, in aerial combat, all that stood between the pilots and use of nuclear weapons was their training, discipline and judgement.

Sagan provides five plausible pathways to how the incident could have led to the Falcon missiles being fired:

> First, if a US interceptor pilot was unable to contact ground control, he might assume that a precursor Soviet strike had been launched and that he should immediately attack any hostile aircraft entering what he believed to be Alaskan territory . . . Second, it is possible that an interceptor pilot might panic if confronted with hostile MIGs and fire his most effective weapon regardless of what his orders were from the command post. Third, if a regional Air Defense commander incorrectly believed that Soviet interceptors entering U.S air space constituted a hostile act and signalled that war was imminent, he could have ordered, acting fully within his authority, the use of the Falcon nuclear-armed missiles. Fourth, there is some possibility that Soviet MIGs, entering Alaskan airspace in a crisis, could be misidentified by officers in the regional command post as Soviet bombers attacking the United States, again producing an authorised, but mistaken, order to fire the Falcon missiles. Finally, it is possible that a Falcon missile could be accidentally launched by the pilot in the tense moments of the confrontation.[86]

Submarines

As noted in Chapter 2, the original plan for *Operation Anadyr* envisaged construction of a Soviet naval base at Mariel, near Havana, accommodating surface ships, nuclear-armed ballistic missile-carrying submarines and diesel-electric torpedo submarines. In September 1962, Khrushchev accepted the advice of the General Staff and cancelled the surface ships. He also cancelled the nuclear-missile-carrying submarines but persevered with the diesel-electric boats.[87] Four Project 641s from the Soviet Northern Fleet were despatched to Cuba. One Project 611 submarine (NATO designation Zulu-class), the B-75, then on patrol off the American coast, was also sent to support the merchant ship *Indigirka*, which was carrying nuclear warheads, including those for the MRBMs. The B-75 was equipped with two nuclear torpedoes.[88] A sixth boat, B-88, a Project 641, sailed from its Kamchatka base for Pearl Harbor. As noted in Chapter 2, it also appears that several submarines equipped with nuclear-armed cruise missiles sailed into the northern Atlantic. The Northern Fleet Project 641 boats were each equipped with one nuclear-armed torpedo (and 21 conventional torpedoes) whose nuclear yield was comparable in yield to the weapons used against Hiroshima and Nagasaki.[89] The nuclear torpedoes were designed for use against large ships or groups of ships, though they were also capable of attacking naval bases or ports. [90]

Details of the Soviet naval deployment to Cuba have emerged from the testimony of surviving Soviet naval officers, together with some archival material. However, as Svetlana Savranskaya has cautioned, given the available evidence, all conclusions should be seen as preliminary, as what has been discovered is only the 'tip of the iceberg'.[91] Various aspects of the command and control procedures on nuclear release await clarification. So too does the suggestion that Khrushchev and senior Soviet admirals were unaware that the submarines they had sent to Cuba were not nuclear-powered, but had diesel-electric engines that required regular recharging at or near the surface.[92] Originally, the submarines were despatched to Mariel. When the blockade was announced they were redirected to patrol in the Sargasso Sea.

There was fierce debate within the Presidium, and in particular between Mikoyan and Malinovsky, over whether to allow the submarines to run the blockade. Fursenko and Naftali's account suggests that while Mikoyan won the argument against proceeding, the submarines nevertheless proceeded.[93]

Sufficient material has emerged to illuminate hitherto unconsidered risks, some of which have been portrayed in highly dramatic fashion. The existence of nuclear weapons on board the submarines was first revealed in Moscow in 1995, though excitement in the West developed when accounts of what happened at sea appeared in time for the fortieth anniversary of the crisis in Cuba in 2002.[94] These events cast particular light on the attempts of the American navy to enforce the blockade by forcing Soviet submarines to surface. Kennedy announced the quarantine on 22 October to come into effect at 10 a.m. on 24 October. At 5 a.m. on 24 October, US navy ships received Submarine Surfacing and Identification Procedures (SSIP), with which they were to police the blockade. These entailed using sonar and explosive charges to signal to the submarines that they should surface. The procedures were not part of peacetime US naval activity and involved use of MK64 practice depth charges by anti-submarine warfare (ASW) helicopters, while ASW surface ships used grenades.[95]

It was as news began to percolate into Washington that key Soviet ships were stopping or turning around, that McNamara began to explain to ExComm how the US navy would make Soviet submarines surface if they breached the quarantine.[96] The explosives were not intended to damage the ships but to signal to them to surface. However, if the submarines continued to breach the quarantine or undertook aggressive actions, General Maxwell Taylor told ExComm, the US navy would attack them. When Kennedy interjected that the submarines were the last thing he wanted to interdict, McNamara emphasized that it would be 'extremely dangerous' to defer an attack on a submarine.[97] The blockade rules of engagement were similar to normal naval procedures in countenancing the use of force in self-defence, and in 'anticipatory self defence' in the face of 'actions which can reasonably be considered as threatening'.[98] The Defense Secretary stated that it was dangerous to limit the discretion of the naval commanders. This is a rather different McNamara to the one depicted in the exchange with Admiral Anderson, the Chief of Naval Operations, depicted in the film *Thirteen Days*. As Joseph Bouchard concludes, while Kennedy and McNamara were anxious to ensure political control, they were sympathetic to the military's concern with protecting their men.[99]

The procedures developed by the navy were approved by McNamara after the blockade came into effect, publicly announced in a Notice to Mariners on 25 October, and communicated to the Soviet government by the US embassy in Moscow (though the Soviets did not acknowledge receipt).[100] The Submarine Surfacing and Identification Procedures were not normal practice. And such were the problems of communication, that not even all the American ASW ships learned of surfacing procedures – one commander requested permission to use real depth charges (at a distance) to surface a Soviet submarine.[101] McNamara's assumption was that the American procedures would be communicated to the Soviet submarines, understood, and accepted. The reality was different. The Project 641 boats needed to be at periscope depth to receive communications. Some of the captains did learn of the American procedures, but at least one appears not to have done when he believed he was coming under attack. Svetlana Savranskaya concludes that all the Soviet captains saw the explosions as hostile acts rather than signalling devices, and each believed their ships had been damaged as a result.[102] Yet none of the Project 641 submarines surfaced in response to the actions of US ASW forces. While three submarines (B-36, B-59 and B-130) surfaced in the presence of US forces it was because they needed to recharge their batteries, not in response to the SSIPs. And with the exception of B-130, whose engines had given up, they were then able to break away from their ASW pursuers. The B-4, although detected and pursued, did not surface in the presence of the US navy.

Were Soviet commanders authorized to fire their nuclear torpedoes at American ships? If not, could they fire them anyway? Available accounts are ambiguous. According to Peter Huchthausen, the Commander-in-Chief of the Soviet Navy, Admiral Gorshkov, told the commander of the submarine brigade, Rear-Admiral Rybalko, that his rules of engagement were clear: 'You will use these weapons if the American forces attack you submerged or force your units to surface and then attack, or upon receipt of orders from Moscow.'[103] When the four Project 641 captains were seen off by the Deputy Commander-in-Chief of the Soviet Navy, Admiral Fokin, they were given more precise orders from the Northern Fleet Chief of Staff, Vice-Admiral Rossokha. Use of the nuclear torpedoes was authorized, 'first, in the event you are attacked with depth bombs and your pressure hull is ruptured; second, if you surface and are taken under fire and hit; and, third, upon orders from Moscow.'[104] Rossokha told the captains to enter these instructions into their logbooks. According to Captain Ketov, the commander of the B-4, Admiral Rossokha also added, 'I suggest to you commanders, that you use the nuclear weapons first, and then you will figure out what to do after that.'[105] Yet, when the captains opened their sealed orders, their written instructions seemingly differed from their oral instructions: 'Torpedoes with atomic weapons may be used only as directed in instructions from the Ministry of Defence or the main Navy Staff.'[106] Ambiguities surround the procedural and technical aspects of arming and launching the nuclear torpedoes. Savranskaya concludes that, 'Although physically the captains could arm and launch the nuclear–tipped torpedo, the procedure of the actual launching was quite complex and required three keys to be initiated.'[107]

Highly dramatic accounts of what happened on several submarines have emerged. On 30 October, the B-130 was partially crippled by serious engine problems and was running out of oxygen when the destroyer, USS *Blandy*, dropped explosives around the submarine. Huchthausen recounts that the commander of B-130, Captain Shumkov, believed real depth charges were being dropped, although his executive officer told him they were hand grenades used as signalling devices.[108] Shortly afterwards, instructions were received from Moscow giving details of the American submarine-surfacing procedures. Shumkov, nevertheless, ordered the loading of the nuclear torpedo, along with other torpedoes, when he was again attacked. Hutchausen's account of these events raises various questions about naval command and control. When Shumkov ordered the nuclear torpedo to be loaded, the special weapons security officer told him that weapons could not be armed without specific instructions from the Main Navy Staff.[109] 'Do as you're told. I'll handle the permission,' Shumkov is reported to have replied, shortly before the special weapons security officer passed out. Hutchausen's account suggests that Captain Shumkov did not intend to fire the weapon, but was apparently concerned that the political officer on board would report any reluctance to do so.

Another dramatic account of events on 27 October came on board the B-59, under Captain Savitsky. According to the communications officer, Vadim Orlov:

> only emergency light was functioning. The temperature in the compartments was 45-50C, up to 60C in the engine compartment. It was unbearably stuffy. The level of CO2 in the air reached a critical practically deadly for people mark. One [of] the duty officers fainted and fell down. Then another one followed, then the third one . . . They were falling like dominoes. But we were still holding on, trying to escape. We were suffering like this for about four hours. The Americans hit us with something stronger than the grenades – apparently with a practice depth bomb. We thought – that's it – the end. After this attack, the totally exhausted Savitsky, who in addition to everything was not able to establish connection with the General Staff, became furious. He summoned the officer who was assigned to the nuclear torpedo, and ordered him to assemble it to battle readiness. 'Maybe the war has already started up there, while we are doing summersaults here' screamed emotional Valentin Grigorievich, trying to justify his order. 'We're going to blast them now! We will die, but we will sink them all. We will not disgrace our Navy!'[110]

Was this the moment when the world really did stand on the brink of nuclear war? Or were Soviet naval command and control procedures and the discipline of Soviet naval personnel sufficient to the task.

According to Orlov, Captain Savitsky was able to 'rein in his wrath' and after consulting Second Captain Arkhipov and Deputy Political Officer Maslennikov, he decided to surface.

From the Soviet side we have an incomplete picture with which to assess the risk that a nuclear torpedo could have been launched (including the risk of an accidental launch). Only one of the four Project 641 captains had experience of firing a nuclear torpedo and there was the possibility that attempts to use the weapons could have ended in disaster for the crews. According to Huchthausen's account, Rybalko also protested to Gorshkov that the range of the blast effects was not understood and that use of the weapons might destroy another submarine.[111]

Yet perhaps the most striking aspect of the encounters between the Soviet and American navies is the fact that in the area of military activity most closely scrutinized and co-ordinated by political leaders, the gap between reality in Washington and reality at sea was stark. Throughout the crisis, the President and his Defense Secretary were adamant about the subordination of military means to political ends. This was exemplified in the oft-quoted exchange between McNamara and Admiral Anderson, concerning the naval blockade, when Defense Secretary insisted that the President would decide when and how to act.[112] The blockade was the exemplar of crisis management and the effective subordination of military means to political goals. In 1987, Paul Nitze stated that '. . . certainly with respect to the seas, we had managed to cause all the Soviet submarines in the vicinity to surface. We had them under control. We had complete local tactical control of the situation.'[113] Yet, it is now clear that none of the submarines surfaced because of USN surfacing procedures, and one did not surface at all in the presence of American forces. The submarine surfacing procedures were improvised arrangements that involved dropping explosive charges on submarines whose crews were assumed to know what the Americans intended. Unbeknownst to American leaders, those submarines carried nuclear ordnance. Contrary to Nitze's assertion, the Americans were not in control of a situation whose potential for inadvertent nuclear escalation they did not understand.

Accidents will happen?

Any discussion of inadvertent nuclear war in 1962 must also consider the possibility of nuclear accidents.[114] In itself, a nuclear accident was a potential disaster.[115] But there was also the risk that, in a crisis, it might lead to inadvertent escalation.[116] As the Assistant Secretary of Defense, John T. McNaughton, stated in 1962: 'The explosion of a nuclear device by accident – mechanical or human – could be a disaster for the United States, for its allies, and for its enemies. If one of these devices accidentally exploded, I would hope that both sides had sufficient means of verification and control to prevent the accident from triggering a nuclear exchange. But we cannot be certain that this would be the case.'[117]

Scott Sagan argues persuasively that accidents are inevitable in complex military organizations, and he provides evidence of break-downs in command and control during the crisis.[118] Yet, in over sixty years, there have been no accidental nuclear detonations (or, if there have been, they have been very successfully hidden). Assessing the risk of nuclear accidents is difficult, not least because much relevant information is strictly classified. Without details of nuclear weapons' design, it is difficult to make assessments of the risk of accidental detonation. Several accidents in the 1950s and 1960s apparently came close to nuclear detonation. In 1956, an American B-47 bomber crashed into a nuclear weapons' storage igloo at RAF Lakenheath, containing three Mark-6 thermo-nuclear bombs. According to the preliminary examination of the bomb disposal officer it was 'a miracle that one mark six with exposed detonators sheared didn't go.'[119] In 1961, a B-52 crashed in North Carolina, carrying two thermo-nuclear weapons. Most of the safety triggers on one were activated. Paul Bracken states that 'had the final interlock been thrown, the nuclear weapon would have detonated', though Sagan quotes an official Pentagon report that suggests two of the six safety devices were still intact.[120]

Accidents that resulted in the release of radioactivity were more likely. SAC experienced two that resulted in the spread of radioactive material. In 1966, a USAF B-52 and a KC-135 tanker collided while refuelling near the village of Palomores in Spain. Conventional explosives on two of the four thermo-nuclear weapons detonated, though none of the nuclear components exploded (a third bomb fell into the sea and was not recovered for nearly three months).[121] The incident fuelled the determination of Robert McNamara to terminate the SAC airborne alert that had operated during the missile crisis. In 1968 a B-52 crashed in Greenland. The high explosive materials on the four Mark-28 thermo-nuclear bombs detonated and the resulting fire spread radioactive plutonium across the ice.[122]

Evidence of Soviet accidents was for many years harder to come by, though the fact that Soviet aircraft did not routinely fly with nuclear weapons provides part of the explanation. Evidence of Soviet naval accidents, however, has accumulated. The story of the first Soviet SSBN was eventually made into a Hollywood film in 2002 which portrayed the accident on K-19's first combat patrol in 1961, when loss of primary cooling on the nuclear reactor led to near-catastrophe.[123] Safety had been compromised in the race to catch up with the Americans, and no back-up cooling systems were installed. Disaster on the boat was only averted by the ingenuity and self-sacrifice of the ship's engineers, many of whom died from radioactive poisoning as a consequence.[124] The accident resulted in the Project 658 SSBNs being withdrawn from service to have back-up systems installed, and it appears that the Soviets were without their seven Project 658 SSBNs during the crisis.[125] The Soviet ICBM programme also experienced serious accidents. In October 1960, the head of the Soviet Rocket Forces, Marshal Nedelin, was among a large number of scientists and military personnel killed when a fully-fuelled R-16 ICBM exploded during preparations for its first test flight.[126] The CIA and SIS were told of this incident in April 1961 by their agent in the GRU, Oleg Penkovsky.[127]

As Blight and Welch argue, 'Inadvertent events are unforeseeable; there is simply no way of accurately gauging the risks associated with these possibilities.'[128] In any counterfactual scenario, accidents appear as random variables. Nevertheless, in a crisis certain activities raise some of the risks. On the other hand, crises concentrate the mind. Sagan himself recounts that SAC's airborne-alerted B-52s flew over

2,088 missions involving 47,000 flying hours, 20 million miles and 4,076 aerial refuellings without a single crash or known weapons safety incident.[129] The rate of accidents actually decreased during the crisis.

Some plausible scenarios can, nevertheless, be discerned where the risk of accident increased as a result of the crisis. One involved the transportation of Soviet nuclear warheads to Cuba on the *Indigirka* and the *Aleksandrovsk*. The Kremlin became concerned at the possible destruction (or capture) of the warheads and when the blockade was due to come into effect, Khrushchev was, in particular, anxious that the *Aleksandrovsk* reach Cuba.[130] The ship was carrying the 24 IRBM warheads and 44 of the Meteor warheads, and only just managed to arrive before the blockade began.[131] The ship docked in La Isabela rather than the intended destination of Mariel where there were appropriate storage depots for the nuclear warheads.[132] The warheads therefore remained on board the ship during the crisis, until the *Aleksandrovsk* left for home on 5 November (carrying all the MRBM and IRBM warheads).[133]

In the event of an American attack on Cuba, air attacks could have jeopardized the security of the warheads. Without understanding of Soviet security protocols, assessing the possibility of a nuclear detonation at La Isabela is extremely difficult. A major fire on board the *Aleksandrovsk* or the *Indigirka*, however, might well have risked radioactive contamination of the port. Furthermore, *Operation Mongoose* was still proceeding. The same morning that Robert Kennedy was told about Soviet missiles, he was co-ordinating sabotage operations against Cuba. While the President had earlier vetoed his brother's proposal to mine Cuban harbours, underwater demolition attacks on Soviet shipping were authorized on 17 October.[134] The CIA decided to suspend *Operation Mongoose* toward the end of the month, though activities on the ground continued into November.[135] One additional possibility was that the ships transporting the warheads could have been attacked by the anti-Castro group, Alpha 66, which had carried out attacks on ships (including a British ship) in September and October.[136]

Conclusion

During the missile crisis, political leaders on both sides actively considered the risk that nuclear war might begin with the actions of junior commanders. Concern at these risks was shared by the military organizations involved, inasmuch as nuclear release procedures were designed to prevent unauthorized use. In 1962, the Americans were moving away from procedural safeguards alone, towards installation of PALs on European-based weapons. This programme had not been completed by October 1962, and various NATO-assigned nuclear weapons operated under procedures that fell far short of what would soon be seen as basic safety standards. The Soviets relied on procedural safeguards that included greater reluctance to mate nuclear charges with delivery systems. Kennedy remained anxious to retain political control over events and was suspicious of existing procedures. He insisted on measures to insure against inadvertence, including precautions to prevent unauthorized retaliation in the event of attack on Jupiter missiles in Europe. The recent literature has shown the concerns of both political leaders about the activities and judgement of their respective military. Yet what is clear is that a number of events and contingencies were beyond the knowledge of political (and military leaders) leaders.

The recent historiography of the crisis has yielded plausible scenarios in which subordinate commanders might have crossed the nuclear threshold. Without further detail about command and control it is difficult to determine how close some of these episodes came to crossing the nuclear threshold, particularly those involving Soviet tactical weapons in Cuba and on submarines around the Caribbean. In the case of Soviet tactical nuclear missiles, the possibility of their use – authorized or unauthorized – would only have arisen in the circumstances of an American invasion. With the submarines, the possibility of inadvertent nuclear war seems greater. The indications are that decisions about whether to use nuclear weapons were taken by a handful of officers in physical and psychological environments that were extremely demanding. None of them chose to cross the nuclear threshold, but some of them may nearly have done so.

With hindsight, we are all owls now. In October 1962, there were a sufficient number of moles to suggest the risk of nuclear war was on the disquieting side of Allison and Zelikow's crack between unlikelihood and impossibility.

CHAPTER 5

Perils of the Land Crabs

The fish are back in the lagoons; the coconut trees are growing coconuts; the guava bushes have fruit on them; the birds are back. As a matter of fact, everything is about the same except the land crabs. They get minerals from the soil, I guess, through their shells, and the land crabs were a little bit hot [radioactive] and there's a little question about whether you should eat a land crab or not.

General Curtis Le May, 1968,
observations on Bikini atoll nuclear test site[1]

Allison and Zelikow's conclusion that the missile crisis is special 'because no other event so clearly demonstrates the awesome crack between the *unlikelihood* and *impossibility* of nuclear war' was noted in Chapter 1.[2] How we calibrate the awesome crack, and how we measure differences between likelihoods and possibilities is inherently subjective. Chapters 3 and 4 have explored how the nuclear threshold might have been crossed. Conclusions were drawn with varying degrees of caution. Most are, inevitably, of an tentative nature. The idea that political leaders would have used nuclear weapons as a rational instrument of national policy remains very unlikely. It is, nevertheless, conceivable that a concatenation of misperceptions, mistakes and misfortune could have led political leaders to authorize the use of nuclear weapons. Pre-emption by either (or both) sides in

113

the straying U-2 scenario, for example, was possible. For Robert McNamara, the risk of inadvertent nuclear war was greater than he realized at the time, when it will be recalled that he had seriously contemplated the possibility that nuclear war was imminent. For Ray Cline, the risk of nuclear war was 'no more than one in a thousand'.[3] Yet, however the risks are assessed, there was the possibility that nuclear weapons might be used and that what Bundy described to Kennedy as 'the moment of thermo-nuclear truth' could arrive.

We still have insufficient understanding of Soviet military capabilities and the attitude of Soviet military leaders to make fully informed assessments on key issues. On the other hand, as Chapter 3 explored, everything that we have learned of Khrushchev's outlook on nuclear war as the crisis developed, suggests that he would have resisted military pressure to initiate attacks that would bring retribution on a colossal scale. As he wrote to Castro on 30 October: 'we are not struggling against imperialism in order to die'.[4] More information exists about the possibility that nuclear weapons could have been used by subordinate commanders, although again, key scenarios are based on limited evidence, in particular concerning Soviet command and control arrangements. Assessing the credibility of scenarios depends on interpretation of the motives and intentions of key actors. The possibility of tactical nuclear warfare in Cuba, for example, presupposes that Kennedy would have invaded had a diplomatic solution not been achieved by 28–30 October. It seems more likely that he would have 'gone the extra mile for peace'. There are, nevertheless, scenarios that may provide more credible paths to the use of nuclear weapons, notably the despatch of nuclear-armed American interceptors in support of the Alaskan U-2 and the deployment of nuclear-armed Soviet submarines in the Caribbean. Here the gap between unlikelihood and impossibility may well have been worryingly wide. Kennedy and Khrushchev sought to end the crisis without escalation to nuclear war, as they clearly recognized what that meant for their own societies and for humankind. Nevertheless, once the nuclear threshold was crossed and escalation accelerated, they would have faced a world beyond experience, in which they would have known that the fate of their societies and indeed the fate of the Earth, was in their hands.

How they would have reacted to the stresses of the 'moment of thermo-nuclear truth' is as incalculable as it would have been crucial. A desire to limit and constrain destruction would surely have endured into the early stages of a nuclear war. How long control and restraint would have been possible is much less clear. The circumstances in which millions of American and Soviet people were being killed would have tested personal rationality to the limit. Whether command and control capabilities would have enabled them to exercise control, and draw back from the brink, is very doubtful.

Had nuclear weapons been used, what then? Unless it is assumed that escalation to all-out nuclear war would have been inevitable, then any answer is inherently speculative. It depends, among other issues, on the types and numbers of weapons used initially and the targets they struck. The risk of escalation would have been greater if intermediate or strategic weapons had been used against the territory of either the Soviet Union or the United States. Whichever country was attacked would need to assure itself that it was indeed under nuclear attack. As explained in Chapter 4, there were several episodes in which indicators of imminent attack were received, and at least one occasion (the Moorestown simulation tape incident) where there was a false attack warning. McNamara was clear that before retaliation took place it was necessary to clearly establish that an attack had occurred.[5] Potentially more difficult was determining who was responsible for the decision, and whether this was a considered act by the adversary political leadership, a subordinate actor or, conceivably, a third party. There was also the possibility that any explosion was the result of an accident. How each side would have interpreted events would also have depended on other military and political decisions and activities that were taking place.

A large variety of scenarios can, therefore, be constructed around recent revelations. In most, the pattern of escalation, and therefore the focus of analysis, is similar. The principal scenarios explored here include Soviet tactical nuclear attack in Cuba; the use of US air-to-air nuclear missiles in a Soviet–US dogfight arising from the Alaskan-U2 incident; Soviet nuclear torpedo attack in the Caribbean/Atlantic; and a Soviet MRBM strike from Cuba. The analysis is drawn from discussions in Chapters 3 and 4 about how the nuclear threshold might have been crossed. Analysis focuses on factors or pressures that would have facilitated escalation and those that would have facilitated control, de-escalation and termination of hostilities. Attention is given to the respective nuclear strategies and operational doctrines of the belligerents; command and control, including delegation and pre-delegation; communication in war; and how decisions would be taken by political (and military) leaders.

The study of the missile crisis has generated insights into the beliefs and actions of the two principal leaders and the behaviour of their governments and militaries. Prima facie these insights from the crisis phase have relevance in a conflict phase. But any discussion of how a nuclear war would have been fought (or terminated) comes with the obvious caveat that we can never know how decision-makers would have reacted. Moreover, in war, contingency is as unpredictable as it is inevitable. Discussion of what might have occurred in the early phases of a conflict may be more pertinent than when escalation began. The greater the escalation, the greater the unpredictability. Only the broadest of generalizations may be possible. Even predictions about the more apocalyptic outcomes are hazardous, especially with more holistic perspectives that move beyond the military, political and humanitarian aspects of nuclear war to economic, environmental and societal collapse.

Retaliation

At the core of all thinking about nuclear deterrence is the concept of retaliation. Neither of Oppenheimer's scorpions will strike first because the other scorpion will retaliate with lethal force. Most would see this as the inescapable existential condition of the Cold War. Yet the central paradox of deterrence is that, while it may be necessary to threaten retaliation in order to deter, if deterrence fails, and the enemy launches an attack designed to destroy the defender, retaliation cannot serve the purpose for which it was created. All-out nuclear retaliation would be a 'blow from the grave', whose primary aim would be a primordial yearning for vengeance. And as we have seen in

Chapter 3, where destruction was seen as inescapable and imminent, there was the possibility of pre-emptive retaliation.

When in 1987 McNamara was asked what the administration would have done if war had come, he replied:

> This is a very important question. Important mainly because I have no idea what the answer is. I'd thought about it and I had discussed it with the President. If we had been attacked with nuclear weapons I am certain that the President would have responded with one, two or maybe ten – something like that. Neither he nor I thought we should respond at all though, until we could determine what had happened. Now I know the SIOP called for a massive response and I also recall that the President said in his speech announcing the quarantine that we'd respond massively. No way would we have done that.[6]

The idea of limited nuclear retaliation, conducted on a discriminate and proportionate basis, was at the heart of McNamara's approach to controlled escalation. In his exchange with Admiral Anderson, McNamara explained that the blockade was a form of communication with the Soviets. It demonstrated both resolve and restraint. Using nuclear weapons could be conceived in similar terms. Discrete and proportionate attacks would demonstrate resolve and, moreover, signal willingness to escalate. Limiting their use would demonstrate restraint and a desire to bring hostilities to an end. For several decades, such propositions were fiercely and extensively debated as the United States and its NATO allies grappled with nuclear strategy in an era of mutually assured destruction. For the Joint Chiefs in 1962, restraint signalled weakness. And from a different perspective, Dean Rusk described the idea of limited nuclear war as 'nonsense', derisively dismissing the suggestion that it was possible to communicate with the Soviets about limiting the use of weapons of mass destruction when American nuclear weapons were about to land on their territory.[7]

Words as Deeds

Communication of a more conventional kind would have been crucial if nuclear war was to be terminated short of an all-out exchange. Among the many memorable scenes in *Dr Strangelove* is one where President Muffley speaks to Premier Kissof on the hotline. Ambassador De Sadeski has supplied Muffley with the number of his mistress's flat, where he is worse the wear for drink. President Muffley has to explain that one of his commanders has gone mad and launched his bombers at their targets in the Soviet Union. Later the American President co-operates in helping Soviet air defences attempt to shoot down the one bomber that has not been recalled. In the other celebrated nuclear war film of the 1960s, *Fail Safe*, the American President also speaks to his adversary on the telephone, and the Americans also provide help to Soviet air defences to shoot down bombers that have mistakenly been launched.[8] Direct telephone communication between Kennedy and Khrushchev in October 1962 did not exist (although it could have been improvised). Kennedy did speak over a recently installed secure telephone to Macmillan. However, it was only after the crisis that a direct real-time communication link was established between the Soviet and American governments. The need for effective and direct communication was indeed a lesson learned from the crisis (although even then, the hotline was a teleprinter link, and connected to the Pentagon, not the White House).

Communications during the crisis were complex and often convoluted. Khrushchev's letter of 26 October took twelve hours to arrive in full in the White House.[9] When Dobrynin sent his enciphered cables to Moscow, including the account of his meeting with Robert Kennedy on 27 October, they were sent via the commercial Western Union cable company, who despatched an employee on a bicycle to collect from the embassy.[10] Kennedy and Khrushchev had previously made extensive use of back-channel communications involving Georgi Bolshakov, a GRU officer working under cover as a TASS journalist. Bolshakov established good relations with Robert Kennedy, and was used to pass messages back and forth between the President and the Premier, on subjects including Berlin, nuclear testing and Cuba.[11] Contrary to previous understanding that, with the discovery of the missiles, Bolshakov became effectively *persona non grata*, Fursenko and Naftali demonstrate that he was used as a conduit after 23 October.[12] They also show that the Americans erroneously believed they had opened another line of communication to Khrushchev via Aleksandr Feklisov (see Chapter 4). Relations with NATO allies were conducted through normal diplomatic means, including personal emissaries from the President to key NATO allies at the start of the crisis. Relations with the British were somewhat different – in addition to Macmillan's telephone calls, David Ormsby-Gore had highly privileged access to the President.[13]

Technical aspects of communication were, of course, only one obstacle to mutual understanding. The meaning of words (and of course actions) exercised political leaders and their advisers. As the crisis reached its climax, ExComm vigorously debated the meaning of Khrushchev's letters of 26 and 27 October, which were mistakenly taken to indicate that Khrushchev was under pressure from hard-liners. Castro's message to Khrushchev was interpreted as a plea for nuclear pre-emption, but it only hastened Khrushchev's determination to reach a deal with Kennedy. The crisis thus provides examples of misunderstandings as well as of unintended consequences that are, of course, to be found in all periods of diplomacy and statecraft.

Deeds as Words

As we have seen, among the more plausible scenarios of nuclear use are those in the skies near Siberia or the seas of the Caribbean. Chapter 3 examined whether an American U-2 flying mistakenly into Soviet air space could have triggered Soviet pre-emption and whether preparations for this could, in turn, have triggered an American pre-emptive attack on the Soviet Union. Chapter 4 examined the risk of inadvertent nuclear use, including the nuclear-armed fighters to support the straying U-2. Various scenarios outlined by Scott Sagan showed how American pilots might have fired their Falcon nuclear-armed air-to-air missiles. What would have happened if they had?

Presumably, the Soviet MiGs would have been destroyed, and Soviet air defence commanders left to work out what had happened. The Falcon missile carried a sub-kiloton yield and its effects would have been limited to the immediate locality. Whether the explosion would have been detected on Soviet territory is by no means certain. The MiGs would presumably have reported that they were engaging the F-102s before they were destroyed. Yet Soviet air defence commanders might have considered or concluded that the American aircraft was a nuclear bomber that had been destroyed in the explosion.

If – and it remains an if – Moscow had learned that a small nuclear explosion had taken place in the skies of Siberia on the night of 26/7 October, how might the Kremlin have reacted? Despite the serious-ness of such an incident, it would have remained only one indicator of imminent American aggression. It would indeed have been possible for the Soviets to correctly deduce what had happened and that some 'damn [American] second lieutenant' had taken the initiative. In these circumstances, Khrushchev's reaction to the attack on his MiGs might well have mirrored Kennedy's reaction to the downing of Major Anderson's U-2. On the other hand, there would have been pressure to take precautionary measures, such as raising the combat readiness of Soviet strategic forces.

Any F-102 pilots who fired nuclear missiles and returned to Alaska would have provided explanation of what happened. When Major Maultsby arrived back safely, he was flown direct to debrief the commander of SAC, General Power. If the pilot(s) had not survived, American air defence would have presumably worked out the likely sequence of events and ExComm would have learned sometime on 27 October. Black Saturday would certainly have become even darker. What would Kennedy have done in these cir-cumstances? ExComm's deliberations that day can be studied in great detail and the growing sense of tension is evident. The immediate reaction would have depended on when exactly the news arrived. If, for example, ExComm learned of the American attack on the Soviet fighters before news of the Soviet SAM attack on the U-2, the latter might have been seen as a possible response to the former. However, what would have been clear was that the crisis was spiralling. Given what we know of how Kennedy's thinking developed that day, would this news have altered his fear of escalation or would it have reinforced his concern that events were moving beyond control and that urgent action was needed to de-escalate the crisis? Surely, it would have been the latter.

Submarines

Chapter 4 discussed accounts of Soviet submarine activities in the Caribbean/Atlantic. In the event of an American attack on Cuba, various circumstances can be imagined in which the submarines might be ordered (or decide) to use their nuclear weapons against major American warships. And in circumstances in which escalation to general war was taking place, the submarines could have attempted to destroy a major American embarkation port or other seaborne city. However, the accounts that depict the greatest risk are those which suggest that the captains of the submarines came close to using their nuclear torpedoes. It was emphasized that a clear picture of this risk has yet to properly emerge. Available accounts, nevertheless, make clear the context in which decisions could have been taken where submariners were under enormous physical strain and psychological stress. A decision to 'sink them all' rather than 'disgrace the navy' seems frighteningly plausible.

If, when the submarine commanders had fired their nuclear torpedoes, they had managed to avoid blowing themselves up, but instead had struck an American warship, the US navy would no doubt have exercised the right of self-defence and immediately attacked the submarine. Similarly, American ASW commanders would presumably have sought to attack any submarine they were tracking, as their rules of engagement allowed them to do. Would President Kennedy have acquiesced or indeed endorsed such action? Or would he have desperately tried to constrain a military response?

Tactical Nuclear War in Cuba

Before considering how escalation might (or might not) have occurred, it is useful to examine the third scenario, concerning the use of Soviet tactical nuclear weapons in Cuba. Would Khrushchev have ordered the use of the tactical weapons in the event of an American invasion of Cuba? It seems clear that in September, he drew a distinction between weapons that would deter the Americans from invading, and those that would be used for fighting them if they did (which he presumably drew when he agreed to send the Meteors). While using nuclear weapons against invading American marines or against Guantánamo may not have crossed the threshold drawn by Kennedy in his 22 October speech, it would have marked a dramatic escalation of the crisis. As Fursenko and Naftali point out, if twenty years earlier Field-Marshal Rommel had had battlefield nuclear missiles, he could have wiped out all five allied landing beaches in Normandy.[14] General Pliyev had eighty Meteors and twelve Lunas at his disposal, though like Rommel he faced an enemy who would have quickly established air superiority.

The discussion in Chapter 4 concluded that the prospect of Soviet tactical use in Cuba was very unlikely. Khrushchev was determined to avoid escalation, and there is no reason to believe that General Pliyev would have disobeyed direct orders from Moscow, and no reason to believe that Soviet command and control procedures were ineffective. Moreover, the warheads were stored well away from the missiles. Khrushchev would have had to calculate that firing nuclear weapons against American troops and ships would not provoke nuclear retaliation against Cuba. And, of course, he would also have had to calculate that it would not provoke nuclear retaliation against the Soviet Union. Khrushchev believed that Kennedy was a pragmatist battling the militarists in the American government. Using nuclear weapons against American forces might have provided the militarists with the pretext for nuclear war.

If an American invasion had begun on or around 30 October (which, if McNamara and Bundy are correct, is unlikely), and surviving nuclear-armed Meteors or Lunas been used (which, for reasons explored in Chapter 4, is very unlikely), would the Americans have retaliated with nuclear weapons?[15] Soviet nuclear attacks would have come as a great shock to Washington. Among the first questions to be asked would have been whether Khrushchev had given the order to fire. When ExComm studied his letter of 27 October, there was much speculation that he had been overruled by a hard-line faction in the Kremlin (something that mirrored Khrushchev's fears about militarists in Washington), though accounts of Soviet decision-making make clear that Khrushchev was fully in charge of Soviet policy throughout.[16] Concern that the hardliners were in control would no doubt have surfaced in assessments of how nuclear weapons had been used, and what response was appropriate.

An equally immediate question would have been whether military commanders were instead responsible. We now know (unlike ExComm at the time) that subordinate Soviet officers took the decision to shoot down Major Anderson's U-2 on 27 October. It is clear that high-level Soviet military communications between Moscow and Havana had not been compromised. So there would have been no way of knowing if Khrushchev (or anyone else in Moscow) had given the order to fire nuclear weapons (unless it was announced). Senior American officials believed that Soviet field commanders had greater autonomy than their Western counterparts. If one or two nuclear weapons had been fired, this might have suggested the actions 'of some damn Soviet second lieutenant'. There would also have been the concern about whether the missile(s) were fired by Soviet or Cuban troops.

Even if Soviet tactical nuclear missiles hit their targets (and the warheads exploded) the use of one or two weapons might not have proved militarily decisive. The essential equation, however, was not military. Retaliation against Cuba was a microcosm of the general argument about nuclear escalation. In the circumstances in which Kennedy had decided to make war on Cuba, the hawks would already have been winning the internal battle in Washington. The nature and form of the arguments and the dispositions of key protagonists can be predicted with some confidence. While the use of nuclear weapons would have caused great shock, the arguments for and against retaliation would have take similar form to debates on the use of force about which we know. The argument would have been forcefully put that if America did not retaliate against the use of nuclear weapons in its own backyard, then the credibility of any American threat to use nuclear weapons anywhere would have been called into question. Analogies of Munich would have loomed large in the President's counsels. So too would the analogy of 1914.

American intelligence eventually identified 6–8 Lunas and, according to Michael Desch, the possibility that the Soviets might use tactical nuclear weapons played an important part in the decision to discard OPLAN 314-61 in favour of OPLAN 316-61, increasing the tempo of operations to reduce the invasion forces' reaction time.[17] When the invasion fleet was being assembled, the Joint Chiefs had wanted to assign Honest John short-range ballistic missiles to the invasion force, but McNamara had refused.[18] Immediate retaliatory options against Cuba would presumably have included nuclear strike aircraft on the US carriers supporting the invasion. Otherwise, SAC bombers would have been reassigned for nuclear missions against Cuba. If America had used nuclear weapons in Cuba how would Khrushchev have responded, in circumstances in which the Americans had already gone to war, and were already fighting and killing Soviet troops? If he had not already moved against Berlin or Turkey, would he not have felt compelled to do so then? So, would Kennedy have responded with nuclear weapons knowing the risk of escalation? Or would he have held back from retaliation in Cuba to make clear that any move on Berlin or Turkey would meet with nuclear attack? Would the American President have stepped onto the second rung of the ladder of escalation? McNamara implies that he would. Garthoff indicates that he would, though he emphasizes that retaliation would have been confined to Cuba and would not have provoked Soviet–American escalation. If Kennedy had chosen to retaliate with nuclear weapons in Cuba he would presumably have done so on a discriminate and proportionate basis. Certainly, he would have attempted to exercise the maximum degree of control over the operation. Many Americans would have wanted to avenge their troops by killing Fidel Castro. However, an attack on Havana –

assuming the Americans believed him to be in Havana – would have caused huge civilian loss of life. So too would an attack on ports handling Soviet shipping, for example Muriel or Isabela. The MRBM sites themselves would presumably have been reduced to ruin by this stage. Finding targets of sufficient military significance, however, would not have been difficult, given the scale of Cuban and Soviet forces deployed.

MRBM strike from Cuba

The MRBMs in Cuba were within range of SAC air bases, ICBM sites and command centres (though whether they were capable of hitting military targets remains in doubt). What they were to be targeted on is unknown. There were 92 million Americans, including 58 cities of 100,000 population, believed to be within range of the missiles.[19] There was no discussion of nuclear strategy or nuclear targeting in ExComm, and McNamara is adamant that no discussions took place between him and the President on using nuclear weapons. Yet the public phase of the crisis began, on 22 October, with a clear statement on nuclear retaliation by President Kennedy, and one which seemingly abandoned his previous attempts to move away from the strategy of Massive Retaliation. In his televised speech on 22 October, Kennedy warned that the United States would 'regard any nuclear missile launched from Cuba against any nation in the western hemisphere as an attack by the Soviet Union on the United States, requiring a full retaliatory response upon the Soviet Union'. The statement was clearly designed to deter the Soviet Union as well as to reassure Latin American opinion at a moment when the Americans were anxious to secure OAS support for the naval blockade. Yet as a basis for action it raised fundamental and perplexing questions about American nuclear strategy.

While the term 'full retaliatory response' was never spelt out, it clearly augured a major nuclear attack on the Soviet Union, and could be readily interpreted to mean full implementation of the SIOP. Given the care with which ExComm considered actions and communications with the Soviets during the crisis, it is remarkable that the

potential consequences of this message were not more fully considered. Reflecting in 1987, McNamara pondered, 'if some damn Soviet
second lieutenant had launched a missile and it destroyed say Atlanta,
would we then have gone to all-out nuclear war? I hope not. But we
never discussed it. We should have, but we didn't.'[20] The former CIA
Deputy Director for Intelligence, Ray Cline, assisted those who
drafted 'the direct threat of nuclear retaliation'. His view was that the
threat was made because the risk of actual nuclear war was so low.
'Had it been otherwise,' he concluded in 1989, it 'would have been
argued at length and probably would have been hedged.'[21]

For Bundy, it will be recalled, the principal reason why Kennedy
needed to respond to the missiles in Cuba was because of his public
statements in September that he would respond. Yet the public threat
of nuclear retaliation could well have been an immeasurably greater
hostage to fortune. The implications for America's allies were potentially enormous. The inclusion of the phrase 'any nation' was designed
to reassure Latin American states, but significantly extended the scope
of American deterrence. Moreover, for the United States to launch 'a
full retaliatory response' against the Soviet Union would surely have
brought nuclear war to Europe. Yet there was no attempt to consult
allies in NATO. In *Danger and Survival*, Bundy attached great importance to the meaning and interpretation of words, and he revisited the
22 October speech, noting areas where there was an 'excess in
rhetoric'.[22] Yet, intriguingly, this did not include the passage where the
threat of retaliation was made, nor did he provide analysis of the one
major public statement on the use of nuclear weapons in the crisis,
beyond cursory dismissal of its significance in a footnote.[23]

Of the scenarios here under discussion, a nuclear conflict that
would begin with an MRBM attack on the United States was among
the least likely. The only credible circumstances in which the MRBMs
might have been fired was if the Soviet Union itself was under attack
or believed it was about to come under attack. In the circumstances of
an American invasion of Cuba the possibility of a launch under attack
would have arisen. The discussion in Chapter 4 suggested, however,
that given the scale of an American attack, and the disposition of
Soviet forces, the prospect of MRBMs being fired was negligible, even

if authorization from Moscow had been granted. The crack between unlikelihood and impossible in this case was probably very thin.

Nevertheless, had MRBMs been fired from Cuba, the Americans would again have needed to assess whether Khrushchev had given the order to fire, and why. Had Khrushchev lost control of his government or himself? Had the military taken over? Was it a 'damn Soviet second lieutenant'? Or a damn Cuban Lieutenant Colonel? Although it is now very clear that the Soviets were in full control of the MRBMs, there were those within ExComm, notably the Chairman of the Joint Chiefs, who worried that the Cubans might be able to fire the missiles at the United States.

Civil–Military Relations

A singular feature of the historiography of the missile crisis concerns how much has been learned of American decision-making. This includes evidence of *how* decisions were made and which advisers were influential at each stage. A key aspect of Kennedy's style of crisis management was to use his senior officials to argue through the options, sometimes in his presence, sometimes not. In this context, the Joint Chiefs were marginalized. Kennedy relied upon the Chairman of the Joint Chiefs, Maxwell Taylor, as well as Defense Secretary McNamara to represent their views on ExComm. The President only met the Joint Chiefs once during the crisis, when they vigorously argued for an attack on Cuba and when Curtis Le May opined that the blockade was 'almost as bad as the appeasement at Munich'.[24] Could Kennedy have kept the military at arm's length once armed conflict began and nuclear weapons had been used? Had consideration been given to using nuclear weapons, Kennedy would surely have needed to argue through the options with Le May and his colleagues.

After the crisis Kennedy confided to an aide that he believed that the military were 'mad'.[25] Throughout the crisis, the Joint Chiefs were consistent in recommending military action against Cuba. Within the JCS, General Earle Wheeler, the Army Chief of Staff, was minuted as saying: 'I never thought I'd live to see the day when I would want to go to war.'[26] Perhaps the best indicator of their desire for war on Cuba was the response of the Joint Chiefs on the 29 October to Khrushchev's announcement that he would withdraw the missiles. They argued that the air strikes should proceed the next day, to be followed by invasion unless 'irrefutable evidence' emerged that the Soviets were dismantling the missiles.[27] Very little is known about discussions – formal or informal – within the Pentagon at this time. Yet support for war on Cuba was not, in itself, an indicator of attitudes to nuclear war on the USSR. And although a request was made to equip the invasion force with tactical nuclear weapons, so far as is known at no point did the Joint Chiefs discuss, and certainly they did not recommend, destroying the MRBMs by means of nuclear attack.

It is a presumption to argue that the Joint Chiefs of Staff would have advocated nuclear escalation or pre-emption. They never disguised the fact that an American disarming attack would preclude all Soviet retaliation, and it is by no means certain that they would have pushed for nuclear pre-emption except where there was clear evidence of Soviet intent to strike. Moreover, there would have been other voices and other counsels in the White House. Nevertheless, it seems reasonable to assume that in certain scenarios the attitude and influence of the military would have been a factor for escalation.

Nuclear Strategy

McNamara has remained confident that Kennedy would not have used nuclear weapons first, and both in and out of office strenuously pursued a strategy for both the United States and NATO that was not based on first use. As we have seen, he felt 'certain' in retrospect that Kennedy would have retaliated 'with one, two or maybe ten' weapons. If nuclear weapons had been used against the United States or its allies, against what targets would America have responded? Curiously, none of the critical oral history conferences explored the issue of nuclear retaliation. In June 1962, McNamara had articulated an approach to fighting a nuclear war that was markedly different from the one Kennedy inherited. The emphasis was on counterforce and controlled escalation. The aim was to avoid the immediate destruction of cities to provide the Soviets with strong incentives against retaliation. The result became known as the 'no-cities strategy', though targeting of cities remained an integral part of the strategy. Soviet cities would be targeted to deter Soviet retaliation against the United States. American attacks would be against military targets. Kennedy himself told senior officials in December 1962:

> The only targets seem to me that really make any sense are at their missiles, firing in order to lessen – to the degree that we can – the amount of megatonnage the United States receives. That makes some sense to us. We should always suggest that . . . they assume we'd fire at their cities if we have to, because that will deter them. But as a practical matter, if the deterrent fails and they attack, what we want to do is be firing at their missile sites. Beyond that, these targets don't seem to me to make much sense.[28]

A disarming first strike had been scrutinized in September 1961, and Kennedy remained focused on the practicalities of how he might order such an attack. McNamara, however, did not support the idea of a disarming first strike because, as he explained in classified testimony to Congress in February 1962, 'Even if we attempted to destroy the enemy nuclear strike capability at its source, using all available resources, some portion of the Soviet force would strike back.'[29]

The rational argument against pre-emption was that the Soviets would retaliate with devastating effect. As Blight and Welch argue, 'No rational calculation would have led them to attempt a pre-emptive strike.'[30] Initiating a nuclear attack on the Soviet Union or the United States remained irrational because retaliation was sufficiently assured. Yet once nuclear weapons began to be used, the logic of mutual deterrence might begin to unravel. If either side believed that, for whatever reason, the adversary was preparing to strike first, the equations could change. The essence of the decision (to coin a phrase) is captured in the words of General Turgidson when he warns President Muffley:

> . . . it is necessary now to make a choice. To choose between two admittedly regrettable but nevertheless *distinguishable* post-war

environments – one where you got *twenty million* people killed and the other where you got *a hundred and fifty million* people killed . . . Mister President, I'm not saying we wouldn't get our hair mussed, but I do say no more than ten to twenty million killed . . . tops . . . depending on the breaks.

This was, of course, a parody of the logic that animated American civilian strategists in thinking about limited nuclear war.[31]

Crucial to many of the calculations was the perception that either side might be preparing to strike first. Potentially, a key warning indicator was the alert and readiness posture of the belligerents. Alerting nuclear forces is a potential source of misperception and escalation.[32] In the crisis itself the alert and readiness postures were asymmetrical. As noted in Chapter 1, the alert condition of United States forces around the globe was raised to DEFCON-3 on 22 October. The number of B-47 and B-52 aircraft on 15-minute ground-alert grew from 652 to 912, and 183 B-47s were dispersed to military and civilian airports around the United States.[33] Two days later, SAC was placed on the unprecedented and unrepeated state of DEFCON-2.[34] The number of B-52 bombers on airborne alert held at their Fail Safe points, *en route* to their targets, increased from 12 to 66. According to Sergei Khrushchev, his father believed the DEFCON-2 alert was bluff, though he still took it into consideration.[35]

Much has been made of Kennedy's attachment to the lessons drawn from Barbara Tuchman's account of how war came in 1914 in her book *The Guns of August*.[36] Yet this did not translate into caution about nuclear alerts. McNamara recognized that there were risks in changing SAC's alert condition, though no consideration was given to them.[37] Instead, the assumption was that an enhanced alert and readiness posture would act as a deterrent.[38] Some of these risks might have arisen from Soviet misperception. Others could have been generated by organizational problems, including greater risk of accidents and unauthorized action.[39] Alerting and dispersing nuclear bombers could have been seen as the equivalent of mobilizing mass armies. Whereas it had taken European armies weeks to mobilize, the nuclear bombers of the Strategic Air Command and Bomber

Command could strike their targets within hours, while IRBMs, SLBMs and ICBMs were some 10–35 minutes' flying time from the Soviet Union. Mutual misperception could have led far more quickly to a catastrophe that was far greater than in August 1914. Yet, although McNamara alluded to risks in changing SAC's alert condition, Kennedy and his senior officials barely paused before raising the US DEFCON alert states, and neither the President nor his colleagues exhibited concern that the Soviets might misinterpret the signal and mistake resolve for imminent aggression.

Harold Macmillan had also read Tuchman's account of the coming of the Great War, in which as a young subaltern in the Grenadier Guards he was wounded in the trenches where so many of his generation perished.[40] The Prime Minister appears to have taken a very different view from the President, whose initial response he privately felt was 'rather panicky'.[41] At the start of the crisis Macmillan signalled support for American mobilization in the Caribbean as an instrument of coercion. Yet he was strongly opposed to mobilization in Europe. On 22 October, his observation to General Norstad that, 'mobilisation had sometimes caused war' had strong echoes of *The Guns of August*. The British nuclear alert and readiness state did not include provision for airborne alerting (as the cost of ensuring bombers were airborne at all times was seen as prohibitive). Although Thor missiles and V-bombers on Quick Reaction Alert were at fifteen minutes' readiness, no attempt was made to disperse the V-bomber force. Even as the crisis reached its climax on 27 October, Macmillan made clear to the Chief of the Air Staff, Sir Thomas Pike, that he 'did not consider the time was appropriate for any overt preparatory steps to be taken such as mobilisation' and he, 'did not wish Bomber Command to be alerted'.[42]

Much remains to be clarified about Soviet command and control. As noted in Chapter 3, Soviet strategic forces were moved to a higher state of nuclear alert than was realized in the West.[43] Was this sufficient for them to consider a pre-emptive launch, either on warning or under attack? Available evidence of Soviet technological capabilities suggests not. There was a central tension (if not a fundamental flaw) in Soviet operational doctrine at this time. The emphasis was on

131

striking first, but by the time the ICBMs were ready to fire they could well have been destroyed. Such conclusions remain tentative, and even with greater insight into Soviet command and control arrangements during the crisis, the $64,000 question of whether retaliation against the United States was possible may only be answered by guesswork. It may well be that, given the size and relative technological backwardness of their strategic forces, the Soviet Union would not have been able to visit assured destruction on the United States (though Western Europe was another matter). Yet the possibility that a handful of missiles or bombers might get through and destroy one or more American cities was another matter.[44]

Decapitation

One specific question concerns what would have happened if an MRBM had struck Washington. The missile would presumably have been detected in flight and its trajectory tracked. Some warning might have reached political authorities, though there would probably have been no time to evacuate the President. Provision had been made for an alternate headquarters at a bunker at Mount Weather, a 434-acre site in the Virginia Mountains, 48 miles from Washington.[45] A separate site had also been established for Congress, under the Greenbrier resort in West Sulphur Springs in West Virginia. Whether in circumstances of an imminent attack, Kennedy would have even attempted to flee would have depended on how he interpreted what was happening. He once told an aide that in a nuclear attack he would remain in the White House.[46] Depending where the missile(s) landed (and assuming any warheads detonated), political and military leaders in Washington would almost certainly have perished, though Alice George recounts that one somewhat optimistic plan existed for helicopter pilots and rescue workers from Olmstead Air Force Base in Pennsylvania to fly into Washington and dig the President out of the White House bunker from under the rubble.[47]

If Kennedy had been killed, the line of Presidential succession ran to the Vice-President, Speaker of the House, president pro tempore of the Senate, and cabinet secretaries in order of the creation of their departments.[48] Discussion of air strike options on 16 October had already raised the possibility of Soviet missiles being fired under attack. If Kennedy had decided on military force after 28 October there would have been detailed consideration of specific scenarios, including a decapitating blow from Cuba. In circumstances where the MRBMs were fired in response to an American attack on Cuba, precautions would presumably have been taken for this contingency to relocate the Vice-President and other senior members of the executive away from Washington. In these circumstances, the destruction of the capital would have meant the Presidency would have passed to Lyndon Johnson.

Predelegation

It is difficult to see a 'bolt from the blue' attack as a credible scenario in October 1962. But in circumstances where evacuation of alternate leaders had not taken place, it is unclear who would have assumed Presidential authority. It is easier to imagine the likely confusion and paralysis that would have gripped Washington. Unless prior to military action a clear policy on retaliation had been decided and communicated, in particular to military commanders, decisions on the use of nuclear war weapons would have rested with the military. On the one occasion that nuclear weapons have been used in war, authority for their use was delegated to the commander of the US strategic air force in the Pacific, General Spaatz.[49] This authority extended to the second and subsequent bombs, which meant no separate Presidential decision was taken when Nagasaki was destroyed. Indeed, it has even been suggested that Truman himself 'did not know about the attack on Nagasaki until after it happened'.[50] However, by 10 August, Truman had second thoughts about delegating authority to his military commanders, and decided that no further operations were to be undertaken without his express order.[51] As the Cold War developed, Truman refused to allow the Pentagon operational control over nuclear weapons, whose nuclear cores were held by the Atomic Energy Commission. Nor was he prepared to consider delegating his authority to his generals.[52]

Truman's successors took a different view. Evidence has emerged that President Eisenhower delegated authority to the military to use nuclear weapons under specified emergency conditions. Arrangements were developed under Eisenhower that provided for predelegation, 'to expend nuclear weapons in defense of the United States, its Territories, possessions and forces when the urgency of time and circumstances does not permit a specific decision by the President or other person empowered to act in his stead'.[53] President Kennedy accepted these when he took office, and had not reviewed or revised them by the time of the missile crisis. Predelegation of nuclear release authority could have been potentially decisive in escalation. In circumstances where Washington was attacked, for example, and the National Command Authority destroyed, CINCSAC would have possessed authority to launch retaliatory attacks on the Soviet Union. It could have been for General Power to decide whether to execute the SIOP. Reflecting on a situation where Washington was the only target hit, the founder of SAC, Curtis Le May, once said he doubted he would have retaliated against the Soviet Union.[54] Whether his successor shared these doubts is unknown. The idea of controlled escalation was fundamental to McNamara's approach to nuclear strategy, and was by 1962 reflected in the SIOP. However, the idea of limited nuclear war was imposed on the military who saw dangers in restraint.

When Kennedy and McNamara reviewed the SIOP they inherited, one aspect that deeply concerned them was that countries other than the Soviet Union were scheduled for oblivion. Most significantly – in both humanitarian and political terms – this included China. Some provision for withholding attacks on other countries was introduced by McNamara,[55] though had SIOP-63 been implemented in full, the People's Republic of China would have been the victim of devastating and unprovoked nuclear bombardment by the United States. There is no indication that Khrushchev consulted Mao on the deployments in Cuba. The Chinese themselves were preparing to attack India over disputed border territory on 25 October. The Chinese leadership had shown interest in and support for Castro's revolution, and during the crisis supported the Soviet/Cuban position. When the Soviets withdrew the missiles from Cuba, Beijing condemned Moscow for 'adventurism and capitulationism'.[56] Yet the Chinese government played no part in the decisions of the Soviet government. In 1961, General Shoup, the Commandant of the US Marine Corps, expressed concern that striking China when it was not at war with the US was 'not the American way'.[57] Had the SIOP been implemented in full, scores of millions of Chinese civilians would have been killed.

One fundamental aspect of seeking to control a nuclear war was to preserve the enemy's ability to manage and terminate military operations. To provide the Soviets with the option of fighting a controlled nuclear war, Moscow was taken off the list of initial targets in late 1961.[58] General Power had previously made clear that 'if you are going to attack a nation, you have to attack its control centres'.[59] The military – and humanitarian – rationale for this was that beheading the behemoth would impair retaliation, constrain damage and reduce casualties. Without specific orders and left to his own judgement, would General Power have looked to proportionate retaliation, or would he would have 'stuck to the plan' and launched a genuinely full retaliatory response? As noted previously, he is reported to have inveighed against the cowardice of Kennedy for shying away from the chance to wage all-out nuclear war on the Soviet Union in October 1962. One of his subordinates, General Horace Wade, commander of SAC's 8th Air Force, said of him:

> General Power . . . was demanding; he was mean; he was cruel, unforgiving, and he didn't have the time of day to pass with anyone. A hard cruel individual . . . I used to worry about General Power. I used to worry that General Power was not stable. I used to worry about the fact that he had control over so many weapons and weapons systems and could, under certain conditions, launch the force. Back in the days before we had real positive control, SAC had the power to do a lot of things, and it was in his hands, and he knew it.[60]

In September 1961 General Power had warned the President that the greatest danger in the next year was a Soviet surprise attack. 'If a general atomic war is inevitable,' he counselled, 'the US should strike first.'[61] How far, and under what circumstances, would he have exercised restraint if the choice had been his?

Since the late 1960s, British procedures for authorization of nuclear retaliation in the event that the United Kingdom was victim of a devastating nuclear attack, apparently involved captains of Polaris and later Trident SSBNs reading a handwritten letter from the Prime Minister deposited in advance in the ship's safe explaining his or her wishes.[62] Would Kennedy have contemplated a 'decision from beyond the grave' in 1962? Would those who received such a message have felt obligated to abide by his wishes or instructions?

If John Kennedy (or Lyndon Johnson) had lived to retain responsibility for the decision whether to retaliate to an MRBM strike, what would they have done? Declaratory American strategy before 22 October augured a controlled and discriminate response. Whether SIOP-63 was sufficiently fine-tuned for such a contingency is extremely doubtful. Indeed, the targeting plans inherited by the Nixon administration, which had themselves been through several revisions since 1962, were deemed inflexible by the incoming Republican administration. One insider quipped that the SIOP had 'five options for massive retaliation'.[63] Henry Kissinger described it as a horror strategy and remarked, 'to only have the option of killing 80 million people is the height of immorality'.[64] In 1962, one thing was certain. Kennedy (and McNamara) would not have simply deferred to military assessments of what was and was not practicable. Kennedy's conduct of the naval blockade and his insistence that the navy adhere to his wishes rather than pre-existing plans and procedures was surely indicative of how he would have acted in war.[65]

Many of the assumptions about the ability of the Americans to control a nuclear exchange were based on unwarranted optimism about their command and control capabilities. Subsequent studies have made clear that, in 1962, effective command and control of nuclear war was a chimera.[66] The breakdown of command could well have fuelled pressure for a disarming attack (if not indeed for an all-out response). A further factor that could have undermined American attempts to use nuclear forces in a controlled and discriminate fashion was the actions of third parties, and in particular the use of British nuclear weapons – the third arachnid in the bottle. The independent use of British nuclear weapons could have seriously undermined any attempt to control escalation and terminate hostilities.[67] In Chapter 3 it was suggested that the UK would have been no more likely to 'go nuclear' over Berlin than the US. A situation in which general war had broken out was different. Certainly once nuclear weapons began exploding on British territory the pressure to use, rather than lose, the British strategic force would have been strong.

By October 1962, the RAF had some 140 operational V-bombers capable of striking the Soviet Union with atomic and thermo-nuclear weapons. Bomber Command also had access to American thermo-nuclear weapons. Although agreements between the British and the Americans specified that bombs could only be transferred on receipt of Presidential authorization, arrangements between the USAF and the RAF were different on the ground. At RAF Marham, for example, 24 Valiant bombers, each armed with two US Mark 5 bombs were deployed during the missile crisis.[68] Moreover, Bomber Command operated the four squadrons of Thor IRBMs, deployed under dual-key arrangements with the USAF. Sixty Thors, each with a 1.45 MT warhead, were based in East Anglia, 10 to 20 minutes' flying time from their targets in Eastern Europe and the Soviet Union. With a range of 1,500 miles, the weapons could strike Moscow.

As noted, to provide the Soviets with the option of fighting a controlled nuclear war Moscow was taken off the US list of initial targets in late 1961.[69] The British, however, appear to have seen Moscow as a key element in their national targeting policy. Later, in the 1970s, 'the Moscow Criterion' formed the entire basis of the British deterrent.[70] By 1962, Bomber Command had a co-ordinated nuclear strike plan with SAC, and a national plan. In February 1962, both the British and the Americans had undertaken to consult with NATO on the use of nuclear weapons. Yet had British strategic nuclear weapons been used, Moscow could well have been a priority.

A further dimension concerns British nuclear predelegation, details of which have now appeared.[71] By 1962, the British had developed arrangements for an alternative government headquarters at

Corsham in Wiltshire (in 1962 code-named Turnstile) and for a designated deputy to the Prime Minister.[72] The alternate seat of government was to oversee survival as well as to act as 'an alternative centre to London for authorising nuclear retaliation'.[73] The Prime Minister, or his designated deputy, could authorize nuclear retaliation (although he could not order military commanders, who owed their allegiance to the Crown and not the government).[74] It was recognized, particularly with the advent of ballistic missiles, that there was the prospect that the political leadership might be killed in a surprise attack. Pre-delegated nuclear authority to the military was therefore agreed.

In September 1962, the Commander-in-Chief of Bomber Command, Air Marshal Cross, was issued with a directive authorizing specified measures if he judged his forces in the UK were about to come under nuclear attack and there had been no strategic warning, or if nuclear bombs had already exploded in the UK. In these circumstances he was authorized to order his bombers airborne 'under positive control' and seek to contact the Prime Minister (or his deputy). He was also to contact the commander of the US 7th Air Division and, in the event of nuclear attacks on Britain, co-ordinate release of nuclear weapons under joint control. In 1962, this covered both American nuclear bombs on RAF bombers and Thor IRBMs. Air Marshal Cross was further told that, 'If enemy nuclear bombs have burst in this country, and action [to make contact with the Prime Minister, his deputy or the Commander of the US 7th division] has proved abortive, you are authorized in the last resort to order on your own responsibility nuclear retaliation by all means at your disposal.'[75] Nuclear retaliation entailed attacks on Soviet cities as well as command and control and other military targets.

Conclusion

'If indeed war should break out,' Khrushchev warned Kennedy in his letter of 26 October, 'then it would not be in our power to stop it, for such is the logic of war.'[76] He could have been right. The possibility that attempts to control and terminate nuclear war would sooner or later have failed was clearly very real. Apocalyptic visions of nuclear Armageddon pervaded popular culture and presumably the nightmares of political leaders at the time. Understanding of climatic catastrophe has subsequently reinforced our understanding of what major or all-out nuclear war would have brought. It is important to recognize the mortal threat to humankind in October 1962, though conveying the almost unimaginable horror and suffering is beyond the vocabulary, if not the imagination, of most commentators. Retreating (or advancing) into the parody of *Dr Strangelove* becomes a way of coping with the ultimate human nightmare.

Apocalyptic thinking is necessary, though it comes with a risk that other plausible nuclear outcomes are discounted. When Julius Caesar crossed the Rubicon in 49 BC he still had many days' march before he reached Rome. Crossing the nuclear threshold in 1962 would not inexorably have led to all-out nuclear war. The die *might* not have been cast. Innumerable scenarios can be drawn involving the use of different types and numbers of nuclear weapons against different targets, some involving retaliation, others not. Assessing the humanitarian and socio-economic consequences would involve a vast and complex study in its own right. Similarly, charting the likely political consequences of such contingencies raises formidably complex questions. At what point, for example, would the institutions of global governance and configurations of global authority have been transformed, and into what?

In Robert O'Connell's counterfactual essay, full-scale nuclear attack on the Soviet Union leads to the disintegration of NATO and expulsion of the United States from the United Nations. Similarly, in Brendon Dubois's *Resurrection Day*, as SAC obliterates the cities and peoples of the USSR and its allies, NATO swiftly disintegrates and America retreats into isolationism, excluded from the UN as a pariah state. In both these representations, American casualties are well below the threshold of General Turgidson's 'getting the hair mussed'. Rather more curiously, Western Europe is spared direct attacks or major casualties from fallout. Indeed in *Resurrection Day*, none of America's allies provide any military support to the United States, and although nuclear attacks are mounted on the Soviet Union from

NATO territory, Western Europe is left unscathed (and in Britain, bizarrely untouched, reactionary elements in the government attempt to seize the post-holocaust moment to reclaim an imperial global ascendancy).

In early-1960s' Whitehall, the Joint Inter-Services Group for the Study of All-Out Warfare (JIGSAW) used scenario-based thinking in developing a concept of 'breakdown'.[77] This was the point at which they believed civil society would collapse under nuclear attack. By then, the British had abandoned any notion of effective civil defence, and were wholly reliant on deterrence. Is there a global equivalent of breakdown? At what point would it have come? How would the complex interactions of environmental, socio-economic, agricultural, political and military changes brought about by nuclear war have wrought fundamental changes in life on Earth? The prospective answers are as imponderable as they are frightening. Yet whether it would mean the risk of Armageddon, or fundamental degradation of life on Earth, or 'merely' levels of carnage and suffering reaching beyond all past wars all put together, the prospect of nuclear war in 1962 remains terrifying. Given the attention which historians and others have devoted to understanding the Cuban missile crisis, if we cannot learn about nuclear weapons from this event, there seems little purpose in studying the past to guide the present or the future. So, Chapter 6 examines whether there are lessons to be learned, and whether they have relevance today.

CHAPTER 6

Silence of the Lambs

First principles. Of each particular thing, ask: what is it in itself, in its own constitution? What is its causal nature?'
Dr Hannibal Lecter, quoting Emperor Marcus Aurelius[1]

What is the 'causal nature' of a thermo-nuclear weapon? What is it 'in itself'? Does it deter? Does it provoke? Does it matter? Is it sufficient to state that it is a weapon of mass destruction or more pertinent to note that in the twentieth century more people perished at the hands of machetes than hydrogen bombs? According to Jonathan Schell, it is 'a striking historical fact, and one that should make us reflect, that the severest crisis of the nuclear age, was *about* the weapons themselves'.[2] Perhaps a similar sentiment occurred to John F. Kennedy on 21 October 1962, when he confided to David Ormsby-Gore that 'the existence of nuclear arms made a secure and rational world impossible. We must somehow find a means to get rid of nuclear weapons.'[3] Or are thermo-nuclear weapons simply artefacts whose meaning and purpose derive from the motivations of those who wield them and the perceptions of those who fear them?

The Cuban missile crisis was the moment in human history when the prospect of nuclear war seemed most real for most people. The crisis has been the most intensely and imaginatively studied crisis of the Cold War, if not of the twentieth century. If the Cuban missile crisis cannot tell us about thermo-nuclear weapons, what (or who) can? So what did people learn from the Cuban missile crisis about the political and military role of nuclear weapons? What should they – or we – learn? And what can be gleaned about the nature and risks of nuclear deterrence? Can we, indeed, learn lessons from events that took place years ago, at the height of the Cold War, for the conduct of political and military affairs in the twenty-first century?

The assumption that we can learn from the past provokes various objections. There are those who contend that the nature of history (or rather historiography) cannot provide us with lessons, because the past is a construct of the present. 'The trouble is there is no such thing as "history"; Sir Michael Howard has observed. 'History is what historians write, and historians are part of the process they are writing about.'[4] The nature and purpose of that process, and of how knowledge is constructed, are moreover contested. Few retain simplistic divisions between objective historical reality and the subjective (or normative) perspectives of the historian. Such considerations merit careful reflection, not least because the possession and development of nuclear weapons remain a matter of enduring controversy. Lessons of nuclear history, moreover, can be readily drawn to fit pre-existing assumptions and perspectives. The lessons that hawks and doves drew from the crisis for the conduct of diplomacy and the management of nuclear arsenals were informed by whether they were hawks or doves to begin with. In one sense, we are all owls now. We have greater understanding of things that decision-makers did not know at the time, and which for decades eluded (or were hidden from) scholars and commentators. Yet greater insight, and in some instances greater consensus on the pattern of events, does not transcend fundamental debate about the utility and legitimacy of weapons of mass destruction. One person's dove remains another person's chicken, just as one person's hawk is another person's lemming.

The idea that we can learn specific 'lessons' from the crisis can also be challenged. Many historians are rightly wary of cherry-picking the evidence. As Michael Howard has warned, 'It is safer to start with the assumption that history, whatever its value in educating the judgement, teaches no "lessons" . . . The past is infinitely various, an inexhaustible storehouse of events from which we can prove anything or its contrary.'[5] And, as McGeorge Bundy noted, 'the task of thinking straight about moments of danger in the nuclear age is much larger than the study of any single episode.'[6] Yet single episodes and historical analogies loom large in debates about crisis management and nuclear weapons, and as Michael Howard observed (in his review of Bundy's book) the missile crisis provides nuclear strategists with 'the only hard evidence of nuclear confrontation they have'.[7] Since then, evidence has emerged about other crises, including the superpower involvement in the 1973 Arab–Israeli war and the confrontations between India and Pakistan.

Applying lessons from the crisis has also extended beyond nuclear crisis management. In December 1990, for example, the former British Prime Minister, Edward Heath, invoked Kennedy's handling of the crisis to advocate creative diplomacy rather than force in the eviction of Iraq from Kuwait.[8] Most recently, Graham Allison used the analogy of Kennedy's handling of the denouement of the missile crisis to suggest an alternative American strategy for Iran's determination to master the nuclear fuel cycle.[9] Whatever doubts historians may have about the hazards of learning from history, political leaders are happy to use (or mis-use) the lessons of the past to meet the needs of the present. Kennedy's reading of Barbara Tuchman's *The Guns of August*, and its impact on the missile crisis provides an exemplar of learning lessons from history.[10] And in pondering the relevance of the missile crisis for the issues of today, it is worth noting that we are about as far from the events of 1962 as Kennedy was from the events of 1914.

Counterfactuals, too, feature in political debate. The case for Britain's retention of its strategic nuclear deterrent has been made with reference to the historical counterfactual that Japan and Germany would not have embarked upon their wars of aggression had they known that the democracies would develop atomic weapons to use against them.[11] Proponents of maintaining the British deterrent have also argued that if Argentina had possessed nuclear weapons in 1982 and Britain had not, the UK might have not responded with force to the seizure of the Falkland Islands.[12] And the general proposition that nuclear weapons kept the peace in Europe rests on the counterfactual proposition that without nuclear weapons the Soviets would have sought to use their conventional superiority for political or military purposes.

Lessons of History: History of Lessons

Writing in 1987, Richard Ned Lebow observed:

> The 'lessons' of the Cuban Missile crisis occupy a central place both in United States foreign policy and in international relations theory. For policymakers, the crisis confirmed a number of tenets about the utility of power in a nuclear world and the ways in which relations with the Soviet Union should best be managed. Theoreticians have thoroughly examined the case for generalizations about crisis decision-making, bargaining theory, and the role of nuclear weapons in foreign policy.[13]

A useful starting point in exploring the lessons of history is the history of lessons. In the immediate years after the crisis, the dominant interpretation of events in the West followed Arthur Schlesinger's depiction of JFK's handling of events: 'It was this combination of toughness and restraint, of will, nerve, and wisdom, so brilliantly controlled, so matchlessly calibrated, that dazzled the world.'[14] Harold Macmillan wrote that, 'While boldly facing the ultimate resort to force, his tactics and his sense of timing were perfect. He was at the same time ready to act, and to allow his adversary the opportunity of retreat.'[15] The lessons were that nuclear crises could be managed, and the threat of force manipulated by wise and careful leaders, to successfully defend and deter.[16] The American war in Vietnam owed much to a belief in the calibration of force that had seemingly worked in 1962. Critical or 'revisionist' interpretations also emerged that condemned the recklessness and risks of Kennedy's behaviour.[17] In the 1970s and 1980s, sophisticated critiques of crisis management gathered pace.[18] Others had a different perspective on Kennedy's management of events. Dean Acheson attributed the outcome to pure 'dumb luck'.[19]

What lessons did the Soviets draw? 'You Americans will never be able to do this to us again,' Soviet Deputy Foreign Minister, Vasily Kuznetsov, is reputed to have said in 1962. Certainly, the Caribbean crisis was one factor in the removal of Nikita Khrushchev, whose successors could hardly be described as impulsive risk-takers.[20] Yet the experience of October 1962 reinforced the determination of the Soviets to pursue their existing build-up of strategic forces, as well as to create 'a blue-water fleet' to project Soviet power and influence. Moreover, although Soviet policy after the crisis involved dialogue and détente with the Americans, it did not entail either disarmament or disengagement from the Third World. Arms control did not mean disarmament. Détente did not mean an end to ideological struggle.

A more radical lesson was drawn in the midst of the crisis by John F. Kennedy: 'We must somehow find a means to get rid of nuclear weapons.'[21] Yet, neither the United States nor the Soviet Union (nor indeed Kennedy, himself, once the crisis was over) saw nuclear disarmament as the lesson to be learned from October 1962. Instead, important arms control measures were pursued, in particular the 1963 Partial Test Ban Treaty, which banned atmospheric testing of nuclear weapons. There was also the hotline agreement, as mundane reality sought to catch up with *Dr Strangelove*. Nevertheless, the 'arms race' continued apace, and technological and political developments soon provided the basis for renewed East–West confrontation.

Writing in the late 1980s, Blight, Nye and Welch conclude that 'though the world of 1962 is becoming increasingly remote, some of its lessons seem timeless.'[22] James Blight argued that the central lesson was that nuclear wars cannot be won and must never be fought.[23] Bundy concluded his analysis in *Danger and Survival*, by quoting John F. Kennedy: 'We must make it our business not to pass this way again.'[24] Bundy and McNamara argued that nuclear crises are not to be managed, but avoided. Were it not for the fact that so many people somehow failed to grasp this point it would be tempting to evoke Basil Fawlty's depiction of his wife appearing on *Mastermind* to answer questions on: 'The Bleeding Obvious'.[25]

In one sense we have not passed this way again. The United States did not mobilize to invade Cuba (though the CIA continued plotting the assassination of Castro at least until 1965).[26] The Soviet Union withdrew all its nuclear forces from Cuba (including its tactical weapons) and did not try to re-introduce land-based nuclear missiles. On the other hand, an attempt was made to base nuclear-armed submarines in Cuba in 1970 when what Raymond Garthoff describes as 'a muffled confrontation of wills' was resolved by diplomacy rather than by blockade or military confrontation.[27] Castro re-established his relationship with Khrushchev, and Cuba eventually went on to play an important role in promoting revolutionary and Soviet foreign policy objectives in Africa.[28]

The Cuban missile crisis is frequently depicted as the end of the most dangerous phase of the Cold War. A better description is that it marked the end of a dangerous phase in Nikita Khrushchev's foreign policy. The reasons for the Berlin and Cuban crises reflected complex issues of East–West relations (as well as East–East and West–West relations). The issue of West Berlin, for example, was inextricably bound up with Soviet perceptions of a militarily resurgent and nuclear-armed Germany. Yet everything that has emerged about Soviet decision-making suggests that the Berlin and Cuban crises owed their origins to Khrushchev's strategic ambitions and political calculations.

Chickens Coming Home to Roost

Yet although détente and arms control led to a more stable political relationship for the next decade, the foundations of this stability were insufficiently robust to withstand the pressures that led to the Second Cold War. In the late 1970s/1980s many familiar ingredients of Soviet–American confrontation were apparent. Americans found a new missile gap in the form of 'the window of opportunity', generated by Soviet ICBM capabilities, as well as Moscow's support for revolutionary forces in the Third World.[29] The Soviets became so concerned about their own vulnerability and about aggressive American intent that they believed Washington was preparing for a nuclear first strike. At one point in November 1983 they apparently mistook a NATO command exercise for genuine nuclear mobilization.[30] The precise military and political configurations may have been different from

1962 but the contexts and pretexts for conflict were, in important respects, rather similar.

Perhaps the most obvious parallel, and the most striking demonstration that no-one seemed to learn one obvious lesson from the Cuban missile crisis, involved deployment of land-based MRBMs within striking range of the adversary's territory. In December 1983, the United States deployed an MRBM (the Pershing-2) in West Germany which the Soviets maintained could destroy Moscow (in about the same time that an R-12 could destroy Washington). The American government insisted that the Pershing-2 had a range of 1,600 km rather 2,500 km and could not reach the Soviet capital. Deterrence, it has been said, is in the eye of the beholder. So too is threat. As we have seen, the United States was prepared to take the world to the brink (or at least towards the brink) of nuclear war in 1962, because they estimated the Soviets had put 33 MRBMs within range of the United States. Twenty years later, NATO deployed 108 MRBMS (and 464 GLCMs) within the range of the Soviet Union. If the lessons of the Cuban missile crisis were about avoiding crises, the history of the Second Cold War suggests some lessons were not learned very well or remembered very long. As noted in Chapter 2, the Soviet deployment in 1962 did not create a crisis simply because of a military threat. And just as in 1962, the Soviets could target ICBMs and strategic bombers on the United States, so in 1983 the United States had many ICBMs, SLBMs and strategic bombers targeted on the USSR. The Soviets may have overestimated the range of the Pershing-2 but not its precision guidance or hard-target killing capability. What most concerned them in 1983 was that the MRBMs could destroy key Soviet command and control centres without which the Soviet scorpion would be blind. To paraphrase Bundy (and mix the metaphor) the Pershing-2 was a cobra because the Soviets believed it was a cobra.

Parallels between 1962 and 1983 should not be overdrawn. There were no thirteen days. Whether we see the events of the 1980s as a crisis depends on how we define a crisis. Historical scrutiny of Soviet behaviour in this period has barely begun, though intriguing comparisons can be made. When, in October 1962, Major Maultsby's U-2 violated Soviet airspace, he was able to turn around and return to safety. In September 1983, the South Korean airliner KAL 007 enjoyed no such luck and was shot down by MiG interceptors, killing all 269 people on board. The most worrying comparison – and certainly one of the most worrying incidents in 1983 – was when Soviet satellite-based detectors picked up the launch of a Minuteman ICBM, followed by four more ICBMs several minutes later.[31] There are parallels with the Moorestown radar incident in 1962 although, in this case, the duty officer at the air defence early-warning centre at Serpukhov-15 decided not to pass on the warning, as more reliable ground radars had not picked up the attack, and because he had been trained to expect a massive ICBM assault rather than a handful of missiles. In contrast to the Americans in 1962, however, the Soviets *did* have a policy of launch-on-warning in 1983. Three weeks earlier, Soviet military authorities had responded to the intrusion of KAL 007 with lethal military force. As Benjamin Fischer argues, 'If the General Staff had reacted as the original air-defense commander had on that occasion, the Soviets might have fired off their nuclear arsenal.'[32] The actions of a Lieutenant Colonel Petrov in not passing on the warning – for which he was removed from his post – is, of course, a striking example of the role of unauthorized action in *reducing* the risk of nuclear war. Perhaps one of the more interesting parallels concerns the lessons learned by Ronald Reagan. Beth Fischer persuasively argues that Reagan's sudden realization of how Soviet paranoia had almost led to disaster led him to review and revise his approach to Soviet–American relations, shortly before Mikhail Gorbachev emerged with his radical vision of global security and nuclear disarmament.[33]

The events of 1962 and 1983 both involved the concept of extended deterrence. Soviet missiles were placed in Cuba to deter an American attack on Cuba (though there were other reasons for the deployment). Extended deterrence was therefore integral to the origins of the crisis (even if this was not accepted by many Americans for many years). The deployment of nuclear missiles in NATO Europe in 1983 was also born of extended nuclear deterrence, although the calculations about the nuclear balance were more complex (or at least convoluted) than twenty years earlier. The genesis of Khrushchev's actions in 1962 was (in part) born of concern for Cuba's security. President Carter's willingness to put nuclear missiles into Western Europe was designed to reassure Western Europeans that changes in both the strategic and theatre nuclear balance had called into question the credibility of extended deterrence. Among the more obvious dissimilarities between 1962 and 1983 was that, whereas the Soviets used secrecy and deception, NATO decisions in 1979 were made public, and moreover led to several years' negotiations over an Intermediate Nuclear Forces (INF) treaty.[34] It was only when these failed that the deployment of Pershing-2s and GLCMs then proceeded.

The lessons of the missile crisis emerged in political and strategic debates of the 1980s. There were those who argued that lessons could not be applied in the 1980s because the strategic relationship between the United States and the Soviet Union had fundamentally altered. In 1962, the United States enjoyed both overwhelming nuclear supremacy and overwhelming naval and conventional superiority in the Caribbean. In the 1980s, when the Soviets had attained a form of strategic parity, enshrined in the SALT process, American nuclear superiority no longer counted for what it had. In the view of Douglas Dillon in 1987, for example: 'It's a totally different world today, and as far as I can see, the Cuban missile crisis has little relevance in today's world.'[35] Other ExCommites disagreed. Kennedy's advisers were as divided in the 1980s as they had been twenty years earlier.

The debates over whether Khrushchev was deterred by overwhelming American nuclear superiority or simply by the threat of nuclear war, and whether Kennedy was deterred by the potential loss of only a handful of American cities, were important in discussions about nuclear superiority and the composition of nuclear deterrence. There was vigorous argument among American students of nuclear strategy. Prominent among the protagonists were the ExCommites, notably Bundy, McNamara and Nitze. Bundy and McNamara became vigorous critics of US nuclear strategy and arms control under Ronald Reagan. Nitze remained wedded to the utility and necessity of American nuclear superiority, and played an important role in the Reagan administration's pursuit of arms control.[36] Bundy argued that the foundation of deterrence was the danger of nuclear war rather than the nuclear superiority that Reagan pursued. In the 1980s, informed European critics of Western strategy drew upon the writings of Bundy, McNamara, *et al*, as they articulated an alternative vision of security in the nuclear age.

The end of the Cold War and the collapse of the Soviet Union have fundamentally transformed the strategic equations and political geometry of world politics. They have not, however, resulted in nuclear disarmament. The differences between the worlds of 2007 and 1987 are even greater than those between 1987 and 1962. Yet, paradoxically, the world we now inhabit bears greater similarity to an earlier period of the Cold War, when the United States had overwhelming nuclear superiority, before the era of Mutual Assured Destruction. Recently, it has been argued that the United States has reached, or is about to reach, a state in which it could launch a disarming nuclear first strike on Russia or China.[37] Whether the Cuban missile crisis belongs to the era of Mutual Assured Destruction, or whether the strategic relationship in 1962 was more opaque and ambiguous, is an issue discussed previously. The political relationship between America and Russia has fundamentally shifted. Yet if there is a return to political confrontation, the 'rise of US nuclear primacy' may portend a return to the calculations of 'use them or lose them', pre-emptive retaliation and the risk of inadvertent nuclear war.

Non-American Ornithology

It is important to recognize in exploring what lessons we might learn that they depend on who 'we' are. How America's allies understood what had happened, for example, raised very different questions than those raised in Washington or Moscow. Similarly, how emerging nuclear powers 'read' the crisis was potentially crucial where nuclear arms races occurred in areas of regional instability. Some students of the India–Pakistan crises have drawn explicitly on Bundy's interpretations and expositions of existential deterrence.[38] And there is evidence that both Indian and Pakistani officials have taken an interest in lessons from the crisis.[39] From what can be discerned these lessons appear to draw on the benefits of minimum deterrence rather than the risks of nuclear inadvertence.

At a general level, the Europeans, like the Soviets, drew lessons from the crisis that encouraged them down paths on which they were already moving. Harold Macmillan, for example, was already wedded to the British deterrent for personal, domestic political and strategic reasons. If he accepted what General Strong told him of Kennedy's intentions to 'go nuclear' regardless of the views of America's allies, it would have only reinforced an already fiercely held view that Britain needed to maintain an independent nuclear deterrent. The failure of Kennedy to consult at the outset of the crisis was a personal and political irritation for Macmillan, though it was offset by their transatlantic telephone conversations, which Macmillan later assiduously talked up. For de Gaulle, likewise, the refusal of the Americans to consult on the imposition of the naval blockade, reinforced pre-existing assumptions about American behaviour, and like the British, reinforced existing determination to develop a national deterrent.[40]

Kennedy's assurance to Khrushchev that he would withdraw the Jupiter IRBMs on condition that the arrangement was kept secret from NATO raises interesting questions about how America's allies would have reacted had they known. Some voices within ExComm suggested that any bilateral arrangement over the Turkish Jupiters would have dire consequences for the alliance. Public revelation would undoubtedly have strengthened European concern about Kennedy's commitment to NATO security (even if the decision was taken to enhance that security by reducing the risk of nuclear war). On the other hand, the essential strategic imperatives and national interests that underpinned the alliance still held sway. Perhaps the most significant revelation which compels revision of European thinking about the transatlantic relationship concerns McNamara's statements that he advised both Kennedy and Johnson never to use nuclear weapons first, and that he believed they accepted that advice. This was, of course, the very opposite of what General Strong conveyed to the Prime Minister in November 1962. It was also the opposite of what McNamara said publicly and to America's NATO allies. McNamara wanted NATO to have sufficient conventional force so that first use of nuclear weapons would not be necessary. Yet even with the development of the strategy known as Flexible Response in 1967, NATO remained wedded to the principle of initiating nuclear war in response to Soviet conventional aggression, and to threatening nuclear escalation should the Soviets not draw back. The idea that President Kennedy might have been deterred from initiating the use of nuclear weapons by the threat of only a single bomb on a single American city called into question the credibility of a NATO strategy predicated on willingness to use nuclear weapons in response to Soviet conventional aggression in Europe. Indeed, for many it would have called into question the very foundation of NATO in the nuclear age. The suggestion that the United States' nuclear guarantee to Western Europe was nothing more than a piece of paper would have been vindication for those in Paris and London who argued for national deterrents, as well as sustenance for those in Bonn who felt West Germany needed nuclear weapons to guarantee its own security.[41]

Whether Khrushchev would have used nuclear weapons in defence of Cuba is one of many $64,000 questions. Up to the climax of the crisis, all his actions, including despatch of the various tactical nuclear weapons, suggest that he would have done. But once the crisis threatened to escalate, the situation is much less clear. To some extent it depends on how his actions are interpreted. Did his anxiety to reach agreement with Kennedy primarily reflect determination to avoid risking war or did he see in Kennedy's response a genuine means of providing security for Cuba? Was the eventual outcome indicative of Khrushchev's determination to preserve the safety of Cuba? Or was his refusal to consult Castro evidence that when push came to shove, romantic attachment to the Cuban revolution would always take second place to the security of the Soviet Union? One credible conclusion is that Khrushchev shared Kennedy's willingness to use nuclear weapons in support of political commitments, which if the moment of thermo-nuclear truth arrived, he would not want to honour. If this interpretation is correct then the Cuban missile crisis suggests that commitment to use nuclear weapons on behalf of an ally against a nuclear adversary is inherently incredible. The evidence, however, is perhaps too fragile (and indeed contested) to draw conclusions that would apply to all leaders in all circumstances. Moreover, the nature and scale of nuclear deployments in 1962 generated its own momentum and its own dangers. The infrastructure of extended deterrence provided its own form of deterrence (and its own risks). Whatever political leaders intended, they could end up facing choices about retaliation and escalation through forces and circumstances beyond their control. Indeed recognition of this helped both men compromise and manoeuvre when inflexibility could have led to conflict and war.

This study has explored two particular schools of thought that point in differing directions in assessing the risk of nuclear war in 1962. The first concerns high-level decision-making, the second, subordinate actors and organizations. The first suggested that the closer the risk of escalation, the more determined Kennedy and Khrushchev were to secure a negotiated settlement. Whether it was the risk of all-out nuclear war or the risk of losing one city to enemy retaliation, the existence of nuclear weapons exercised a particular hold on political leaders. Two caveats need to be entered here. First, the initial responses of Kennedy to the discovery of the missiles and of Khrushchev to the blockade were belligerent, and could have led to escalation. The second concerns circumstances in which either one state believed the other was gearing for attack. The straying U-2 provides a clear example of where the Soviets might have reasoned that their retaliation had to be got in first, even though it would have meant committing suicide out of fear of death. There was also the possibility that if the United States believed the Soviets were preparing to act in this way, they would have considered pre-emption. For the Soviets, pre-emption was a means of assuring their attack. For the Americans, pre-emption was a means of reducing (and conceivably eliminating) destruction in the United States (though not Europe). General Turgidson offered President Muffley the choice between 150 and 20 million dead. General Le May could well have offered 'distinguishable post-war environments' with a much lower level of devastation.

The fact that both leaders drew back from the brink because they understood the horrors of the abyss, nevertheless provides support

argue that the existence of nuclear weapons is a
nst their use. American 'doves' maintain that while
ns have no value other than to deter the use of other
ons, they nevertheless do deter the use of nuclear
weapons. Within the American aviary there was agreement on the
concept, if not the composition, of nuclear deterrence. As a group of
prominent owls have argued, 'If a little nuclear deterrence goes a long
way, some may be necessary.'[42] Here, European ornithology differs
somewhat from that found in North America. While at the height of
the Second Cold War anti-nuclear Europeans and pro-freeze
Americans found common cause, and while the views of Bundy and
McNamara on No-First Use resonated with (and were much quoted
by) advocates of alternative defence, various threads of European
opinion rejected nuclear deterrence itself. In Britain, there was greater
intellectual and ideological bio-diversity than in the United States.
Nevertheless, some things have changed, and McNamara himself
came to embrace zero-tolerance of nuclear weapons, and together
with James Blight, argued eloquently and passionately the case for a
nuclear-free world.[43]

One commonly held view among British anti-nuclear protesters in
the 1980s was that American political leaders wanted to start a nuclear
war in Europe. These views reflected a particular interpretation of
NATO strategy and were animated by the pronouncements of
President Reagan and senior officials within his administration. The
general conclusion to be drawn from the missile crisis was that the
closer to confrontation, the greater the recognition of nuclear reality.
The case of Fidel Castro, however, is an important corrective to the
assumption that particular conceptions of rationality govern political
behaviour in all cases and for all time. Castro's attitude has been
compared with the leaders of various nuclear threshold states (frequently labelled 'rogue states'), who like Castro have an antagonistic
relationship with Washington.[44] Proliferation pessimists have used his
example to argue the risks and dangers of nuclear proliferation.[45] Yet
it was also argued in Chapter 3 that Castro's views on fighting nuclear
wars, while potentially frightening in the context of the crisis, bear
comparison with the attitudes, policies and strategies pursued by

Western leaders and officials at various stages of the Cold War. Rationality, too, is in the eye of the beholder. The implications of Castro's views for nuclear deterrence are discussed below.

One Foot in the Grave?

The second strand of historiographical enquiry concerns the operational level of nuclear weaponry. Close scrutiny of various near misses and alternative outcomes has suggested that in some cases the risk of nuclear use was tangible and the possibility of escalation was real. The problems of assessing these risks have nevertheless been emphasized. Careful scrutiny of specific scenarios has been made, and attention given both to establishing the plausibility of counterfactuals, and to adjudicating possible outcomes. Conclusions were reached that episodes such as Penkovsky's final warning and the Moorestown radar's detection of an MRBM attack seem more dramatic than they were dangerous, although it was also noted that the potential significance of these and other near misses was if they were part of a concatenation of misperceptions, miscalculations and mistakes.

Similarly, the suggestion that Soviet MRBMs could be launched under attack against the United States by commanders in Cuba can be virtually discounted. Initial USAF assessments of the effectiveness of an American air strike almost certainly erred on the side of caution. The CIA's more robust assessment later in the week was more accurate. Neither assessment took account of the fact that the warheads for the missiles were stored some fifty miles away and kept under (presumably) rigorous procedural safeguards. The MRBM 'launch under attack' scenario was, of course, posited on the assumption of a decision by Kennedy to destroy the missiles, which would most probably have involved an invasion. There remains disagreement on whether Kennedy would have opted to use force, and certainly the view that he would not have attacked as early as 29/30 October seems convincing.

In all these assessments and adjudications two factors need to be borne in mind. First, knowledge and understanding of events is often constrained, particularly in the field of command and control.

General Turgidson's counsel to 'hold off on a judgement like that until all the facts are in' is surely prudent. The debate about pre-delegated authority for the use of Soviet tactical nuclear weapons in Cuba is a salutatory reminder of the hazards of single-source history (especially where the source in question may have a specific agenda). Yet there is now a settled historical consensus on the fact that the Soviets deployed tactical nuclear forces in Cuba, and that warheads for these and for the longer-range missiles had arrived. Of course, settled historical consensuses have a habit of becoming unsettled. And it is worth noting that if the moment when Captain Savitsky was dissuaded from firing his nuclear torpedo was the moment when nuclear weapons came closest to being used, it took forty years for this to become known. It is also, moreover, worth reflecting on the views of the group of North American scholars whose contribution to understanding and debate about the crisis has been so immense, when they comment that '. . . at each step our appreciation of the irreducible element of mystery surrounding this seminal historical event has only grown stronger'. [46]

What cannot be known and will always remain a matter for speculation is what would have happened if the nuclear threshold had been crossed. Would nuclear retaliation have occurred and escalation ensued? Such speculation is unavoidable in assessing the danger of nuclear war and the role of nuclear weapons in the crisis. In his compelling psychological assessment of the crisis, James Blight outlines a model of adaptive behaviour that portrays how Kennedy and Khrushchev each moved from shock to outrage to belligerence to circumspection to fear to caution. [47] If nuclear weapons had exploded in the Sargasso Sea or in the skies of Siberia or on Guantánamo Bay, would the trajectory from initial shock to eventual caution have been swift enough to prevent nuclear escalation? Would indeed the same psychological pattern have been replicated?

In a moment of self-deprecation (and insight), Adlai Stevenson suggested that it was important to have a 'nuclear coward' in the room when decisions with nuclear consequences were being taken. Whether decisions to foreswear retaliation or forgo escalation would have been acts of cowardice or courage is a matter of perspective. In his role as spokesperson for John F. Kennedy's mind, McNamara tells us that the President would never have used nuclear weapons first. Bundy is less certain, inasmuch as he believes no-one knew what Kennedy would have done had the Soviets moved on West Berlin in 1961. McNamara is, however, convinced that the President would have retaliated against Soviet nuclear attack. Kennedy went to the grave without providing recollections and reflections for posterity. Thanks to his duplicity in secretly recording meetings in his office, some of his words and arguments are helpfully preserved. McNamara (this time in his role as witness to history) explains that there were no discussions about what to do if nuclear war broke out. There were, in fact, several stages when specific nuclear issues were considered within ExComm – discussion of an air attack on the missiles on 16 October considered whether missiles would be launched under attack, and whether Khrushchev would be deterred from an attack from Cuba by American strategic forces; on 23 October, provision for civil defence against nuclear attack in the south-east of the United States was reviewed; and on 22 and 27 October attention focused on what should be done if Jupiter missiles in Turkey were attacked as a Soviet response to an American assault on Cuba.

One of many areas where there is a paucity of information concerns what discussions – formal and informal – took place in the Pentagon and among the Joint Chiefs about nuclear war. And the same goes for comparable Soviet decision-makers. Nevertheless, the fact that the crisis was over before detailed discussion of nuclear options constrains our understanding of how Kennedy saw his choices. Some clues exist. In a discussion with senior officials in December 1962 concerning the use of nuclear weapons in war, for example, Kennedy himself drew a distinction between declaratory threats to destroy Soviet cities (which were necessary to deter the Soviets), and attacks on their nuclear forces (designed to limit the damage to the United States, to the degree that was possible). This is certainly consistent with McNamara's interpretations, though how far we can deduce what Kennedy would have done remains inevitably problematic.

157

Retrospective Prophecies

This study's exploration of scenarios in which nuclear weapons might have been used has been attempted with a degree of circumspection. A relatively conservative approach has been taken in constructing counterfactual scenarios, using what historians refer to as the minimum rewrite of history. Attempts have been made to minimize the possible 'rewriting of history' by focusing on one change in the pattern of events. A more radical (and imaginative) approach would be to abandon minimum rewrites and explore concatenations of events and circumstances that might have precipitated the use and escalation of nuclear weapons. No incident or event took place in a vacuum. Black Saturday was Black Saturday because of a combination of contexts and incidents.

If the Cuban missile crisis was the most dangerous event in human history, a case can certainly be made that Saturday, 27 October was the most dangerous day in the life of the planet. What if things had been worse? What if the F-102s had engaged the MiG-19s in the skies of Siberia and fired their nuclear missiles, and as a consequence Soviet ICBMs had been brought to combat readiness? What if American intelligence had somehow detected this? What if the KGB had chosen Saturday, 27 October to telephone the US embassy and activate Oleg Penkovsky's warning that war was imminent? And that around the same time Captain Shumkov and his comrades had decided to fire their nuclear torpedo at an American warship? What if JFK had been suffering from acute back pain and a depressive or psychotic reaction to the concoction of drugs his physician had given him?[48] And if Khrushchev had taken to the vodka? There are so many variables and so many potentially plausible concatenations.

It is tempting to use this approach to quickly reach the conclusion that the possibility of inadvertent nuclear war was very real. Certainly there was a risk although, as this study has attempted to show, the risks of crossing the threshold and the risks of escalation are best assessed separately. The lessons of the missile crisis are nevertheless ambiguous. In various ways, nuclear weapons were part of the reason for the crisis, though they were also part of how the crisis was resolved. Had nuclear weapons been used in specific scenarios they would have been central to whether the crisis then escalated. Distilling these complexities and ambiguities into simple formulae that can be applied across time and place is hazardous. Moreover, while October 1962 may have been the nearest we came to nuclear war, it was not sufficiently close to be able to fully assess the nostrums of deterrence. Furthermore, our knowledge and understanding of events are still insufficient to reach considered judgements on some aspects.

One of the textual reference points in this study has been McGeorge Bundy's *Danger and Survival*. While the present account provides neither the authoritative panorama of Bundy's work, nor the insight of an insider in the highest counsels of nuclear decision-making, it has been able to draw upon other perspectives and, moreover, the extensive research that has emerged since Bundy published his *magnum opus*. *Danger and Survival* is also an apt reference point because the author seeks to explore the choices of decision-makers and the 'what ifs?' of alternative decisions. Bundy's aim was, nevertheless, to draw from history for the conduct of contemporary affairs.

In 2007, and for the first time in nearly two decades, there is now active consideration of nuclear weapons' issues in the United Kingdom. This has been prompted by the Blair government's announcement that consideration is necessary about whether (and how) to replace the Trident system when it begins to become obsolescent in the 2020s. A Trident replacement will provide a British strategic force into the 2050s. To paraphrase Bundy, we now face choices about the bomb in the first hundred years. It would be hazardous to seek specific lessons from the events of 1960s for the circumstances of the 2040s. Nevertheless, the experience of the crisis enables explorations of general propositions about nuclear deterrence.

Central to arguments in favour of deterrence is the assumption of rationality – the assumption that political leaders will always embrace the scorpions, so to speak. The views of Castro clearly challenge that. Moreover, the development of strategies and deployments of weapons for much of the Cold War reflected differing, and often contending, conceptions of deterrence, which were often tangential to Oppenheimer's arachnids. For the early decades of the Cold War, British nuclear strategy exhibited ambiguity if not unresolved disagreement and confusion.[49] The move toward a dedicated sea-based deterrent has resolved some contradictions and ambiguities. Providing that British submarines remain invulnerable, a number of concerns about inadvertence raised by episodes in 1962 would not be relevant. 'Use them or lose them' should not be an issue with SSBNs. On the other hand, the Trident D-5 SLBM, has a counterforce capability, so an adversary equipped with more vulnerable forces could face the 'use them or lose them' dilemma that loomed in 1962. Deterrence and threat are both in the eye of the beholder. The general proposition that nuclear weapons may deter *and* provoke (or rather deter in one context and provoke in another) may hold even where invulnerable retaliatory forces form the basis of one side's deterrent. Newly emerging nuclear states may have weapons, force structures and command and control arrangements that may be more comparable to those that existed in 1962. Command and control is perhaps the most crucial, if least transparent, aspect of nuclear history. The lack of transparency is further emphasized by the fact that we do not know exactly which enemies we are preparing against.

The argument that differing forms of rationality (and differing forms of irrationality) may undermine conceptions of deterrence is an important lesson from the crisis. What al-Qaeda will look like in thirty or forty years' time is almost impossible to assess. Western nuclear states have sought to apply the principles of deterrence to the threats that have emerged. The British government's White Paper on the future of the UK deterrent, states that: 'Any state that we can hold responsible for assisting a nuclear attack on our vital interests can expect that this would lead to a proportionate response.'[50] Recent enunciations of French nuclear strategy provide similar warnings.[51] The credibility of such postures depends, among other things, on the effectiveness of intelligence in identifying the relationship between terrorists and their sponsor. The experience of the war on Iraq illuminates some of the more obvious pitfalls in such endeavours. Yet however credible the threat to the sponsoring state, it is difficult to imagine this would influence those who intend to use weapons of mass destruction themselves. Indeed, there is a more frightening prospect – that those who wish to use such weapons may actively seek to provoke nuclear retaliation. Whether this is described as irrational or recognized as a different and more terrifying form of rationality, depends in part on the motives and objectives of those involved. Yet in abstract terms – and all debates about nuclear deterrence in 2050 are abstract – it may be that the possession of nuclear weapons directly increases the risk of weapons of mass destruction being used against the British people.

Armageddon: A Missed Opportunity?

Had nuclear weapons been used in October 1962, how might attitudes toward nuclear weapons have changed? Apocalyptic outcomes would have been beyond experience, imagination and redemption. Yet scenarios of tactical nuclear warfare or 'discriminate and proportionate' retaliation were conceivable. In such circumstances, how might attitudes toward nuclear disarmament have developed? Could the limited use of thermo-nuclear weapons have mobilized world opinion – or opinion in the principal nuclear weapons states themselves – behind disarmament? What would it have taken (or will it take) to create the political conditions for nuclear disarmament? How many thermo-nuclear explosions does it take to make a paradigm shift?

Napoleon is reputed to have once asked of Marshal Ney: 'Is he lucky?' Perhaps, if Napoleon had taken a keener interest in Marshal Ney's professional competence, the Battle of Waterloo would have turned out rather differently (along with the course of European history). Dean Acheson's claim that the outcome of the missile crisis was attributable to 'plain dumb luck' reflected his own hubris at the fact that Kennedy ignored his arguments for war on Cuba. Yet *Fortuna* did not just nest with the hawks. As Robert McNamara concluded after a lifetime's reflection on the crisis: 'I want to say – and this very important – at the end we lucked out! It was luck that prevented nuclear war!'[52] The suggestion that the principal lesson of the Cuban missile crisis is that we need luck may not appear of great and immediate value to hard-pressed and hard-nosed decision-makers. But to put it another way: the avoidance of nuclear war cannot be allowed to depend upon a state of perpetual serendipity. Nuclear weapons may deter in some situations. They may also provoke in others. And as the Cuban missile crisis suggests, they may create risks that nuclear war may happen despite the best efforts of political leaders to prevent it. Robert McNamara compellingly argues that:

> Human beings are fallible. We know we all make mistakes. In our daily lives, mistakes are costly, but we try to learn from them. In conventional war, they cost lives, sometimes thousands of lives. But if mistakes were to affect decisions relating to the use of nuclear forces, there would be no learning period. They would result in the destruction of nations. I believe, therefore, it can be predicted with confidence that the indefinite combination of human fallibility and nuclear weapons carries a very high risk of a potential nuclear catastrophe.[53]

As John F. Kennedy said, 'the existence of nuclear weapons [makes] a secure and rational world impossible. We must somehow find a means to get rid of nuclear weapons.'[54]

Notes

Chapter 1

1 J. Robert Oppenheimer, 'Atomic Weapons and American Policy', *Foreign Affairs* 31/4 (July 1953), p. 529.
2 See, for example, Philip Brenner, 'Thirteen Months: Cuba's Perspective on the Missile Crisis', in James A. Nathan (ed.), *The Cuban Missile Crisis Revisited* (New York: St Martin's Press, 1992), pp. 187–217.
3 Ray S. Cline, 'Commentary: The Cuban Missile Crisis', *Foreign Affairs* 68/4 (Fall 1989), p. 191. Cline's assessment reflected unwillingness to accept uncorroborated Soviet testimony about nuclear warheads in Cuba. He acknowledged that the presence of warheads increased the risk of nuclear war, so, with archival corroboration, he presumably would have considered the risk greater than a thousand to one.
4 Paul Nitze, *From Hiroshima to Glasnost: At the Center of Decision* (New York: Grove Weidenfeld, 1989), p. 205.
5 Robert S. McNamara, *Blundering into Disaster: Surviving the First Century of the Nuclear Age* (London: Bloomsbury, 1987), p. 11.
6 Robert Kennedy, *13 Days, The Cuban Missile Crisis* (London: Pan Books, 1969), p. 27.
7 Don Munton and David A. Welch, *The Cuban Missile Crisis: A Concise History* (Oxford: Oxford University Press, 2006), p. 1.
8 Raymond L. Garthoff, *A Journey Through the Cold War: A Memoir of Containment and Coexistence* (Washington DC: The Brookings Institution, 2001), p. 168.
9 McGeorge Bundy, *Danger and Survival: Choices About the Bomb in the First Fifty Years* (New York: Random House, 1988), p. 391.
10 Graham T. Allison, Albert Carnesale, and Joseph S. Nye, Jr. (eds), *Hawks, Doves and Owls: An Agenda for Avoiding Nuclear War* (London: W. W. Norton, 1985), p. 9.

11 Bundy, *Danger and Survival*, p. 380.

12 *Dr Strangelove or How I Learned to Stop Worrying and Love the Bomb* (Columbia Pictures, Director: Stanley Kubrick, 1964). For a written version, see Peter George, *Dr Strangelove or How I Learned to Stop Worrying and Love the Bomb* (Oxford: Oxford University Press, 1988). For discussion of the relevance of the film to understanding nuclear issues, see Dan Lindley, 'What I Learned since I Stopped Worrying and Studied the Movie: A Teaching Guide to Stanley Kubricks's "Dr Strangelove"', *Political Science and Politics* 34/3 (September 2001), pp. 663–7.

13 Richard Rhodes, *The Making of the Atomic Bomb* (London: Penguin, 1988 [1986]), pp. 640–1.

14 Harry S. Truman, handwritten journal, 25 July 1945, cited in Gar Alperovitz, *The Decision to Use the Bomb* (London: HarperCollins, 1995), p. 527.

15 Diaries of Henry Wallace, quoted in Rhodes, *Making of the Atomic Bomb*, p. 743.

16 Interview in James G. Blight and David A. Welch, *On the Brink: Americans and Soviets Reexamine the Cuban Missile Crisis* (New York: The Noonday Press, 1990), p. 182.

17 Ibid, p. 50.

18 Graham Allison, *Essence of Decision, Explaining the Cuban Missile Crisis* (Boston: Little, Brown and Company, 1971). A revised co-authored version appeared in 1999: Graham Allison and Philip Zelikow, *Essence of Decision: Explaining the Cuban Missile Crisis* (New York: Longman, 1999).

19 See, for example, Robert Jervis, Richard Ned Lebow and Janice Gross Stein, *Psychology and Deterrence* (Baltimore: Johns Hopkins University Press, 1985).

20 See in particular, Albert Carnesale, Paul Doty, Stanley Hoffman, Samuel P. Huntingdon, Joseph S. Nye, Jr. and Scott D. Sagan, *Living with Nuclear Weapons* (New York: Bantam, 1983) and Allison, Carnesale and Nye, *Hawks, Doves and Owls*; Richard Ned Lebow, *Nuclear Crisis Management: A Dangerous Illusion* (London: Cornell University Press, 1987) and Bruce Blair, *The Logic of Accidental Nuclear War* (Washington DC: The Brookings Institution, 1993).

21 Allison, Carnesale and Nye, *Hawks, Doves and Owls*, p. 210.

22 For discussions of the nuclear taboo, see Nina Tannenwald, 'Stigmatizing the Bomb: Origins of the Nuclear Taboo', *International Security* 29/4 (Spring 2005), pp. 5–49 and George H. Quester, *Nuclear First Strike: Consequences of a Broken Taboo* (Baltimore: Johns Hopkins University Press, 2006).

23 For discussion, see John Lewis Gaddis, *We Now Know, Rethinking the Cold War* (Oxford: Clarendon Press, 1997) and Marc Trachtenberg, *History and Strategy* (Princeton, New Jersey: Princeton University Press, 1991).

24 John Mueller, *The Retreat From Doomsday: The Obsolescence of Major War* (New York: Basic Books, 1989).

25 Edward Thompson, 'Notes on Exterminism, The Last Stage of Civilisation', in Edward Thompson *et al*, *Exterminism and Cold War* (London: Verso, 1982), pp. 1–33. For a different critical perspective on nuclear weapons, Soviet–American relations and Third World conflict, see Fred Halliday, 'The Sources of the New Cold War', in ibid, pp. 289–328.

26 Fred Kaplan, *The Wizards of Armageddon* (Stanford: Stanford University Press, 1991), p. 269; see also *idem*, 'JFK's First Strike Plan', *Atlantic Monthly* (October 2001), pp. 81–6; Desmond Ball gives an estimate of 360–425 million dead, *Politics and Force Levels: The Strategic Missile Program of the Kennedy Administration* (London: University of California Press, 1980), p. 190.

27 See R. P. Turco, O. B. Toon, T. P. Ackerman, J. B. Pollack and C. Sagan, 'Climate and Smoke: An Appraisal of Nuclear Winter', *Science* 222 (1983), pp. 128–392 and Carl Sagan, 'Nuclear War and Climatic Catastrophe: Some Policy Implications', *Foreign Affairs* (Winter 1983/4), pp. 257–92. For a summary of the concept of 'nuclear winter', see Alan Robock, 'Nuclear Winter', in Stephen H. Schneider, *Encyclopaedia of Weather and Climate, Vol. 2* (New York: Oxford University Press, 1996), pp. 53–46.

28 Oppenheimer, 'Atomic Weapons', p. 529.

29 House of Commons, *Official Record*, 1 March 1955, col. 1899.

30 McNamara, *Blundering into Disaster*, p. 175.

31 'Nuclear Notebook: Global Nuclear Stockpiles, 1945–2006', *Bulletin of the Atomic Scientists* 62/4 (July/August 2006), p. 66.

32 R. S. Norris, A. S. Burrows, and R. W. Fieldhouse, *Nuclear Weapons Databook, Volume V* (Boulder: Westview, 1994), pp. 63–5. The British possessed 205 nuclear weapons in 1962 including 100 thermo-nuclear Yellow Sun Mk 2s. To these should be added the 60 Thors and 72 American bombs assigned under Project E. For details of Project E, see Stephen Twigge and Len Scott, *Planning Armageddon: Britain, United States and the Command of Nuclear Forces, 1945–1964* (Amsterdam: Routledge, 2000), pp. 100–2, 126–7, 323–5.

33 McNamara, *Blundering Into Disaster*, p. 8.

34 According to Steven Zaloga, at the time of the crisis there were six launch pads for the R-7A missiles (the longer-range variant of the R-7,

NATO designation SS-6), two for the untested R-9A (NATO designation SS-8), and about twenty R-16 (NATO designation SS-7), Steven Zaloga, *The Kremlin's Nuclear Sword: The Rise and Fall of Russia's Strategic Nuclear Forces 1945–2000* (London: Smithsonian Institution Press, 2002), p. 82. General Dimitri Volkogonov provided the figure of 20 ICBMs in 1989, based on access to Soviet archives, Bruce J. Allyn, James G. Blight and David A. Welch, *Back to the Brink: Proceedings of the Moscow Conference on the Cuban Missile Conference, January 27–28, 1989*, CSIA Occasional Paper No 9 (Lanham, Maryland: University of America Press, 1992), pp. 52–3; Richard Ned Lebow and Janice Gross Stein, *We All Lost the Cold War* (Princeton, New Jersey: Princeton University Press, 1994), p. 35.

35 According to Zaloga, Soviet intercontinental bomber strength in 1962 comprised 104 Tupolev Tu-95M (NATO designation Bear) turboprop bombers and 78 Myasishchev 3M (NATO designation Bison) turbojet bombers, *Kremlin's Nuclear Sword*, p. 77.

36 Raymond Garthoff states that, at the time of the crisis, there were 97 Soviet submarine-based nuclear missiles whose significance he discounts, as they 'were all in Soviet waters and unavailable for early commitment, in addition to being highly vulnerable', Raymond L. Garthoff, *Reflections on the Cuban Missile Crisis* (Washington DC: The Brookings Institution, 1989), p. 208n.

37 Scott D. Sagan, *The Limits of Safety: Organisations, Accidents, and Nuclear Weapons* (Princeton, New Jersey: Princeton University Press, 1993), p. 62. The figure for SLBMs comprises seven (of nine) Polaris SSBNs deployed at this time, each carrying 16 Polaris missiles.

38 Lebow and Stein, *We All Lost*, p. 517 n. 39.

39 Desmond Ball, 'The Development of the SIOP 1960–1983', in Desmond Ball and Jeffrey Richelson, (eds), *Strategic Nuclear Targeting* (London: Cornell University Press, 1986), p. 66.

40 Richard K. Betts, 'A Golden Nuclear Age? The Balance Before Parity', *International Security* 11/3 (Winter 1986–87), pp. 3–32.

41 Robert McNamara, McGeorge Bundy, Dean Rusk, Ted Sorensen, Roswell Gilpatrik and George Ball, 'The Lessons of the Cuban Missile Crisis', *Time* (27 September 1982); see also Bundy, *Danger and Survival*, pp. 391–462.

42 Interview in Blight and Welch, *On the Brink*, pp. 147–8; for Nitze's analysis of the crisis, see *From Hiroshima to Glasnost*, pp. 214–38.

43 Institute for Strategic Studies (ISS), *The Communist Bloc and the Western Alliances: Military Balance 1962–1963* (London: IISS, 1962), p. 3.

44 Norman Polmar and John D. Gresham, *DEFCON-2: Standing on the Brink of Nuclear War during the Cuban Missile Crisis* (Hoboken, New Jersey: John Wiley & Sons, 2006), p. 15.

45 Betts, 'Golden Nuclear Age', p. 27.

46 The Davy Crockett recoilless rocket launcher had a maximum range of 2.5 miles and was armed with a variable sub-kiloton yield warhead, Mathew Byrd, *Political Firepower: Nuclear Weapons and the US Army 1945–1973* (PhD, University of Wales, Aberystwyth, 1999), pp. 203–5, 274. In response to the situation in Berlin, McNamara decided at the end of 1961 to send 171 Davy Crocketts to Europe, Trachtenberg, *History and Strategy*, p. 224.

47 Robert S. McNamara, 'The Military Role of Nuclear Weapons: Perceptions and Misperceptions', *Foreign Affairs* 62/1 (October 1983), p. 62.

48 Sherman Kent, 'The Cuban Missile Crisis of 1962: Presenting the Photographic Evidence Abroad', *Studies in Intelligence* 10/2 (Spring 1972), p. 23.

49 Ernest R. May and Philip D. Zelikow (eds), *The Kennedy Tapes: Inside the White House During the Cuban Missile Crisis* (Cambridge, MA: Harvard University Press, 1997), p. 100.

50 Philip Nash, *The Other Missiles of October: Eisenhower, Kennedy, and the Jupiters 1957–1963* (London: University of North Carolina Press, Chapel Hill, 1997), pp. 118–19.

51 Ibid, p. 3.

52 Sheldon M. Stern, *Averting 'The Final Failure': John F. Kennedy and the Secret Cuban Missile Crisis Meetings* (Stanford: Stanford University Press, 2003), p. 92.

53 Timothy Naftali and Philip Zelikow (eds), *The Presidential Recordings, John F. Kennedy, The Great Crises, Volume Two, September–October 21, 1962* (London: W. W. Norton, 2001), p. 62.

54 For accounts, see Kaplan *Wizards of Armageddon*, pp. 161–73, 248–9, 286–90; Lawrence Freedman, *Intelligence and the Soviet Strategic Threat* (Basingstoke: Macmillan, 1986), pp. 62–80; and John Prados, *The Soviet Estimate: US Intelligence Analysis and Soviet Strategic Forces* (Princeton, New Jersey: Princeton University Press, 1986), pp. 111–26. For the US intelligence estimate that buried the missile gap in September 1961, see Kevin C. Ruffner (ed.), *Corona: America's First Satellite* (Washington DC: CIA Center for the Study of Intelligence, 1995), pp. 127–55.

55 Ball, *Politics and Force Levels*, pp. 41–161.

56 David Coleman, 'Camelot's Nuclear Conscience', *Bulletin of the Atomic Scientists* 62/3 (May/June 2006), p. 43.

57 Polmar and Gresham, *DEFCON-2*, p. 19.
58 John Lewis Gaddis, *Strategies of Containment* (Oxford: Oxford University of Press, 1982), pp. 149–50.
59 For discussion of Massive Retaliation, see Lawrence Freedman, *The Evolution of Nuclear Strategy* (Basingstoke: Palgrave Macmillan, 2003), pp. 72–85; Kaplan, *Wizards of Armageddon*, pp. 174–84.
60 For accounts of the development of SIOP-62, see David Alan Rosenberg, 'The Origins of Overkill: Nuclear Weapons and American Strategy, 1945–1960', *International Security* 7/4 (Spring 1983), pp. 3–71; Ball, 'The Development of the SIOP', pp. 57–83; and Scott D. Sagan, 'SIOP-62: The Nuclear War Plan Briefing to President Kennedy', *International Security* 12/1 (Summer 1987), pp. 22–51. For general discussion, see Peter Pringle and William Arkin, *SIOP: Nuclear War from the Inside* (London: Sphere Books, 1983).
61 For development of the SIOP under Kennedy, see Ball, *Politics and Force Levels*, pp. 179–211, Kaplan, *Wizards of Armageddon*, pp. 263–85 and Deborah Shapley, *Promise and Power: The Life and Times of Robert McNamara* (Boston, MA: Little, Brown and Company, 1993), pp. 109–11.
62 Jane Stromseth, *The Origins of Flexible Response* (London: Macmillan, 1988), pp. 49–51.
63 'Radio-TV Address of the President to the Nation, October 22, 1962', in Laurence Chang and Peter Kornbluh (eds), *The Cuban Missile Crisis, 1962: A National Security Archive Documents Reader* (New York: The New Press, 1992), p. 153.
64 Peter Hennessy, *The Secret State: Whitehall and the Cold War* (London: Penguin, 2003), pp. 145-6.
65 Gaddis, *We Now Know*, pp. 242–3. When the Soviet leader issued his threat, Harriman laughed and told him he was far too sensible to have a war, whereupon Khrushchev agreed with him.
66 Vladislav M. Zubok and Hope M. Harrison, 'The Nuclear Education of Nikita Khrushchev', in John Lewis Gaddis, Philip H. Gordon, Ernest R. May and Jonathan Rosenberg, *Cold War Statesmen Confront the Bomb: Nuclear Diplomacy since 1945* (Oxford: Oxford University Press, 1999), pp. 141–68; see also Vladislav Zubok and Constantine Pleshakov, *Inside the Kremlin's Cold War: From Stalin to Khrushchev* (Harvard University Press, 1996), pp. 174 *et seq.*, and two acclaimed recent biographies of Khrushchev: William Taubman, *Khrushchev: The Man, His Era* (London: Free Press, 2005) and Aleksandr Fursenko and Timothy Naftali, *Khrushchev's Cold War: The Inside Story of an American Adversary* (London: W. W. Norton, 2006), *passim*.
67 Jerrold L. Schecter and Peter S. Deriabin, *The Spy Who Saved the World:*

How a Soviet Colonel Changed the Course of the Cold War (New York: Charles Scribner's Sons, 1992), pp. 190–1, 247, 312, 328, 376–7. Copies of *Voyennaya Mysl* articles have been declassified and are available in the US National Archive and at the CIA website: http://www.foia.cia.gov/penkovsky.asp. For discussion of Penkovsky's role in the missile crisis, see Len Scott, 'Espionage and the Cold War: Oleg Penkovsky and the Cuban Missile Crisis', *Intelligence and National Security* 14/3 (Autumn 1999), pp. 23–47.

68 Michael R. Beschloss, *Kennedy v Khrushchev: The Crisis Years 1960–63* (London: Faber and Faber, 1991), p. 371,

69 James G. Blight and David A. Welch, 'Risking "The Destruction of Nations": Lessons of the Cuban Missile Crisis for New and Aspiring Nuclear States', *Security Studies* 4/4 (Summer 1995), p. 811.

70 Ibid, pp. 811–50; Scott D. Sagan, 'More Will be Worse', in Scott D. Sagan and Kenneth N. Waltz, *The Spread of Nuclear Weapons: A Debate* (London: W. W. Norton, 1995), pp. 78–9.

71 James G. Blight, Joseph S. Nye and David A. Welch, 'The Cuban Missile Crisis Revisited', *Foreign Affairs* 66/1 (Fall 1987), p. 188.

72 Allison and Zelikow, *Essence of Decision*, p. 394.

73 Barton Bernstein, 'Understanding Decisionmaking, US Foreign Policy and the Cuban Missile Crisis: A Review Essay', *International Security* 25/1 (Summer 2000), p. 161.

74 E. H. Carr, *What is History?* (Harmondsworth, Middlesex: Pelican, 1978 [1961]), p. 102. For criticism of Carr, see Philip E. Tetlock and Geoffrey Parker, 'Counterfactual Thought Experiments: Why We Can't Live Without Them & How We Must to Learn With Them', in Philip E. Tetlock, Richard Ned Lebow and Geoffrey Parker (eds), *Unmaking the West: 'What-If' Scenarios That Rewrite World History* (Michigan: University of Michigan Press, 2006), pp. 28–33. For a robust defence of counterfactual approaches, see Niall Ferguson, 'Virtual History: Toward a Chaotic Theory of the Past', in *idem* (ed.), *Virtual History, Alternatives and Counterfactuals* (Basingstoke: Picador, 1997), pp. 1–90.

75 Philip E. Tetlock and Aaron Belkin, 'Counterfactual Thought Experiments', in Philip E. Tetlock and Aaron Belkin, *Counterfactual Thought Experiments in World Politics: Logical, Methodological and Psychological Perspectives* (Princeton, New Jersey: Princeton University Press, 1996), p. 3.

76 Allison and Zelikow, *Essence of Decision*, p. 383.

77 See Tetlock and Belkin, 'Counterfactual Thought Experiments', pp. 1–38 and Richard Ned Lebow and Janice Gross Stein, 'Back to the Past:

Counterfactuals and the Cuban Missile Crisis', in Tetlock and Belkin, *Counterfactual Thought Experiments*, pp. 119–48.

78 Tetlock and Belkin, 'Counterfactual Thought Experiments'.

79 Ibid.

80 May and Zelikow, *Kennedy Tapes*, p. 581.

81 Robert Jervis, *Perception and Misperception in International Politics* (Princeton, New Jersey: Princeton University Press, 1976), pp. 58–113.

82 See for example, Allison and Zelikow, *Essence of Decision*, pp. 394–6.

83 See Blight and Welch, *On the Brink*; Allyn, Blight and Welch, *Back to the Brink*; and James G. Blight, Bruce J. Allyn and David A. Welch, *Cuba on the Brink: Castro, the Missile Crisis, and the Soviet Collapse* (New York: Pantheon Books, 1993). For explanation of the psychological underpinnings of critical oral history, see James G. Blight, *Shattered Crystal Ball: Fear and Learning in the Cuban Missile Crisis* (Savage, Maryland: Rowman & Littlefield Publishers, 1992), pp. 12–14, 79. For an overview of issues arising from recent research, see Len Scott and Steve Smith, 'Lessons of October: Historians, Political Scientists, Policy-makers and the Cuban Missile Crisis', *International Affairs* 70/4 (October 1994), pp. 659–84.

84 See for example, Mark Kramer, 'Tactical nuclear weapons, Soviet command authority, and the Cuban missile crisis', *Cold War International History Project Bulletin* Issue 3 (Fall 1993), pp. 40, 42–6 and James G. Blight, Bruce J. Allyn and David Welch, 'Kramer Vs. Kramer, Or How Can You Have Revisionism in the Absence of Orthodoxy?', *Cold War International History Project Bulletin* Issue 3 (Fall 1993), pp. 41, 47–50. *The Cold War International History Project Bulletin* provides invaluable opportunities for debates of this kind; Mark Kramer, Bruce J. Allyn, James G. Blight, and David A. Welch, 'Correspondence: Remembering the Cuban Missile Crisis: Should We Swallow Oral History?', *International Security* 15/1 (Summer 1990), pp. 212–18; Raymond L. Garthoff, 'Some Observations on Using the Soviet Archives', *Diplomatic History* (Spring 1997), pp. 243–57; Marc Trachtenberg, 'Commentary: New Light on the Cuban Missile Crisis', *Diplomatic History* 14/2 (Spring 1990), pp. 241–7.

85 See in particular, Aleksandr Fursenko and Timothy Naftali, *'One Hell of a Gamble': Khrushchev, Castro, Kennedy and the Cuban Missile Crisis 1958–1964* (London: John Murray, 1997) which is based on access to the archives of the Presidium, the KGB, Soviet Military Intelligence (GRU), the Ministry of Defence and the Ministry of Foreign Affairs. Subsequent archival disclosures formed the basis for their more recent study, *Khrushchev's Cold War*, which provides important new insights and revelations.

86 See, for example, the criticism of May and Zelikow's *Kennedy Tapes*, by former JFK Presidential Library historian, Sheldon M. Stern, 'The Published Cuban Missile Crisis Transcripts: Rounds One, Two and Beyond', in *idem*, *Averting 'The Final Failure'*, pp. 427–40.

87 Blight, *Shattered Crystal Ball*.

Chapter 2

1 Dmitri Volkogonov, *The Rise and Fall of the Soviet Empire: Political Leaders from Lenin to Gorbachev* (HarperCollins, 1998), p. 236.

2 Bundy, *Danger and Survival*, p. 424.

3 Ibid, p. 453.

4 Volkogonov, *Rise and Fall*, p. 236.

5 Bundy, *Danger and Survival*, p. 424.

6 For summaries and reassessments of Khrushchev's reasoning see Allison and Zelikow, *Essence of Decision*, pp. 78–109, 201–17; Blight and Welch, *On the Brink*, pp. 116–21; Lebow and Stein, *We All Lost*, esp. pp. 51–93; May and Zelikow, *Kennedy Tapes*, pp. 666–82; Taubman, *Khrushchev*, pp. 529–57; Fursenko and Naftali, *Khrushchev's Cold War*, pp. 429–31, 433–7.

7 Nikita Khrushchev (introduction, notes and commentary by Edward Crankshaw; translated by Strobe Talbott), *Khrushchev Remembers* (Boston: Little, Brown and Company, 1970; quotation from paperback edition, Aylesbury, Bucks: Sphere Books, 1971), p. 455.

8 Fursenko and Naftali, *Khrushchev's Cold War*, pp. 429–31, 433–7.

9 Fursenko and Naftali, '*One Hell of a Gamble*', pp. 11–16.

10 Tom Paterson, *Kennedy's Quest for Victory: American Foreign Policy 1961–3* (Oxford: Oxford University Press, 1989), p. 140.

11 Fursenko and Naftali, '*One Hell of a Gamble*', pp. 142–3.

12 Arthur M. Schlesinger Jr., *Robert Kennedy and His Times* (Boston: Houghton, Mifflin, 1978), p. 532.

13 Garthoff, *Reflections*, p. 32. For discussion of CIA action against Cuba under Kennedy, see Aiyaz Husain, 'Covert Action and US Cold War Strategy in Cuba, 1961–62', *Cold War History* 5/1 (February 2005), pp. 23–53. See also Philip Zelikow, 'American Policy and Cuba, 1961–1963,' *Diplomatic History* 24/2 (Spring 2000), pp. 317–34.

14 Interim Report: Alleged Assassination Plots Involving Foreign Leaders, 94th congress 1st session Senate Report No. 94-465 20 (Washington DC: US Government Printing Office, 1975).

15 For critical scrutiny of the suggestion that the Kennedys knew of the CIA's relationship with the Mafia, see J. A. Wolske, 'Jack, Judy, Sam,

Bobby, Johnny, Frank . . . : An Investigation into the Alternate History of the CIA-Mafia Collaboration to Assassinate Fidel Castro, 1960–1997', *Intelligence and National Security* 15/4 (Winter 2000), pp. 104–30.

16 Blight, Allyn and Welch, *Cuba on the Brink*, pp. 43–6.

17 Ibid, p. 45.

18 Nick Cullather, *Secret History: The CIA's Classified Account of its Operations in Guatemala 1952–1954* (Stanford: Stanford University Press, 1999). For British perspectives, see John W. Young, 'Great Britain's Latin American Dilemma: The Foreign Office and the Overthrow of "Communist" Guatemala, June 1954', *The International History Review* VIII/4 (November 1986), pp. 573–92.

19 For details, see Guto Thomas, 'Trade and Shipping to Cuba 1961–1963: An Irritant in Anglo-American Relations', (University of Wales, Aberystwyth, PhD, 2001).

20 Garthoff, *Reflections*, pp. 31, 60.

21 For discussion see Bruce J. Allyn, James Blight and David A. Welch, 'Essence of Revision: Moscow, Havana, and the Cuban Missile Crisis', *International Security* 14/3 (Winter 1989/90), pp. 144–7; James Hershberg, 'Before "The Missiles of October": Did Kennedy Plan a Military Strike Against Cuba?', *Diplomatic History* 14/4 (Spring 1990), pp. 163–98, reprinted in Nathan, *Cuban Missile Crisis*, pp. 237–80; and Husain, 'Covert Action.'

22 Anatoli I. Gribkov and William Y. Smith, *Operation Anadyr: US and Soviet Generals Recount the Cuban Missile Crisis* (Chicago: Edition Q, 1994), pp. 113–26. On US invasion planning, see Michael Desch, '"That Deep Mud in Cuba", The Strategic Threat and US Planning for a Conventional Response During the Missile Crisis', *Security Studies* 1/2 (Winter 1991), pp. 317–51 and Hershberg, 'Before "The Missiles"'.

23 Allyn, Blight and Welch, *Back to the Brink*, p. 7.

24 Bundy, *Danger and Survival*, pp. 381–2.

25 Fursenko and Naftali, *'One Hell of a Gamble'*, pp. 155–6; Fursenko and Naftali, *Khrushchev's Cold War*, p. 424.

26 Lebow and Stein summarize views of key former officials: Sergei Khrushchev, Georgiy Kornienko, Aleksandr Alekseev and Sergo Mikoyan believed the primary purpose was to protect Cuba; Georgiy Shakhnazarov and Dmitri Volkogonov (as well as Fidel Castro) believed the primary concern was the strategic balance, while Aleksei Adzhubei and Leonid Zamyatin believed 'psychological equality' was the goal in order to compel fundamental changes in US foreign policy, *We All Lost*, pp. 60–1.

27 Fursenko and Naftali, '*One Hell of a Gamble*', p. 182.

28 Fursenko and Naftali, *Khrushchev's Cold War*, pp. 429–31.

29 Taubman, *Khrushchev*, p. 529; for discussion, see pp. 529–53.

30 Fursenko and Naftali, *Khrushchev's Cold War*, pp. 431, 609 n.63.

31 Fursenko and Naftali, '*One Hell of a Gamble*', pp. 166–97.

32 Lebow and Stein, *We All Lost*, pp. 73–4, n.313; Taubman, *Khrushchev*, pp. 543–4.

33 Blight, Allyn and Welch, *Cuba on the Brink*, p. 72.

34 Fursenko and Naftali, '*One Hell of a Gamble*', p. 188.

35 Fursenko and Naftali, *Khrushchev's Cold War*, p. 473; Zaloga, *Kremlin's Nuclear Sword*, p. 84.

36 Svetlana V. Savranskaya, 'Soviet Submarines in the Cuban Missile Crisis', in Lyle J. Goldstein, John B. Hattendorf and Yuri M. Zhukov, Special Issue of *Journal of Strategic Studies* 28/2 (April 2005), pp. 233–59; Fursenko and Naftali, '*One Hell of a Gamble*', pp. 188–9; Gribkov and Smith, *Operation Anadyr*, pp. 27–8.

37 May and Zelikow, *Kennedy Tapes*, p. 667. For discussion, see Lebow and Stein, 'Back to the Past', pp. 136–7 and Munton and Welch, *Cuban Missile Crisis*, p. 38.

38 Fursenko and Naftali, '*One Hell of a Gamble*', pp. 194–6.

39 Blight, Allyn and Welch, *Cuba on the Brink*, pp. 207, 208.

40 See Lebow and Stein, 'Back to the Past', pp. 128–9.

41 May and Zelikow, *Kennedy Tapes*, pp. 71–2; Stern, *Avoiding 'The Final Failure'*, pp. 74–5.

42 For the conclusion that, 'a shorter crisis time might well have lead to relatively severe military option choices', see Stuart J. Thorson and Donald A. Sylvan, 'Counterfactuals and the Cuban Missile Crisis', *International Studies Quarterly* 26/4 (December 1982), pp. 539–71.

43 Blight, Allyn and Welch, *Cuba on the Brink*, p. 208. Emphasis in original.

44 Fursenko and Naftali, *Khrushchev's Cold War*, p. 435.

45 Kennedy, *13 Days*, pp. 30–1. Dobrynin recounts how he told Moscow of what he had said and received no correction, Anatoly Dobrynin, *In Confidence: Moscow's Ambassador to America's Six Cold War Presidents* (London: University of Washington Press, 1995), p. 74. Fursenko and Naftali's account suggests that Bolshakov may have stuck to the formula about defensive missiles, '*One Hell of a Gamble*', pp. 197, 219.

46 May and Zelikow, *Kennedy Tapes*, p. 169.

47 Andrei Gromyko, *Memories* (London: Hutchinson, 1988), p. 177; Dobrynin confirmed the detail, but distanced himself from Gromyko's behaviour in the meeting. And he remained indignant at not having

been told the truth by Moscow, Dobrynin, *In Confidence*, pp. 71–95.

48 Beschloss, *Kennedy v. Khrushchev*, p. 457.

49 Ibid, p. 481.

50 Stevenson was unaware of the truth and briefly considered resignation when he discovered it, ibid, p. 115.

51 Daniele Ganser, *Reckless Gamble: The Sabotage of the United Nations in the Cuban Conflict and the Cuban Missile Crisis of 1962* (New Orleans: University Press of the South), pp. 13–85.

52 W. Scott Lucas, *Divided We Stand: Britain, the US and the Suez Crisis* (London: Sceptre, 1996), p. 268.

53 Nash, *Other Missiles*, pp. 156–8.

54 Bundy, *Danger and Survival*, p. 434.

55 John McCone, Memorandum for the President, 28 February 1963, in M. S. McAuliffe (ed.), *CIA Documents on the Cuban Missile Crisis 1962* (Washington DC: CIA, 1992), pp. 373–4.

56 Max Holland, 'A Luce Connection: Senator Keating, William Pawley, and the Cuban Missile Crisis', *Journal of Cold War Studies* 1/3 (Fall 1999), pp. 139–67.

57 For details, see Munton and Welch, *Cuban Missile Crisis*, pp. 34–7.

58 Allison and Zelikow, *Essence of Decision*, p. 338.

59 Ibid, p. 207. An even more ingenious theory is proffered by Servando Gonzalez, who contends that not only were no nuclear warheads ever sent, but that Khrushchev's real motivation was to provoke the Americans into getting rid of Castro and in so doing bring international opprobrium upon themselves, see Servando Gonzalez, *The Nuclear Deception: Nikita Khrushchev and the Cuban Missile Crisis* (Oakland, California: Spooks Books, 2003), p. 39 *et seq*.

60 May and Zelikow, *Kennedy Tapes*, p. 51.

61 Ibid, p. 57.

62 Blight and Welch, *On the Brink*, pp. 54–7, 125–6.

63 Fursenko and Naftali, 'One Hell of a Gamble', pp. 204–6.

64 Bundy, *Danger and Survival*, p. 393.

65 Beschloss, *Kennedy v Khrushchev*, p. 420.

66 Fursenko and Naftali, *Khrushchev's Cold War*, pp. 452–4.

67 Bundy, *Danger and Survival*, p. 410.

68 May and Zelikow, *Kennedy Tapes*, p. 92.

69 Blight and Welch, *On the Brink*, p. 43.

70 Lebow and Stein, 'Back to the Past', pp. 128–9, 136–7.

71 For details, see Fursenko and Naftali, 'One Hell of a Gamble', pp. 188, 210, 242. Naftali and Fursenko state the range of the Lunas was 31 miles, ibid, p. 242; Gribkov states it was 20–5 miles, *Operation Anadyr*, p. 4.

72 Fursenko and Naftali, '*One Hell of a Gamble*', pp. 213–14.

73 Ibid, pp. 211–13; *idem*, 'The Pitsunda Decision: Khrushchev and Nuclear Weapons', *Cold War International History Project Bulletin* Issue 10 (March 1998), pp. 223–7; see also *idem*, 'New Evidence on the Cuban Missile Crisis: Khrushchev, Nuclear Weapons, and the Cuban Missile Crisis', *Cold War International History Project Bulletin* Issue 11 (Winter 1998), pp. 251–62.

74 Fursenko and Naftali, '*One Hell of a Gamble*', p. 211 and Gribkov and Smith, *Operation Anadyr*, pp. 27–8. Both employ this distinction and explicitly use the term 'deterrence' to explain the MRBM deployment.

75 Allison and Zelikow, *Essence of Decision*, p. 87.

76 Mark Kramer, 'The Cuban Missile Crisis and Nuclear Proliferation', *Security Studies* 5/1 (Autumn 1995), p. 176.

77 Fursenko and Naftali, '*One Hell of a Gamble*', p. 311.

78 See Glenn Snyder, *Deterrence and Defense* (Princeton: Princeton University Press, 1961).

79 Blight, Allyn and Welch, *Cuba on the Brink*, p. 251.

80 Gribkov and Smith, *Operation Anadyr*, p. 28.

81 Ibid.

82 Fursenko and Naftali, '*One Hell of a Gamble*', pp. 310–15.

83 Gribkov and Smith, *Operation Anadyr*, p. 4.

84 Intelligence Memorandum, 'Evaluation of Offensive Threat in Cuba' with cover memorandum, 'Carter to Members of United States Intelligence Board, 21 October 1962', McAuliffe, *CIA Documents*, p. 237.

85 Dino A. Brugioni (ed. Robert F. McCort), *Eyeball to Eyeball, The Inside Story of the Cuban Missile Crisis* (New York: Random House, 1991), pp. 174–5.

86 Garthoff, 'New Evidence', p. 252.

87 Special National Intelligence Estimate 85-3-62, 'The Military Buildup in Cuba', 19 September 1962, in McAuliffe, *CIA Documents*, p. 93.

88 Zaloga, *Kremlin's Nuclear Sword*, p. 86.

89 According to Polmar and Gresham, US intelligence underestimated the range of the Soviet MRBMs and IRBMs by over 20%, *DEFCON-2*, p. xxiii.

90 Allyn, Blight and Welch, *Back to the Brink*, p. 161.

91 Zaloga, *Kremlin's Nuclear Sword*, p. 79.

92 May and Zelikow, *Kennedy Tapes*, p. 338.

93 Zaloga, *Kremlin's Nuclear Sword*, p. 42; Garthoff puts the figure at 700 nautical miles, *Reflections*, p. 37n; the British intelligence community believed the range was 650 nautical miles, NA: CAB 129/111, JIC (62) 93 (Final), 'Cuba: The Threat Posed by Soviet Missiles', 26 October 1962.

94　Matthias Uhl and Vladimir I. Ivkin, '"Operation Atom": The Soviet Union's Stationing of Nuclear Missiles in the German Democratic Republic, 1959', *Cold War International History Project Bulletin* 12/13 (Fall/Winter 2001), pp. 299–306. See also Fursenko and Naftali, *Khrushchev's Cold War*, pp. 194, 208, 211. Western intelligence had also been told by Oleg Penkovsky that warheads for R-11 missiles were deployed in East Germany. CIA: 'Meeting 1 (London) 20 April 1961', paras 40–1, http://www.foia.cia.gov/penkovsky.asp, doc. 149.

95　Uhl and Ivkin, '"Operation Atom"', p. 306 n.33.

96　Bundy, *Danger and Survival*, p. 411.

97　Stern, *Averting 'The Final Failure'*, pp. 159–75.

98　Thomas G. Paterson and William J. Brophy, 'October Missiles and November Elections: The Cuban Missile Crisis and American Politics, 1962', *The Journal of American History* 73/1 (June 1986), pp. 87–119.

99　Richard Ned Lebow, 'Domestic Politics and the Cuban Missile Crisis: The Traditional and Revisionist Interpretations Reevaluated', *Diplomatic History* 14/4 (Fall 1990), pp. 471–92. A revised version of this article was published as 'The Traditional and Revisionist Interpretations Reevaluated', in Nathan, *Cuban Missile Crisis Revisited*, pp. 161–86.

100　David Lowenthal, 'US Cuban Policy: Illusion and Reality', *National Review*, 29 January 1963, p. 63, quoted in Arnold L. Horelick, 'The Cuban Missile Crisis: An Analysis of Soviet Calculations and Behavior', *World Politics* 16/3 (April 1964), p. 364 n.4.

101　Blight and Welch, *On the Brink*, p. 163.

102　Stern, *Averting 'The Final Failure'*, pp. 80–1.

103　Ibid, p. 92.

104　May and Zelikow, *Kennedy Tapes*, p. 92.

105　L. V. Scott, *Macmillan, Kennedy and the Cuban Missile Crisis: Political, Military and Intelligence Aspects* (Basingstoke: Macmillan, 1999), p. 64.

106　Garthoff, *Reflections*, p. 204.

107　Raymond L. Garthoff, 'The Military Significance of the Soviet Missile Bases in Cuba', 27 October 1962, reproduced in Garthoff, *Reflections*, p. 202.

108　Bundy, *Danger and Survival*, p. 452.

109　Ibid, p. 412.

110　Lebow and Stein, *We All Lost*. See also, Alexander L. George, 'The Cuban Missile Crisis: Peaceful Resolution through Coercive Diplomacy', in Alexander L. George and William E. Simons, *The Limits of Coercive Diplomacy* (Oxford: Westview, 1994), pp. 111–32. For a critical constructivist analysis of the nature of American reactions to the Soviet missiles, see Jutta Weldes, *Constructing National Interests: the United States and the Cuban Missile Crisis* (Minnesota: University of Minnesota Press, 1999).

111 For differing assessments see Lebow and Stein, *We All Lost*, pp. 45–6, 71, 98–102 and Taubman, *Khrushchev*, pp. 498–500.

112 For differing perspectives, see Allison and Zelikow, *Essence of Decision*, pp. 99–108; Bruce J. Allyn, James G. Blight, and David A. Welch, *Afterword from Cuba on the Brink: Castro, the Missile Crisis, and the Soviet Collapse* (Lanham: Rowman and Littlefield, 2002), pp. 8–9. http://www.watsoninstitute.org/pub/CotBafter.pdf

113 For the view of Gromyko, see Allyn, Blight and Welch, *Back to the Brink*, p. 147; for those of Troyanovsky see Taubman, *Khrushchev*, pp. 537–8.

114 Fursenko and Naftali, *Khrushchev's Cold War*, pp. 440–4, 450–1, 458–60.

115 May and Zelikow, *Kennedy Tapes*, p. 59.

116 Bundy, *Danger and Survival*, p. 452. Emphasis in original.

117 Ibid, p. 450.

118 Ibid, p. 452.

Chapter 3

1 Khrushchev to Kennedy, 26 October 1962, May and Zelikow, *Kennedy Tapes*, p. 490.

2 Theodore Sorensen, *Kennedy* (New York: Harper and Row, 1965), p. 779.

3 See in particular the analysis of Lebow and Stein, *We All Lost, passim*. For accounts of the resolution of the crisis, see Fursenko and Naftali, *'One Hell of a Gamble'*, pp. 257–89; *idem, Khrushchev's Cold War*, pp. 483–92; May and Zelikow, *Kennedy Tapes*, pp. 472–629; Stern, *Averting 'The Final Failure'*, pp. 260–383; and Taubman, *Khrushchev*, pp. 567–77.

4 For perspectives on this, see Blight, *Shattered Crystal Ball*, Bundy, *Danger and Survival* and Trachtenberg, *History and Strategy*.

5 Fursenko and Naftali, *Khrushchev's Cold War*, pp. 483–4.

6 Khrushchev to Kennedy, 27 October 1962, May and Zelikow, *Kennedy Tapes*, p. 506.

7 Arthur M. Schlesinger Jr., *A Thousand Days – John F. Kennedy in the White House* (London: Andre Deutsch, 1965), p. 709; Roger Hilsman, *To Move A Nation* (New York: Dell Publishing Co. [1964] 1967), pp. 223–4; Elie Abel, *Missiles of October: The Story of the Cuban Missile Crisis 1962* (London: MacGibbon and Kee, 1966), pp. 184–5.

8 Kennedy, *13 Days*, pp. 104–6.

9 Schlesinger, *Robert Kennedy*, pp. 521–4.

10 Allyn, Blight and Welch, *Back to the Brink*, pp. 92–3.

11 For reasons understandable to those with an intimate knowledge of the novels of Anthony Trollope (i.e. McGeorge Bundy), this became known as the Trollope ploy.

12 May and Zelikow, *Kennedy Tapes*, p. 604.

13 For discussion, see James Hershberg, 'Anatomy of a Controversy: Anatoly Dobrynin's Meeting with Robert Kennedy, Saturday 27 October 1962', *Cold War International History Project Bulletin*, Issue 5 (Spring 1995), pp. 75, 77–80.

14 Lebow and Stein, *We All Lost*, pp. 523–6.

15 Dobrynin, *In Confidence*, pp. 86–9.

16 Bundy, *Danger and Survival*, p. 438.

17 Lebow and Stein, *We All Lost*, p. 525.

18 Ibid, p. 526.

19 *Foreign Relations of the United States* (FRUS): 'Memorandum from Attorney General Kennedy to Secretary of State Rusk', 30 October 1962, *Cuban Missile Crisis and Aftermath, Vol. XI 1961–1963*, p. 270.

20 For the view that Robert Kennedy was not delivering an ultimatum, see Blight, *The Shattered Crystal Ball*, pp. 124–9, 142. For the view that he was, see George, 'Cuban Missile Crisis', pp. 121–4.

21 Fursenko and Naftali, *'One Hell of a Gamble'*, pp. 283–4. For discussion, see Chapter 4.

22 Ibid, p. 284.

23 Lebow and Stein, *We All Lost*, p. 525.

24 Nikita S. Khrushchev (translated by Jerrold Schecter and Vyacheslav Luchkov), *Khrushchev Remembers: The Glasnost Tapes* (Boston MA: Little, Brown and Company, 1990).

25 Ibid, p. 179.

26 The Americans also had Honest John tactical ballistic missiles in Turkey, Robert S. Norris, 'Where They Were', *Bulletin of the Atomic Scientists* 55/6 (November/December 1999).

27 Kennedy, *13 Days*, p. 107.

28 NA: FO 371/162404, Ormsby-Gore to Caccia, 7 November 1962, AK 1261/586.

29 Bundy, *Danger and Survival*, p. 427; Blight and Welch, *On the Brink*, p. 263.

30 Scott, *Macmillan, Kennedy*, pp. 168–71.

31 Blight and Welch, *On the Brink*, pp. 83–4, 113–15.

32 Mark J. White, 'Dean Rusk's Revelation: New British Evidence on the

Cordier Ploy', *The Society for Historians of American Foreign Relations Newsletter* 25/3 (September 1994), p. 6; see also *idem, The Cuban Missile Crisis* (Basingstoke: Macmillan, 1996), pp. 202–3. For a different interpretation see Raymond L. Garthoff, 'Some Reflections on the History of the Cold War', *The Society for Historians of American Foreign Relations Newsletter* 26/3 (September 1995), pp. 1–3.

33 NA: FO 371/162387, Dean to FO, 25 October 1962.

34 NA: PREM 11/3689 Ormsby-Gore to Macmillan, Prime Minister's Personal Telegram T.500/62 23 October 1962. Initially, Ormsby Gore hesitated before reporting this back to London, believing that no-one in the administration, aside from Robert Kennedy, was aware of JFK's thinking, ibid.

35 Blight and Welch, *On the Brink*, pp. 113–15.

36 See May and Zelikow, *Kennedy Tapes*, pp. 197–203; for Stevenson's memo to Kennedy outlining his opposition to an air strike, see 'UN Ambassador Adlai Stevenson's opinions against an airstrike on Cuba, October 17, 1962', in Chang and Kornbluh, *Cuban Missile Crisis*, pp. 119–20.

37 McNamara, *Blundering into Disaster*, p. 176.

38 Stern, *Averting 'The Final Failure'*, p. 123.

39 Blight and Welch, *On the Brink*, pp. 147–8. The suggestion that it would have been reasonable for the Soviets to attack the UK seems rather bizarre, not least because Britain was a nuclear weapons state. Presumably, Nitze had simply conflated the Jupiters with the Thors.

40 For accounts, see Lawrence Freedman, *Kennedy's Wars: Berlin, Cuba, Laos and Vietnam* (Oxford: Oxford University Press, 2000), pp. 45–120; Fursenko and Naftali, *'One Hell of a Gamble'*, *passim*; Taubman, *Khrushchev*, pp. 396–528, *passim*; Trachtenberg, *History and Strategy*, pp. 169–234.

41 For accounts of the summit, see Beschloss, *Kennedy v Khrushchev*, pp. 191–231, and Fursenko and Naftali, *Khrushchev's Cold Wars*, pp. 360–4.

42 Bernard Brodie, *War and Politics* (London: Cassell, 1973), p. 431.

43 Allison and Zelikow, *Essence of Decision*, p. 348.

44 Freedman, *Kennedy's Wars*, pp. 62–71.

45 Ibid, pp. 94–5. For an account of the development of Berlin contingency planning between the US, UK and France, and then within NATO, see Sean M. Maloney, 'Berlin Contingency Planning: Prelude to Flexible Response, 1958–63', *Journal of Strategic Studies* 25/1 (March 2002), pp. 99–134.

46 Bundy, *Danger and Survival*, p. 375.

47 Ibid, p. 375.

48 Acheson, 'Wishing Won't Hold Berlin', *Saturday Evening Post* 1959, quoted in Bundy, *Danger and Survival*, pp. 375–6.
49 Kaplan, 'JFK's First Strike Plan', pp. 81–6.
50 Stern, *Averting 'The Final Failure'*, p. 167.
51 Ibid, pp. 200–1; Alice L. George, *Awaiting Armageddon: How Americans Faced the Cuban Missile Crisis* (Chapel Hill: University of North Carolina Press, 2003), pp. 62–7.
52 Blight and Welch, *On the Brink*, p. 195.
53 Scott, *Macmillan, Kennedy*, pp. 39–40.
54 NA: PREM 11/3972, Note for the Record [of a meeting between Prime Minister, Foreign Secretary and General Strong, Director of the Joint Intelligence Bureau], 19 November 1962. Emphasis in original. I am grateful to Ben Fenton for drawing my attention to this document.
55 Ibid.
56 Ibid.
57 The North Atlantic Treaty, 4 April 1949, http://www.nato.int/docu/basictxt/treaty.htm
58 Freedman, *Kennedy's Wars*, p. 49.
59 McNamara, 'Military Role of Nuclear Weapons', p. 79; Bundy, *Danger and Survival*, p. 376.
60 Blight and Welch, *On the Brink*, pp. 147–8.
61 Ian Clark, *Nuclear Diplomacy and the Special Relationship: Britain's Deterrent and America, 1957–1962* (Oxford: Oxford University Press, 1994), p. 328.
62 Ibid, p. 335.
63 Quoted in ibid, p. 15.
64 Sagan, *Limits of Safety*, pp. 111–13. This account reflects several misconceptions of British command and control; see Twigge and Scott, *Planning Armageddon*, pp. 122–9.
65 Nigel Ashton, *Kennedy, Macmillan and the Cold War: The Irony of Interdependence* (Basingstoke: Palgrave Macmillan, 2002), pp. 63, 73–5.
66 NA: 'Cuba', Memorandum by the Lord Chancellor, C(62)170, 25 October 1962, CAB 129/111.
67 Alistair Horne, *Macmillan 1957–1986, Volume II of the Official Biography* (London: Macmillan, 1989), pp. 370–5.
68 Peter Hennessy, *The Prime Minister: The Office and its Holders since 1945* (London: Allen Lane, 2000), pp. 102–3.
69 NA: CAB 134/940, 'The Defence Implications of Fallout from a Hydrogen Bomb' [The Strath Report], HDC (535) 3. For discussion, see Matthew Grant, 'Civil Defence Policy in Cold War Britain, 1945–68' (University of London PhD, 2006), esp. pp. 137–43.

70   NA: CAB 134/2039, 'Assessment of the Effects of Attack on the United Kingdom', Note by the Home Office, 5 April 1960, HDR (60)8. For discussion, see Grant, 'Civil Defence Policy', pp. 191–220.

71   NA: DEFE 32/7, 'Record of a Conversation between the Chief of the Air Staff, First Sea Lord and the Chief of the Imperial General Staff held in the Ministry of Defence at 1430, Saturday, 27 October 1962', Annex to COS 1546/29/10/62.

72   NA: DEFE 13/212, Record of a meeting between the MOD and the COS on 28 October 1962, MM/COS (62)7.

73   McNamara, 'Military Role of Nuclear Weapons', p. 72. See Earl Mountbatten, Lord Noel-Baker, Lord Zuckerman, *Apocalypse Now?* (Nottingham: Spokesman, 1980).

74   *Department of Defense Dictionary of Military and Associated Terms* (Washington DC: DOD, 12 April 2001 amended 16 October 2006), p. 421. For discussion of preventive and pre-emptive war, see Freedman, *Evolution of Nuclear Strategy*, pp. 117–30.

75   *Dictionary of Military Terms*, p. 425. Richard Betts further distinguishes between surprise attack, pre-emption and prevention. 'Surprise Attack and Preemption', Allison, Carnesale and Nye, *Hawks, Doves and Owls*, pp. 54–79.

76   Quoted in Michael Walzer, *Just and Unjust Wars: a Moral Argument with Historical Illustrations* (London, Penguin [1977] 1984), p. 74.

77   Scott D. Sagan, 'The Perils of Proliferation: Organization Theory, Deterrence Theory and the Spread of Nuclear Weapons', *International Security* 18/4 (Spring 1994), pp. 78–9.

78   Richard L. Aldrich, *The Hidden Hand: Britain, America and Cold War Secret Intelligence* (London: John Murray, 2001) pp. 10–11, 327–33.

79   Kennedy, *13 Days*, p. 117. Whether the officer meant preventive or preemptive war is unclear. For discussion of US debates about preventive war, see Scott D. Sagan, *Moving Targets: Nuclear Strategy and National Security* (Princeton, New Jersey: Princeton University Press, 1989), pp. 19–22. For the KGB's concern that the Pentagon was preparing for preventive war in 1960, see Fursenko and Naftali, *'One Hell of a Gamble'*, pp. 51–2.

80   Lebow and Stein, *We All Lost*, p. 509 n.64.

81   William Burr and Jeffrey T. Richelson, 'Whether to "Strangle the Baby in the Cradle": The United States and the Chinese Nuclear Program, 1960–64', *International Security* 25/3 (Winter 2000/1), pp. 54–99.

82   Ibid, p. 68.

83   Scott Sagan and Jeremi Suri, 'The Madman Nuclear Alert: Secrecy Signaling and Safety in October 1969', *International Security* 27/4 (Spring 2003), pp. 176–7.

84 See Freedman, *Evolution of Nuclear Strategy*, pp. 243–7; Stephen M. Meyer, 'Soviet Nuclear Weapons', in Ashton B. Carter, John D. Steinbruner and Charles A. Zracket (eds), *Managing Nuclear Operations* (Washington DC: The Brookings Institution, 1987), pp. 470–531; Lebow and Stein, *We All Lost*, p. 40.

85 Raymond L. Garthoff, 'BMD and East-West Relations', in Ashton B. Carter and David N. Schwarz (eds), *Ballistic Missile Defence* (Washington: The Brookings Institution, 1984), pp. 290–1; see also Michael McGwire, *Military Objectives in Soviet Foreign Policy* (Washington DC: The Brookings Institution, 1987), pp. 50–1.

86 For discussion of the development of Soviet doctrine, see Stephen M. Meyer, 'Soviet Perspectives on the Paths to Nuclear War', in Allison, Carnesale and Nye, *Hawks, Doves and Owls*, pp. 167–205; *idem*, in Carter, *Managing Nuclear Operations*, pp. 470–531; and Freedman, *Evolution of Nuclear Strategy*, pp. 53–9, 105–7, 136–45, 243–57.

87 Sagan, *Limits of Safety*, pp. 135–40; see also Polmar and Gresham, *DEFCON-2*, pp. 7–8, 151–2, 190–1.

88 Hilsman, *To Move A Nation*, p. 221.

89 Lebow and Stein, *We All Lost*, pp. 139–40.

90 Ibid, p. 445 n.188.

91 May and Zelikow, *Kennedy Tapes*, p. 634.

92 Sagan, *Limits of Safety*, p. 141.

93 Zaloga, *Kremlin's Nuclear Sword*, p. 87.

94 Sagan, *Limits of Safety*, pp. 142–5; Blair, *Logic of Accidental*, pp. 23–4.

95 Oral history, Lieutenant General David A. Burchall, quoted in Trachtenberg, *History and Strategy*, p. 249. McNamara denied he responded in this fashion.

96 Freedman, *Kennedy's Wars*, p. 97.

97 Ibid, p. 98.

98 *FRUS*, 1961–1963, Volume VIII: Memorandum of Conversation with President Kennedy, 20 September, 1961, p. 130.

99 Sagan, *Limits of Safety*, p. 133.

100 Ibid, pp. 122–34.

101 Ibid, pp. 127–30.

102 Ibid, pp. 130–1.

103 Ibid, pp. 78–80.

104 Fursenko and Naftali, *'One Hell of a Gamble'*, pp. 272–3.

105 For Castro's message to Khrushchev, see Blight, Allyn and Welch, *Cuba on the Brink*, pp. 481–2. For discussion, see Fursenko and Naftali, *'One Hell of a Gamble'*, pp. 272–3.

106 Blight, Allyn and Welch, *Cuba on the Brink*, pp. 20–2.

107 Khrushchev, *Glasnost Tapes*, p. 183

108 Khrushchev to Castro, 30 October 1962, in Blight, Allyn and Welch, *Cuba on the Brink*, p. 486–7.

109 Castro to Khrushchev, 31 October 1962, in ibid, p. 490.

110 Fursenko and Naftali, *'One Hell of a Gamble'*, p. 273; for Castro's reflections at the 1992 Havana conference and discussion, see Blight, Allyn and Welch, *Cuba on the Brink*, pp. 73–4, 108–13, 361–5.

111 Ibid, pp. 252–3.

112 Ibid, p. 22.

113 Blight and Welch, 'Risking "The Destruction of Nations"', p. 844.

114 Martin Westlake (with Ian St John), *Kinnock, The Biography* (London: Little, Brown and Company, 2001), p. 378.

115 Stromseth, *Origins of Flexible Response, passim.*

116 Robert E. Osgood, *The Entangling Alliance* (Chicago: Chicago University Press, 1962), p. 110.

117 Annette Messemer, 'Konrad Adenauer: Defence Diplomat on the Backstage', in Gaddis *et al, Cold War Statesmen*, p. 244.

118 Christoph Bluth, *Britain, Germany and Western Nuclear Strategy* (Oxford: Oxford University Press, 1995), pp. 33–4.

119 Denis Healey, 'The Bomb That Didn't Go Off', *Encounter* (1954). Healey later 'bitterly regretted' his endorsement of limited nuclear war, *idem, The Time of My Life* (London: Michael Joseph, 1989), p. 238.

120 Sorensen, *Kennedy*, p. 789.

121 Bundy, *Danger and Survival*, p. 455.

122 Coleman, 'Camelot's Nuclear Conscience', p. 42.

Chapter 4

1 Allison, Carnesale and Nye, *Hawks, Doves and Owls*, pp. 209–10.

2 John F. Kennedy, *Why England Slept* (Westpost, CT: Greenwood Press Reprint, 1981).

3 Robert Kennedy, *13 Days*, pp. 124–5.

4 Scott Sagan, 'Nuclear Alerts and Crisis Management', *International Security* 9/4 (Spring 1985), p. 108.

5 Garthoff, *Reflections*, p. 62. In the film, *Thirteen Days*, President Kennedy angrily discovers SAC is at DEFCON-2, *Thirteen Days* (New Line, Director: Roger Donaldson, 2000). With regard to the airborne alert, Sagan explains that 'civilian officials not only made the final decision to implement the SAC airborne alert, but that they also required that the individual SAC bomber routes be approved by political authorities in order to ensure that flights would not accidentally fly into or approach

Soviet air space', Sagan, *Limits of Safety*, p. 68. Changes to the DEFCON alert state were also fully approved by political authorities.

6 Sagan, *Limits of Safety*, p. 69.

7 Fursenko and Naftali, '*One Hell of a Gamble*', p 258. The authors state that the change in alert condition was detected at 10 p.m. though the actual change took place at 10 a.m.

8 Blight, Allyn and Welch, *Cuba on the Brink*, pp. 56–63.

9 Ibid, pp. 60–1, 71, 259.

10 Kramer, 'Tactical nuclear weapons', p. 42.

11 Ibid, pp. 40, 42–6 and Blight, Allyn and Welch, 'Kramer Vs. Kramer,' pp. 41, 47–50.

12 Gribkov and Smith, *Operation Anadyr*, pp. 4-7.

13 Fursenko and Naftali, '*One Hell of a Gamble*', pp. 211–12, 217.

14 Blight, Allyn and Welch, *Cuba on the Brink*, p. 90. These inaccuracies were corrected in his contribution to Gribkov and Smith, *Operation Anadyr*, pp. 4–7.

15 Gribkov and Smith, *Operation Anadyr*, pp. 4–7.

16 Fursenko and Naftali, '*One Hell of a Gamble*', p. 212; Mark Kramer, 'The Lessons of the Cuban Missile Crisis for Warsaw Pact Nuclear Operations', *Cold War International History Project Bulletin* Issue 5 (Spring 1995), p. 110; Gribkov and Smith, *Operation Anadyr*, pp. 5–6.

17 Fursenko and Naftali, '*One Hell of a Gamble*', pp. 242–3; Fursenko and Naftali, *Khrushchev's Cold War*, pp. 468–74.

18 Ibid, pp. 472–3.

19 For Malinovsky's telegrams to Pliyev and discussion of issues, see Svetlana Savranskaya, 'Tactical Nuclear Weapons in Cuba: New Evidence', *Cold War International History Project Bulletin* Issue 14/15 (Winter 2003/Spring 2004), pp. 385–98.

20 Peter A. Huchthausen, *October Fury* (New York: John Wiley, 2002), pp. 148–54.

21 See Aleksandr Fursenko and Timothy Naftali, 'Using KGB Documents: The Scali-Feklisov Channel in the Cuban Missile Crisis', *Cold War International History Project Bulletin* Issue 5 (Spring 1995), pp. 58, 60–2.

22 'John Scali's Notes of First Meeting with Soviet Embassy Counselor Alexandr Fomin, October 26, 1962', in Chang and Kornbluh, *Cuban Missile Crisis*, p. 184.

23 Alexander Feklisov and Sergei Kostin, *The Man Behind the Rosenbergs: by the KGB Spymaster who was the Case Officer of Julius Rosenberg, and helped resolve the Cuban Missile Crisis* (New York: Enigma Books, 2001), pp. 362–402.

24 Fursenko and Naftali, *Khrushchev's Cold War*, pp. 484–5.

25 For background on Kennedy's attitude toward the military, see Stern, *Averting 'The Final Failure'*, pp. 1–14. See also Robert Dallek, *John F. Kennedy: An Unfinished Life 1917–1963* (London: Penguin, 2004), pp. 87–108, 344–6, 516–17.

26 Stern, *Averting 'The Final Failure'*, p. 186.

27 May and Zelikow, *Kennedy Tapes*, pp. 356–7.

28 Oral history, quoted in Joseph Bouchard, *Command in Crisis: Four Case Studies* (New York: Columbia University Press, 1991), pp. 100–1.

29 Stern, *Averting 'The Final Failure'*, p. 182.

30 Bouchard, *Command in Crisis*, pp. 107–8; May and Zelikow, *Kennedy Tapes*, pp. 297–9.

31 Brugioni, *Eyeball to Eyeball*, pp. 463–4.

32 Bouchard, *Command in Crisis*, p. 108.

33 Brendon DuBois, *Resurrection Day* (London: Little, Brown and Company, 1999), pp. 358–61, 367–70.

34 Schecter and Deriabin, *Spy Who Saved the World*, p. 263.

35 Ibid, p. 262.

36 When the episode was first disclosed by Garthoff he indicated that his contemporaneous source had suggested the phone call was made on 22 October, Raymond L. Garthoff, *Reflections on the Cuban Missile Crisis* (Washington DC: The Brookings Institution, 1987), pp. 39–41.

37 Hennessy, *Secret State*, pp. 42–3.

38 Schecter and Deriabin, *Spy Who Saved the World*, p. 337.

39 CIA: John A. McCone, 'Memorandum', 5 November 1962 (courtesy of the US Information and Privacy Coordinator); Schecter and Deriabin, *Spy Who Saved the World*, pp. 346–7.

40 Garthoff, *Reflections* (1989), pp. 64–5. Note: all subsequent references are to the 1989 edition of the book.

41 Schecter and Deriabin, *Spy Who Saved the World*, p. 74, *et seq.* Another motive for this offer may well have been to impress Western intelligence with his commitment to their cause.

42 Oldfield to Maury, 27 October 1961, quoted in Schecter and Deriabin, *Spy Who Saved the World*, p. 285.

43 CIA, 'Memorandum for the Record: Conversation with Mr Helms Re [Penkovsky] Report on Large-Scale Soviet Military Preparations', 26 September 1961, doc. 113.

44 Sagan, *Limits of Safety*, pp. 146–50; see also Blight and Welch, *On the Brink*, pp. 208–9.

45 Fursenko and Naftali, *'One Hell of a Gamble'*, pp. 277–8; Blight and Welch, *On the Brink*, pp. 338–40; Blight, Allyn and Welch, *Cuba on the Brink*, pp. 101–23.

46 See Peter Stein and Peter Feaver, *Assuring Control of Nuclear Weapons: The Evolution of Permissive Action Links* (Cambridge, Mass.: CSIA, University Press of America, 1987) and Peter Feaver, *Guarding the Guardians: Civilian Control of Nuclear Weapons in the United States* (Ithaca, New York: Cornell University Press, 1992), pp. 191–3.

47 Kramer, 'Lessons of the Cuban Missile Crisis', pp. 59, 112–15.

48 Gribkov and Smith, *Operation Anadyr*, p. 63.

49 Kramer, 'The Cuban Missile Crisis and Nuclear Proliferation', p. 177.

50 Blight and Welch, *On the Brink*, p. 195.

51 'Memorandum of meeting attended in Secretary Ball's conference room', 17 October 1962, McAuliffe, *CIA Documents*, p. 160.

52 May and Zelikow, *Kennedy Tapes*, p. 184.

53 Robert L. O'Connell, 'The Cuban Missile Crisis: Second Holocaust', in Robert Cowley (ed.) *What If? America: Eminent Historians Imagine What Might Have Been* (Chatham: Pan Macmillan, 2004), pp. 261–4.

54 Blight and Welch, *On the Brink*, pp. 209–10.

55 May and Zelikow, *Kennedy Tapes*, p. 63.

56 Ibid, p. 195.

57 John McCone, 'Memorandum of Meeting with the President, Attorney General, Secretary McNamara, General Taylor, and McCone, 10 am – 10/21/62', McAuliffe, *CIA Documents*, pp. 241–2.

58 Raymond L. Garthoff, 'US Intelligence in the Cuban Missile Crisis', *Intelligence and National Security* 13/3 (Autumn 1998), p. 40. There were 36 warheads and 42 missiles deployed. Six of the missiles were for training purposes.

59 May and Zelikow, *Kennedy Tapes*, p. 206.

60 Blight and Welch, *On the Brink*, p. 211. Gribkov states that only half the 36 R-12s were ready to be fuelled, a process, he states, that would take eighteen hours, Gribkov and Smith, *Operation Anadyr*, p. 63.

61 Fursenko and Naftali, *'One Hell of a Gamble'*, p. 217.

62 Ibid, p. 217; Gribkov and Smith, *Operation Anadyr*, pp. 45–6.

63 Stern, *Averting 'The Final Failure'*, p. 282. Emphasis in original.

64 Gribkov and Smith, *Operation Anadyr*, p. 7.

65 Ibid, *Operation Anadyr*, p. 64.

66 Bundy, *Danger and Survival*, p. 423.

67 The figure for Cuban forces was provided by the former Chief of Staff of the Cuban army, General Sergio del Valle in 1989, Allyn, Blight and Welch, *Back from the Brink*, p. 106.

68 For exposition of the American legal position, see Abram Chayes, *The Cuban Missile Crisis* (London: Oxford University Press, 1974).

69 May and Zelikow, *Kennedy Tapes*, p. 266. Kennedy's assumption that a

declaration of war absolved the United States from the charge that it was acting illegally would obviously have been vigorously contested.

70 Horne, *Macmillan*, p. 380. Emphasis in original.

71 For discussion, see Blight, Allyn and Welch, *Cuba on the Brink, passim*, Philip Brenner, 'Cuba and the Missile Crisis', *Journal of Latin American Studies* 22/1 (February 1990), pp. 115–42; *idem*. 'Thirteen Months' and Jorge I. Dominguez, 'The @#$%& Missile Crisis: (Or What Was "Cuban" about U.S. Decisions during the Cuban Missile Crisis?)', *Diplomatic History* 24/2 (Spring 2000), pp. 305–15.

72 The actual shooting of the Cuban scenes was done in the Philippines. For assessment of the film, see Munton and Welch, *Cuban Missile Crisis*, pp. 2–3, 110–11. For a sympathetic review, see Ernest R. May, 'Thirteen Days in 145 Minutes', *National Forum* 81/2 (Spring 2001), pp. 34–7. For an incisive and critical review, see Philip Brenner, 'Turning History on its Head', National Security Archive, http://www.gwu.edu/~nsarchiv/nsa/cuba_mis_cri/brenner.htm, pp. 1–6.

73 Blight, Allyn and Welch, *Cuba on the Brink*, p. 362. Emphasis in original.

74 Twigge and Scott, *Planning Armageddon*, pp. 123–5 The normal readiness state of the Thors involved 65% of the missiles at fifteen minutes' readiness, ibid, p. 111 The figure for the Jupiters is based on Dean Rusk's briefing to the President, which made clear that 80% of the Jupiters were normally held at 15 minutes' readiness, Dean Rusk, 'Memorandum for the President: Political and Military Considerations Bearing on Turkish and Italian IRBMs', 9 November 1962, John F. Kennedy Library: NSF: RS: NATO, Weapons, Cables, Turkey, Box 226.

75 NA: AIR8/2307, Air Marshal Sir Edmund Hudleston, 'The Future of Thor', Note by the VCAS, AC (61)44, 2 August 1961.

76 Twigge and Scott, *Planning Armageddon*, pp. 111, 141 n. 62. The missiles could only be held at two minutes' readiness for two hours before the fuel had to be removed and a six-hour recovery period instigated, ibid.

77 Twigge and Scott, *Planning Armageddon*, pp. 112, 142 n.70.

78 Blight, Allyn and Welch, *Cuba on the Brink*, p. 262.

79 Feaver, *Guarding the Guardians*, pp. 180–2.

80 *FRUS*: Minutes of the 505th mtg of the NSC, 20 October 1962, *FRUS, 1961–1963 vol XI: Cuban Missile Crisis and Aftermath*, p. 134.

81 Stern, *Averting 'The Final Failure'*, pp. 144–6.

82 May and Zelikow, *The Kennedy Tapes*, p. 223.

83 Gaddis, *We Now Know*, pp. 273–4.

84 Sagan, *Limits of Safety*, pp. 135–42. According to Polmar and Gresham two F-102s were involved, Polmar and Gresham, *DEFCON-2*, pp. 151.

85 Ibid, p. 152.

86 Sagan, *Limits of Safety*, p. 140.

87 Fursenko and Naftali, *'One Hell of a Gamble'*, pp. 213–14.

88 Savranskaya, 'Soviet Submarines', p. 238. Fursenko and Naftali state that the B-75 carried two R-11f SLBMs, Fursenko and Naftali, *Khrushchev's Cold War*, p. 462.

89 Huchthausen, *October Fury*, p. 70.

90 Pavel Podvig (ed.), *Russian Strategic Nuclear Forces* (London: The MIT Press, 2004), p. 236.

91 Savranskaya, 'Soviet Submarines', p. 251

92 Alexander Mozgovoi, *Kubinskaya Samba Kvarteta Foxtrotov* [The Cuban Samba of the Foxtrot Quartet] (Moscow: Voennyi Para, 2002), p. 62, quoted in Savranskaya, 'Soviet Submarines', p. 239; Savranskaya, 'Soviet Submarines', pp. 247–9. According to Fursenko and Naftali, Mikoyan was aware that the boats in question were diesel-electric when he argued in the Presidium against proceeding, Fursenko and Naftali, *Khrushchev's Cold War*, p. 478.

93 Fursenko and Naftali, *Khrushchev's Cold War*, pp. 478–80.

94 See National Security Archive: http://www.nsarchive.org/nsa/ cuba_mis_cri/press1.htm; Huchthausen, *October Fury*.

95 Bouchard, *Command in Crisis*, p. 123.

96 Stern, *Averting 'The Final Failure'*, pp. 211–14.

97 Ibid, p. 213.

98 Bouchard, *Command in Crisis*, pp. 104–5.

99 Ibid, p. 132.

100 Savranskaya, 'Soviet Submarines', pp. 249–50; for details of the US proclamation announcing their instigation, see Bouchard, *Command in Crisis*, p. 121. A Notice to Mariners was a standard means by which maritime nations warned others of navigation hazards, ibid.

101 Bouchard, *Command in Crisis*, p. 125.

102 Savranskaya, 'Soviet Submarines', p. 251.

103 Huchthausen, *October Fury*, p. 19. The provenance of the reconstructed conversation is not specified.

104 Ibid, p. 53. The dialogue is consistent with the recollections of Captain Ketov, commander of the B-4, Savranskaya, 'Soviet Submarines', p. 240.

105 Ibid.

106 Huchthausen, *October Fury*, p. 65; Mozgovoi states that orders had to come from the Defence Minister, *Kubinskaya Samba*, p. 71, quoted in Savranskaya, 'Soviet Submarines', p. 240

107 Savranskaya, 'Soviet Submarines', p. 252.

108 Huchthausen, *October Fury*, pp. 202–19. For discussion of this account, see Savranskaya, 'Soviet Submarines', pp. 243–4.

109 Huchthausen, *October Fury*, pp. 209–10.
110 William Burr and Thomas S. Blanton, *The Submarines of October, National Security Archive Electronic Briefing Book No 75*, 31 October 2002, note 16, http://www.gwu.edu/
111 Huchthausen, *October Fury*, p. 19.
112 For McNamara's reconstruction of the exchange, over thirty years after the event, see Blight and Welch, *On the Brink*, pp. 63–4. The exchange comprised questions from the Defense Secretary about what the navy intended, culminating in Admiral Anderson's statement that he proposed to fire into the rudder of a tanker to force it to stop. McNamara made clear that no such action would take place without his express permission, and after Anderson remarked that the navy had been running blockades since the time of John Paul Jones, McNamara brought closure by asking Anderson whether he understood that he was not to act without political permission. 'The tight-lipped response was "yes"', ibid, p. 64. See also the account in Abel, *Missiles of October*, pp. 142–5. For a different version in which Admiral Anderson gains the rhetorical upper hand over Secretary McNamara, see Brugioni, *Eyeball to Eyeball*, pp. 473–4.
113 Interview, Blight and Welch, *On the Brink*, p. 147. For a more nuanced but similar perspective on the effectiveness of the US ASW operation, see George, 'Cuban Missile Crisis', pp. 117–20.
114 An official 1993 American definition of a nuclear accident is, 'An unexpected event involving nuclear weapons or nuclear components that results in any of the following: a) accidental or unauthorized launching, firing, or use by U.S. forces or U.S supported Allied forces of a nuclear-capable weapons system; b) an accidental, unauthorized or unexplained nuclear detonation; c) non-nuclear detonation or burning of a nuclear weapon or nuclear component; d) radioactive contamination; e) jettisoning of a nuclear weapon or nuclear component; f) public hazard, actual or perceived', U.S. Defense Department Directive 5230.16, 'Nuclear Accident and Incident Public Affairs (PA) Guidance', issued 20 December 1993, http://www.cnn.com/SPECIALS/cold.war/experience/the.bomb/broken.arrows/intro.html For the purpose of this discussion, unauthorized is distinguished from accidental.
115 For discussion, see Shaun Gregory, *The Hidden Costs of Deterrence: Nuclear Weapons Accidents* (London: Brassey's UK, 1990).
116 Ibid, pp. 100–3.
117 Center for Defense Information, http://www.milnet.com/cdiart.htm#7
118 Sagan, *Limits of Safety*, pp. 53–155.

119   General James Walsh to General Curtis Le May, 27 July 1956, http://www.cnn.com/SPECIALS/cold.war/experience/the.bomb/broken.arrows/intro.html

120   Bracken, 'Accidental Nuclear War', p. 40; Sagan, *Moving Targets*, p. 144

121   Sagan, *Limits of Safety*, p. 178.

122   Ibid, p. 180. Sagan argues that had the aircraft crashed on the nearby Thule early warning installation there was a risk that the incident could have led to accidental war, see ibid, pp. 181–9.

123   K-19: *The Widowmaker* (Paramount Pictures, Director: Kathryn Bigelow, 2002). See also Peter A. Huchthausen, K-19: *The Widowmaker: The Secret Story of the Soviet Nuclear Submarine* (Washington DC: National Geographic Society, 2002).

124   When details of the incident, and how it was covered up, eventually became known, the former Soviet President, Mikhail Gorbachev, nominated the submariners for a Nobel Peace Prize on the grounds that a nuclear accident could have precipitated nuclear war. Gorbachev's scenario was unlikely for several reasons, though the heroism of the crew, in particular its engineers, was indisputable.

125   Polmar and Gresham, *DEFCON-2*, pp. 19, 156–7.

126   Podvig, *Russian Strategic Nuclear Forces*, p. 125; Zaloga, *Kremlin's Nuclear Sword*, p. 66.

127   Schecter and Deriabin, *Spy Who Saved the World*, pp. 70–2.

128   Blight and Welch, *On the Brink*, p. 213.

129   Sagan, *Limits of Safety*, pp. 67–8.

130   Fursenko and Naftali, *'One Hell of a Gamble'*, p. 276.

131   Ibid, p. 247.

132   Ibid, pp. 254–5, 276.

133   Ibid, p. 276; Gribkov and Smith, *Operation Anadyr*, p. 46.

134   Fursenko and Naftali, *'One Hell of a Gamble'*, pp. 227–8.

135   Stern, *Averting 'The Final Failure'*, p. 206; Fursenko and Naftali, *'One Hell of a Gamble'*, pp. 287–8; Chang and Kornbluh, *Cuban Missile Crisis*, pp. 380–1.

136   Garthoff, *Reflections*, p. 31.

Chapter 5

1   Lewis Chester, Godfrey Hodgson and Bruce Page, *An American Melodrama: The Presidential Campaign of 1968* (New York: The Viking Press, 1969), pp. 799–800. I am grateful to R. Gerald Hughes for drawing my attention to this quotation.

2   Allison and Zelikow, *Essence of Decision*, p. 394.

3 Cline, 'Cuban Missile Crisis', p. 191.

4 Blight, Allyn and Welch, *Cuba on the Brink*, pp. 486–7.

5 Blight and Welch, *On the Brink*, p. 195.

6 Ibid.

7 Ibid, pp. 180–1.

8 *Fail Safe* (Columbia Pictures, Director: Sidney Lumet, 1964), based on the novel by Eugene Burdick and Harvey Wheeler, *Fail Safe* (New York: Dell, 1963).

9 Bundy, *Danger and Survival*, pp. 443–4.

10 Allyn, Blight and Welch, *Back to the Brink*, p. 86. At the Moscow conference Dobrynin felt the need to emphasize that the person on the bicycle was a 'black man'.

11 Beschloss, *Kennedy v Khrushchev*, pp. 152–7, *et seq.*

12 Fursenko and Naftali, *'One Hell of a Gamble'*, pp. 249–52, 299–300.

13 On David Ormsby-Gore's role, see Scott, *Macmillan, Kennedy*, esp. pp. 113–20, 183–4.

14 Fursenko and Naftali, *'One Hell of a Gamble'*, p. 243.

15 As the nuclear-configured Ilyushin-28 bombers were still in their crates, there was little chance they could have been assembled and used in time once hostilities began.

16 Fursenko and Naftali, *'One Hell of a Gamble'*, pp. 273–7.

17 Desch, '"That Deep Mud"', p. 333.

18 Blight, Allyn and Welch, *Cuba on the Brink*, p. 255.

19 May and Zelikow, *Kennedy Tapes*, p. 338.

20 Blight and Welch, *On the Brink*, p. 195.

21 Cline, 'Cuban Missile Crisis', p. 191.

22 Bundy, *Danger and Survival*, p. 457.

23 Ibid, p. 688 n. 6.

24 May and Zelikow, *Kennedy Tapes*, p. 178.

25 Schlesinger, *Robert Kennedy*, p. 524.

26 National Archive, Washington DC: 'Transcripts of Meetings of the Joint Chiefs of Staff, October–November 1962,' p. 13. See also comment of May and Zelikow, *Kennedy Tapes*, p. 203n.

27 See May and Zelikow, *Kennedy Tapes*, p. 635. This recommendation was not endorsed by General Taylor. For discussion, see Gribkov and Smith, *Operation Anadyr*, pp. 147–9.

28 Coleman, 'Camelot's Nuclear Conscience', p. 45.

29 Sagan, *Moving Targets*, p. 32. This assessment was based on an overestimation of the Soviet ICBM force.

30 Blight and Welch, *On the Brink*, p. 206.

31 See, for example, Henry Kissinger, *Nuclear Weapons and Foreign Policy*

(New York: Harper, 1957). For discussion of limited war, see Freedman, *Evolution*, pp. 89–113.

32 See Scott D. Sagan, 'Nuclear Alerts and Crisis Management', *International Security* 9/4 (Spring 1985); see also Bruce Blair, 'Alerting in Crisis and Conventional War', in Carter, Steinbruner and Zracket, *Managing Nuclear Operations*, pp. 75–120; *idem*, *Logic of Accidental Nuclear War*.

33 Sagan, *Limits of Safety*, pp. 62–3.

34 For explanation of the DEFCON system, see Sagan, *Limits of Safety*, pp. 62–5.

35 Taubman, *Khrushchev*, p. 567.

36 Kennedy, *13 Days*, pp. 65–6, 124–5.

37 May and Zelikow, *Kennedy Tapes*, p. 87.

38 Trachtenberg, *History and Strategy*, pp. 240–1.

39 For discussion, see Sagan, *Limits of Safety*, pp. 66–7.

40 Horne, *Macmillan*, p. 383.

41 Scott, *Macmillan, Kennedy*, p. 137.

42 NA: DEFE 32/7, 'Record of a Conversation between the Chief of Air Staff, First Sea Lord and the Chief of the Imperial General Staff held at the Ministry of Defence at 1430, Saturday 27 October 1962', Annex to COS 1546/29/10/62.

43 For accounts, see Meyer, 'Soviet Nuclear Operations', pp. 470–531, *idem*, 'Soviet Perspectives on the Paths to Nuclear War', in Allison, Carnesale and Nye, *Hawks, Doves and Owls*, pp. 167–205.

44 In *Resurrection Day*, American cities are destroyed by MRBMs from Cuba, a Soviet-missile firing submarine, and five low-flying Tu-95 bombers that reach the United States and drop three thermo-nuclear bombs around New York, ibid, pp. 147–9, 161–2.

45 George, *Awaiting Armageddon*, pp. 42–53.

46 Ibid, p. 52. The same sentiment was expressed by Dean Rusk in 1987, when he suggested that evacuation plans that separated officials from their families were 'psychologically impossible', interview, Blight and Welch, *On the Brink*, p. 184.

47 George, *Awaiting Armageddon*, p. 44.

48 Walter Slocombe, 'Preplanned Operations', in Carter, Steinbruner and Zracket, *Managing Nuclear Operations*, p. 133.

49 Rhodes, *Making of the Atomic Bomb*, p. 691.

50 Stanley Goldberg, 'Nagasaki', in Kai Bird and Lawrence Lifschultz (eds), *Hiroshima's Shadow* (Stony Creek, Connecticut: The Pamphleteers Press, 1998), p. 405.

51 Rhodes, *Making of the Atomic Bomb*, p. 743.

52 Bundy, *Danger and Survival*, p. 384.

53 For discussion of US archival material on predelegation, see National Security Archive, 'First Documented Evidence That U.S. Presidents Predelegated Nuclear Weapons Release Authority to the Military', http://www.gwu.edu/~nsarchiv/news/19980319.htm. See also Feaver, *Guarding the Guardians*, pp. 47–54.

54 Richard H. Kohn and Joseph P. Harahan, 'U.S. Strategic Air Power, 1948–1962: Excerpts from an Interview with Generals Curtis Le May, Leon W. Johnson, David A. Burchinal, and Jack J. Catton', *International Security* 12/4 (Spring 1988), pp. 85–6.

55 Ball, 'Development of the SIOP', p. 63.

56 Garthoff, *Reflections*, p. 166.

57 Kaplan, *Wizards of Armageddon*, p. 270. For discussion of recently declassified documents on the SIOP, see William Burr, National Security Archive Electronic Briefing Book No. 130, 'The Creation of SIOP-62 More Evidence on the Origins of Overkill', posted 13 July 2004, http://www.gwu.edu/~nsarchiv/NSAEBB/NSAEBB130/index.htm.

58 Ball, *Politics and Force Levels*, p. 191.

59 Bruce G. Blair, *Strategic Command and Control: Redefining the Nuclear Threat* (Washington DC: The Brookings Institution, 1985), p. 79.

60 Sagan, *Limits of Safety*, p. 150.

61 Memorandum of Conversation with President Kennedy, 20 September, 1961.

62 Hennessy, *Secret State*, pp. 208–10.

63 William Burr, 'The Nixon Administration, the "Horror Strategy," and the Search for Limited Nuclear Options, 1969–1972', Prelude to the Schlesinger Doctrine', *Journal of Cold War Studies* 7/3 (Summer 2005), p. 41.

64 Ibid, p. 48.

65 Bouchard, *Command*, pp. 100–4.

66 For discussion of the development of US command and control, see Paul Bracken, *The Command and Control of Nuclear Forces* (London: Yale University Press, 1983); Blair, *Strategic Command*; idem, *Logic of Accidental*; and Feaver, *Guarding the Guardians*.

67 For discussion of what is termed 'catalytic war', see Henry S. Rowen, 'Catalytic Nuclear War', in Carnesale *et al*, *Hawks, Doves, Owls*, pp. 148–63.

68 Twigge and Scott, *Planning Armageddon*, pp. 126–7.

69 Ball, *Politics and Force Levels*, p. 191.

70 See John Baylis, 'British Nuclear Doctrine: The "Moscow Criterion" and the Polaris Improvement Programme', *Contemporary British*

History 19/1 (Spring 2005), pp. 53–65, and John Baylis and Kristan Stoddart, 'Britain and the Chevaline Project: The Hidden Nuclear Programme, 1967–82', *Journal of Strategic Studies* 26/4 (December 2003), pp. 124–55.

71 NA: AIR 8/2530, 'Supplementary Directive to Air Marshal Sir Kenneth Cross', 25 September 1962, reproduced as Appendix 2 in Twigge and Scott, *Planning Armageddon*, pp. 321–2; for discussion see ibid, pp. 85–9.

72 Hennessy, *Secret State*, pp. 137, 160–4, 186–205, 224–5; Twigge and Scott, *Planning Armageddon*, pp. 83–5, 210–12.

73 Hennessy, *Secret State*, p. 187.

74 For discussion, see ibid, pp. 199–200.

75 'Supplementary Directive', p. 322.

76 Khrushchev to Kennedy, 26 October 1962, May and Zelikow, *The Kennedy Tapes*, p. 486.

77 Hennessy, *Secret State*, pp. 151–4.

Chapter 6

1 Thomas Harris, *The Silence of the Lambs* (London: Mandarin, 1991 [1988]), p. 217.

2 Jonathan Schell, *The Abolition* (London: Picador, 1984), p. 128. Emphasis in original.

3 Ormsby-Gore to Macmillan, 23 October 1962.

4 Michael Howard, *The Lessons of History* (Oxford: Oxford University Press, 1993), p. 11.

5 Ibid.

6 McGeorge Bundy, Foreword to Blight and Welch, *On the Brink*, p. xiv.

7 Michael Howard, 'Nuclear Danger and Nuclear History', *International Security* 14/1 (Summer 1989), p. 180.

8 House of Commons, *Official Record*, 11 December 1990, col. 843.

9 Graham Allison, 'Iran's Nuclear Bomb: Acquiesce or Attack?' HuffingtonPost.com http://news.yahoo.com/s/huffpost/20070128/cm_huffpost/039800 27 January 2007.

10 For depiction of the missile crisis as a 'success story' in applying lessons of history, see Richard E. Neustadt and Ernest R. May, *Thinking in Time: The Uses of History for Decision Makers* (New York: The Free Press, 1986), pp. 1–16.

11 Julian Lewis, 'Disarmament versus Peace', in Brian Wicker (ed.) *Britain's Bomb: What Next?* (London: SCM Press, 2006), pp. 23–4.

12 Oliver Kamm, 'If Our Enemies Have Nuclear Weapons, So Must We', in Wicker, *Britain's Bomb*, pp. 75–6 and Julian Lewis, 'Disarmament v.

peace in the twenty-first century', *International Affairs* 82/4 (July 2006), p. 671.

13 Richard Ned Lebow, 'The Cuban Missile Crisis: Reading the Lessons Correctly', *Political Science Quarterly* 98/3 (Fall 1983), p. 431.

14 Schlesinger, *Thousand Days*, p. 716.

15 Harold Macmillan, Foreword to Kennedy, *13 Days*, p. 18.

16 See, for example, Irving L. Janis, *Victims of Groupthink: A Psychological Study of Foreign-Policy Decisions and Fiascos* (Boston: Houghton Mifflin Company, 1972), pp. 138–66.

17 See Lebow, 'Traditionalist and Revisionist Interpretations'.

18 See, for example, Robert Jervis, *The Meaning of the Nuclear Revolution: Statecraft and the Prospect of Armageddon* (London: Cornell University Press, 1989); Lebow, *Nuclear Crisis Management* and Ken Booth. *Strategy and Ethnocentrism* (Ithaca, New York: Croom Helm, 1979).

19 Dean Acheson, quoted in Blight and Welch, *On the Brink*, p. 219.

20 Charles E. Bohlen, *Witness to History, 1929–1960* (New York: W. W. Norton, 1973), pp. 495–6. For a different version of his comment, see Garthoff, *Reflections*, pp. 133–4.

21 Ormsby-Gore to Macmillan, 23 October 1962.

22 Blight, Nye and Welch, 'The Cuban Missile Crisis Revisited', p. 188.

23 Blight, *Shattered Crystal Ball*.

24 Bundy, *Danger and Survival*, p. 462

25 'Basil the Rat', *Fawlty Towers*, 25/10/79.

26 Garthoff, *Reflections*, p. 138.

27 Raymond L. Garthoff, *Détente and Confrontation: American–Soviet Relations from Nixon to Reagan* (Washington DC: The Brookings Institution, 1985), p. 76. For details of the episode see Raymond L. Garthoff, 'Handling the Cienfuegos Crisis', *International Security* 8/1 (Summer, 1983), pp. 46–66.

28 See James G. Blight and Philip Brenner, *Sad and Luminous Days: Cuba's Struggle with the Superpowers after the Missile Crisis* (Oxford: Rowman and Littlefield, 2002).

29 For a detailed and authoritative overview, see Garthoff, *Détente and Confrontation*.

30 Benjamin B. Fischer, *A Cold War Conundrum: the 1983 Soviet War Scare* (Washington DC: CIA Center for the Study of Intelligence, 1997), p. 4. For an overview, see *idem*, 'The Soviet–American War Scare of the 1980s', *International Journal of Intelligence and CounterIntelligence* 19/3 (Fall, 2006), pp. 480–518.

31 Fischer, 'Soviet–American War Scare', pp. 503–4; Zaloga, *Kremlin's Nuclear Sword*, pp. 199–201.

32 Fischer, 'Soviet–American War Scare', p. 504.

33 Beth A. Fischer, *The Reagan Reversal: Foreign Policy and the End of the Cold War* (London: University of Missouri Press, 1997).

34 For discussion, see Strobe Talbott, *Deadly Gambits: The Reagan Administration and the Stalemate in Nuclear Arms Control* (London: Pan, 1985).

35 Blight and Welch, *On the Brink*, p. 23.

36 See Strobe Talbott, *The Master of the Game: Paul Nitze and the Nuclear Peace* (New York: Alfred A. Knopf, 1988).

37 Keir A. Lieber and Daryl G. Press, 'The Rise of Nuclear Primacy', *Foreign Affairs* 85/2 (March/April 2006) and *idem*, 'The End of Mad? The Nuclear Dimension of US Primacy', *International Security* 30/4 (Spring 2006), pp. 7–44.

38 Sumit Ganguly and Devin T. Hagerty, *Fearful Symmetry: India–Pakistan Crises in the Shadow of Nuclear Weapons* (New Delhi: Oxford University Press, 2005), p. 9. See also Rajesh M. Basrur, *Minimum Deterrence and India's Nuclear Security* (Stanford: Stanford University Press, 2006), pp. 39–40.

39 T. V. Paul (ed.) *The India–Pakistan Conflict: An Enduring Rivalry* (Cambridge: Cambridge University Press, 2005), p. 124.

40 For an overview of French nuclear and defence policy see, J. F. V. Keiger, *France and the World Since 1870* (London: Arnold, 2001), pp. 68–77, 179–81. See also, Philip H. Gordon, 'Charles de Gaulle and the Nuclear Revolution', in Gaddis *et al*, *Cold War Statesmen*, pp. 216–35.

41 See R. Gerald Hughes, *Britain, Germany and the Cold War: The Search for a European Détente 1949–1967* (London: Routledge, 2007), pp. 67, 71–2, 102.

42 Blight, Nye and Welch, 'Cuban Missile Crisis Revisited', p. 187.

43 Robert S. McNamara and James G. Blight, *Wilson's Ghost: Reducing the Risk of Conflict, Killing, and Catastrophe in the 21st Century* (New York: Public Affairs, 2001).

44 Blight and Welch, 'Risking "The Destruction of Nations"', pp. 841–2. Among the countries listed as a rogue states is Libya. The suggestion that Colonel Gaddafi can be so compared to Castro is belied by his renunciation of nuclear weapons under IAEA safeguards.

45 Ibid.

46 Blight, Allyn and Welch, 'Kramer Vs. Kramer,' p. 49.

47 Blight, *Shattered Crystal Ball*, p. 170.

48 Michael Beschloss recounts that Kennedy was regularly injected with a concoction of drugs by his unorthodox private physician, which included amphetamines known to cause impaired judgement and depressive reactions, Beschloss, *Kennedy v. Khrushchev*, pp. 189–93.

49 See John Baylis, *Ambiguity and Deterrence: British Nuclear Strategy 1945–1964* (Oxford: Oxford University Press, 1995).

50 *The Future of the United Kingdom's Nuclear Deterrent* Cm 6994 (London: HMSO, 2006), p. 19.

51 David S. Yost, 'France's New Nuclear Doctrine', *International Affairs* 82/4 (July 2006), pp. 701–21.

52 James G. Blight and Janet M. Lang, *The Fog of War: Lessons from the Life of Robert S. McNamara* (Oxford: Rowman and Littlefield, 2005), p. 60.

53 Robert McNamara, 'War in the Twentieth Century', in John Baylis and Robert O'Neill, *Alternative Nuclear Futures: The Role of Nuclear Weapons in the Post-Cold War World* (Oxford: Oxford University Press, 2000), p. 178.

54 Ormsby-Gore to Macmillan, 23 October 1962.

Bibliography

Books

Place of publication is London unless otherwise stated.

Abel, E. *The Missiles of October, The Story of the Cuban Missile Crisis* (MacGibbon and Kee, 1966).

Acosta, T. D. *October 1962: The 'Missile' Crisis as Seen From Cuba* (Pathfinder Press, 2002).

Aldrich, R. L. *The Hidden Hand: Britain, America and Cold War Secret Intelligence* (John Murray, 2001).

Allison, G. T. *Essence of Decision, Explaining the Cuban Missile Crisis* (Boston: Little, Brown and Company, 1971).

Allison, G. T., Carnesale, A., and Nye, J. S. Jr. (eds) *Hawks, Doves and Owls: An Agenda for Avoiding Nuclear War* (W. W. Norton, 1985).

Allison, G. and Zelikow, P. *Essence of Decision: Explaining the Cuban Missile Crisis* (New York: Longman, 1999).

Allyn, B. J., Blight, J. G. and Welch, D. A. *Back to the Brink: Proceedings of the Moscow Conference on the Cuban Missile Conference, January 27–28, 1989*, CSIA Occasional Paper No. 9 (Lanham, Maryland: University of America Press, 1992).

Allyn, B. J., Blight, J. G. and Welch, D. A. *Afterword from Cuba on the Brink: Castro, the Missile Crisis, and the Soviet Collapse* (Lanham: Rowman and Littlefield, 2002).

Alperovitz, G. *The Decision to Use the Bomb* (HarperCollins, 1995).

Andrew, C. *For the President's Eyes Only: Secret Intelligence and the American Presidency From Washington to Bush* (HarperCollins, 1995).

Ashton, N. *Kennedy, Macmillan and the Cold War: The Irony of Interdependence* (Basingstoke: Palgrave Macmillan, 2002).

Ball, D. *Politics and Force Levels: The Strategic Missile Program of the Kennedy Administration* (Berkeley: University of California Press, 1980).

Ball, D. and Richelson, J. (eds) *Strategic Nuclear Targeting* (Ithaca, New York: Cornell University Press, 1986).

Ball, G. *The Past Has Another Pattern: Memoirs* (W. W. Norton, 1982).

Basrur, R. M. *Minimum Deterrence and India's Nuclear Security* (Stanford: Stanford University Press, 2006).

Baylis, J. *Ambiguity and Deterrence: British Nuclear Strategy 1945–1964* (Oxford: Clarendon Press, 1995).

Baylis, J. and O'Neill, R. *Alternative Nuclear Futures: The Role of Nuclear Weapons in the Post-Cold War World* (Oxford: Oxford University Press, 2000).

Beschloss, M. R. *Kennedy v. Khrushchev, The Crisis Years 1960–63* (Faber and Faber, 1991).

Bird, K. and Lifschultz, L. (eds), *Hiroshima's Shadow* (Stony Creek, Connecticut: The Pamphleteers Press, 1998).

Blair, B. G. *Strategic Command and Control: Redefining the Nuclear Threat* (Washington DC: The Brookings Institution, 1985).

—— *The Logic of Accidental Nuclear War* (Washington DC: The Brookings Institution, 1993).

Blight, J. G. *Shattered Crystal Ball: Fear and Learning in the Cuban Missile Crisis* (Savage, Maryland: Rowman & Littlefield Publishers, 1992).

Blight, J. G. and Welch, D. A. *On the Brink: Americans and Soviets Reexamine the Cuban Missile Crisis* (New York: Noonday Press, 1990).

Blight, J. G., Allyn, B. J. and Welch, D. A. *Cuba on the Brink: Castro, the Missile Crisis and the Soviet Collapse* (New York: Pantheon Books, 1993).

Blight, J. G. and Kornbluh, P. *Politics of Illusion: The Bay of Pigs Invasion Reexamined* (Lynne Rienner, 1998).

Blight, J. G. and Brenner, P. *Sad and Luminous Days: Cuba's Struggle with the Superpowers after the Missile Crisis* (Oxford: Rowman and Littlefield, 2002).

Blight, J. G. and Lang, J. M. *The Fog of War: Lessons from the Life of Robert S. McNamara* (Oxford: Rowman and Littlefield, 2005).

Bluth, C. *Britain, Germany and Western Nuclear Strategy* (Oxford: Oxford University Press, 1995).

Bohlen, C. E. *Witness to History, 1929–1960* (New York: W. W. Norton, 1973).

Booth, K. *Strategy and Ethnocentrism* (Croom Helm, 1979).

—— (ed.) *Statecraft and Security* (Cambridge: Cambridge University Press, 1998).

Bouchard, J. *Command in Crisis: Four Case Studies* (New York: Columbia University Press, 1991).

Bracken, P. *The Command and Control of Nuclear Forces* (New Haven: Yale University Press, 1983).

Brugioni, D. A. (ed. Robert F. McCort), *Eyeball to Eyeball, The Inside Story of the Cuban Missile Crisis* (New York: Random House, 1991).

Bundy, M. *Danger and Survival: Choices About the Bomb in the First Fifty Years* (New York: Random House, 1988).

Burlatsky, F. *Khrushchev and the First Russian Spring* (Weidenfeld and Nicolson, 1991).

Burr, W. and Blanton, T. S. *The Submarines of October, National Security Archive Electronic Briefing Book No 75*, 31 October 2002, note 16, http://www.gwu.edu/

Carnesale, A., Doty, P., Hoffman, S., Huntingdon, S. P., Nye, J. S. and Sagan, S.D. *Living with Nuclear Weapons* (New York: Bantam, 1983).

Carr, E. H. *What is History?* (Harmondsworth, Middlesex: Pelican, 1978 [1961]).

Carter, A. B. and Schwarz, D. N. (eds) *Ballistic Missile Defence* (Washington DC: The Brookings Institution, 1984).

Carter, A. B., Steinbruner J. D and Zracket, C. A. (eds) *Managing Nuclear Operations* (Washington DC: The Brookings Institution, 1987).

Chang, L. and Kornbluh, P. (eds) *The Cuban Missile Crisis, 1962 – A National Security Archive Documents Reader* (New York: The New Press, 1992).

Chayes, A. *The Cuban Missile Crisis* (Oxford: Oxford University Press, 1974).

Clark, I. *Nuclear Diplomacy and the Special Relationship, Britain's Deterrent and America* (Oxford: Oxford University Press, 1994).

Cowley, R. (ed.) *What If? America: Eminent Historians Imagine What Might Have Been* (Chatham: Pan Macmillan, 2004).

Cullather, N. *Secret History: The CIA's Classified Account of its Operations in Guatemala 1952–1954* (Stanford: Stanford University Press, 1999).

Dallek, R. *John F. Kennedy: An Unfinished Life 1917–1963* (Penguin, 2004).

Dinerstein, H. S. *The Making of the Cuban Missile Crisis* (Baltimore: Johns Hopkins University Press, 1976).

Divine, R. A. (ed.) *The Cuban Missile Crisis* (New York: Marcus Wiener, 1988).

Dobrynin, A. *In Confidence: Moscow's Ambassador to America's Six Cold War Presidents* (Seattle: University of Washington Press, 1995).

DuBois, B. *Resurrection Day* (Little, Brown and Company, 1999).

Feaver, P. *Guarding the Guardians: Civilian Control of Nuclear Weapons* (Ithaca, New York: Cornell University Press, 1992).

Feklisov, A. and Kostin, S. *The Man Behind the Rosenbergs: by the KGB Spymaster who was the Case Officer of Julius Rosenberg, and helped resolve the Cuban Missile Crisis* (New York: Enigma Books, 2001).

Ferguson, N. (ed.) *Virtual History, Alternatives and Counterfactuals* (Basingstoke: Picador, 1997).

Finkelstein, N. H. *Thirteen Days/Ninety Days: The Cuban Missile Crisis* (Lincoln: Authors Guild Backinprint.Com Edition, 2000).

Fischer, Benjamin B. *A Cold War Conundrum: the 1983 Soviet War Scare* (Washington DC: CIA Center for the Study of Intelligence, 1997).

Fischer, Beth A. *The Reagan Reversal: Foreign Policy and the End of the Cold War* (Columbia: University of Missouri Press, 1997).

Foreign Relations of the United States, 1961–1963, Vol. XI, Cuban Missile Crisis and Aftermath (Washington: United States Government Printing Office, 1996).

Foreign Relations of the United States, 1961–1963, Vol. X, Cuba 1961–1962 (Washington DC: United States Government Printing Office, 1997).

Frankel, M. *High Noon in the Cold War: Kennedy, Khrushchev, and the Cuban Missile Crisis* (New York: Random House, 2004).

Freedman, L. *Intelligence and the Soviet Strategic Threat* (Basingstoke: Macmillan, 1986).

—— *Kennedy's Wars: Berlin, Cuba, Laos and Vietnam* (Oxford: Oxford University Press, 2000).

—— *The Evolution of Nuclear Strategy* (Basingstoke: Palgrave Macmillan, 2003).

Fursenko, A. and Naftali, T. *'One Hell of a Gamble': Khrushchev, Castro, Kennedy and the Cuban Missile Crisis 1958–1964* (John Murray, 1997).

—— *Khrushchev's Cold War: The Inside Story of an American Adversary* (W. W. Norton, 2006).

Gaddis, J. L. *Strategies of Containment* (Oxford: Oxford University Press, 1982).

—— *We Now Know: Rethinking the Cold War* (Oxford: Clarendon Press, 1997).

—— *The Cold War* (Allen Lane, 2006).

Gaddis, J. L., Gordon, P. H., May, E. R. and Rosenberg, J. *Cold War Statesmen Confront the Bomb: Nuclear Diplomacy since 1945* (Oxford: Oxford University Press, 1999).

Ganguly S. and Hagerty, D. T. *Fearful Symmetry: India–Pakistan Crises in the Shadow of Nuclear Weapons* (New Delhi: Oxford University Press, 2005).

Ganser, D. *Reckless Gamble: The Sabotage of the United Nations in the Cuban Conflict and the Cuban Missile Crisis of 1962* (New Orleans: University Press of the South).

Garthoff, R. L. *Détente and Confrontation: American–Soviet Relations from Nixon to Reagan* (Washington DC: The Brookings Institution, 1985).

—— *Reflections on the Cuban Missile Crisis* (Washington DC: The Brookings Institution, 1989).

—— *A Journey Through the Cold War: A Memoir of Containment and Coexistence* (Washington DC: The Brookings Institution, 2001).

George, Alexander L. and Simons, W. E. *The Limits of Coercive Diplomacy* (Oxford: Westview, 1994).

George, Alice L. *Awaiting Armageddon: How Americans Faced the Cuban Missile Crisis* (Chapel Hill: The University of North Carolina Press, 2003).

George, P. *Dr Strangelove or How I Learned to Stop Worrying and Love the Bomb* (Oxford: Oxford University Press, 1988).

Gonzalez, S. *The Nuclear Deception: Nikita Khrushchev and the Cuban Missile Crisis* (Oakland, California: Spooks Books, 2003).

Gregory, S. *The Hidden Costs of Deterrence: Nuclear Weapons Accidents* (Brassey's UK, 1990).

Gribkov, A. I. and Smith, W. Y. *Operation Anadyr: US and Soviet Generals Recount the Cuban Missile Crisis* (Chicago: Edition Q, 1994).

Gromyko, A. *Memories* (Hutchinson, 1988).

Haydon, P. T. *The 1962 Cuban Missile Crisis: Canadian Involvement Reconsidered* (Toronto: Canadian Institute of Strategic Studies, 1993).

Hennessy, P. *The Prime Minister: The Office and its Holders since 1945* (Allen Lane, 2000).

—— *The Secret State: Whitehall and the Cold War* (Penguin, 2003).

Herring, E. *Danger and Opportunity* (Manchester: Manchester University Press, 1995).

Hilsman, R. *To Move A Nation* (New York: Dell Publishing Co. [1964] 1967).

—— *The Cuban Missile Crisis: The Struggle Over Policy* (Westport, CT: Praeger, 1996).

Horne, A. *Macmillan 1894–1956, Volume I of The Official Biography* (Macmillan, 1988).

—— *Macmillan 1957–1986, Volume II of The Official Biography* (Macmillan, 1989).

Howard, M. *The Lessons of History* (Oxford: Oxford University Press, 1993).

Huchthausen, P. A. *October Fury* (New York: John Wiley, 2002).

—— *K-19: The Widowmaker: The Secret Story of the Soviet Nuclear Submarine* (Washington DC: National Geographic Society, 2002).

Hughes, R. G. *Britain, Germany and the Cold War: The Search for a European Détente 1949–1967* (Routledge, 2007).

Institute for Strategic Studies (ISS), *The Communist Bloc and the Western Alliances: Military Balance 1962–1963* (ISS, 1962).

Ivanov, Y. (with Sokolov, G.) *The Naked Spy* (Blake, 1992).

Janis, I. L. *Victims of Groupthink: A Psychological Study of Foreign-Policy Decisions and Fiascos* (Boston: Houghton Mifflin Company, 1972).

Jervis, R. *Perception and Misperception in International Politics* (Princeton, New Jersey: Princeton University Press, 1976).

—— *The Meaning of the Nuclear Revolution: Statecraft and the Prospect of Armageddon* (Ithaca, New York: Cornell University Press, 1989).

Jervis, R., Lebow, R. N. and Stein, J. G. *Psychology and Deterrence* (Baltimore: Johns Hopkins University Press, 1985).

Kaplan, F. *The Wizards of Armageddon* (Stanford: Stanford University Press, 1991).

Keiger, J. F. V. *France and the World Since 1870* (Arnold, 2001).

Kennedy, J. F. *Why England Slept* (Westpost, CT: Greenwood Press Reprint, 1981).

Kennedy, R. F. *13 Days, The Cuban Missile Crisis 1962* (Pan Books, 1969).

Khrushchev, N. (introduction, notes and commentary by Edward Crankshaw; translated by Strobe Talbott), *Khrushchev Remembers* (Boston: Little, Brown and Company, 1970).

—— (edited/translated by Schecter, J. L. and Luchkov, V. V.), *Khrushchev Remembers: The Glasnost Tapes* (Little, Brown and Company, 1990).

Lebow, R. N. *Nuclear Crisis Management: A Dangerous Illusion* (Ithaca, New York: Cornell University Press, 1987).

Lebow R. N. and Stein, J. G. *We All Lost the Cold War* (Princeton, New Jersey: Princeton University Press, 1994).

Lechuga, C. *Cuba and the Missile Crisis* (New York: Ocean Press, 2001).

McAuliffe, M. S. (ed.) *CIA Documents on the Cuban Missile Crisis 1962* (Washington DC: Central Intelligence Agency, 1992).

McGwire, M. *Military Objectives in Soviet Foreign Policy* (Washington DC: The Brookings Institution, 1987).

Macmillan, H. *At the End of the Day, 1961–1963* (Macmillan, 1973).

McNamara, R. S., *Blundering into Disaster: Surviving the First Century of the Nuclear Age* (Bloomsbury, 1987).

McNamara R. S. and Blight, J. G. *Wilson's Ghost: Reducing the Risk of Conflict, Killing, and Catastrophe in the 21st Century* (New York: Public Affairs, 2001).

May, E. R. and Zelikow, P. D. (eds) *The Kennedy Tapes: Inside the White House During the Cuban Missile Crisis* (Cambridge, Mass: Harvard University Press, 1997).

Menaul, M. *Countdown – Britain's Strategic Nuclear Forces* (Robert Hale, 1980).

Miller, R. G. (ed.) *Seeing Off the Bear: Anglo-American Air Power Cooperation During the Cold War* (Washington DC: Royal Air Force Historical Society/Air Force Historical Foundation, 1995).

Mueller, J. *The Retreat From Doomsday: The Obsolescence of Major War* (New York: Basic Books, 1989).

Munton, D. and Welch, D. A. *The Cuban Missile Crisis: A Concise History* (Oxford: Oxford University Press, 2006).

Bibliography

Naftali, T. (ed.) *The Presidential Recordings, John F. Kennedy, The Great Crises, Volume One, July 30–August 1962* (W. W. Norton, 2001).

Naftali, T. and Zelikow, P. (eds) *The Presidential Recordings, John F. Kennedy, The Great Crises, Volume Two, September – October 21, 1962* (W. W. Norton, 2001).

Nash, P. *The Other Missiles of October: Eisenhower, Kennedy, and the Jupiters 1957–1963* (Chapel Hill, North Carolina: University of North Carolina Press, 1997).

Nathan, J. A. (ed.) *The Cuban Missile Crisis Revisited* (New York: St Martin's Press, 1992).

—— *Anatomy of the Cuban Missile Crisis* (Greenwood Press, 2001).

Neustadt R. E. and May, E. R. *Thinking in Time: The Uses of History for Decision Makers* (New York: The Free Press, 1986).

Newhouse, J. *The Nuclear Age: From Hiroshima to Star Wars* (Michael Joseph, 1989).

Nitze, P. *From Hiroshima to Glasnost: At the Center of Decision* (New York: Grove Weidenfeld, 1989).

Norris, R. S., Burrows, A. S. and Fieldhouse, R. W. *Nuclear Weapons Databook, Volume V* (Boulder, Colorado: Westview Press, 1994).

Oliver, K. *Kennedy, Macmillan and the Nuclear Test Ban Debate, 1961–1963* (Macmillan, 1997).

Osgood, R. E. *The Entangling Alliance* (Chicago: Chicago University Press, 1962).

Paterson, T. G. (ed.) *Kennedy's Quest for Victory: American Foreign Policy, 1961–1963* (Oxford: Oxford University Press, 1989).

—— *Contesting Castro: The United States and the Triumph of the Cuban Revolution* (Oxford: Oxford University Press, 1994).

Paul, T. V. (ed.) *The India–Pakistan Conflict: An Enduring Rivalry* (Cambridge: Cambridge University Press, 2005).

Pavlov, Y. *Soviet–Cuban Alliance 1959–1991* (Transaction Publishers, 1994).

Podvig, P. (ed.) *Russian Strategic Nuclear Forces* (Cambridge, Mass: The MIT Press, 2004).

Polmar, N. and Gresham, J. D. *DEFCON-2: Standing on the Brink of Nuclear War during the Cuban Missile Crisis* (Hoboken, New Jersey: John Wiley & Sons, 2006).

Pope, R. R. *Soviet Views on the Cuban Missile Crisis: Myth and Reality in Foreign Policy Analysis* (Washington DC: University Press of America, 1982).

Prados, J. *The Soviet Estimate: US Intelligence Analysis and Soviet Strategic Forces* (Princeton, New Jersey: Princeton University Press, 1986).

Pringle, P. and Arkin, W. *SIOP: Nuclear War from the Inside* (Sphere Books, 1983).

Quester, G. H. *Nuclear First Strike: Consequences of a Broken Taboo* (Baltimore: The John Hopkins University Press, 2006).

Rabe, S. G. *Eisenhower and Latin America: The Foreign Policy of AntiCommunism* (Chapel Hill: The University of North Carolina Press, 1988).

—— *The Most Dangerous Area in the World: John F. Kennedy Confronts Communist Revolution in Latin America* (Chapel Hill: The University of North Carolina Press, 1999).

Reeves, R. *President Kennedy: Profile of Power* (New York: Simon and Schuster, 1993).

Reeves, T. C. *A Question of Character: A Life of John F. Kenendy* (Arrow, 1991).

Rhodes, R. *The Making of the Atomic Bomb* (Penguin, 1986).

Risse-Kappen, T. *Cooperation Among Democracies: The European Influence on U.S. Foreign Policy* (Princeton, New Jersey: Princeton University Press, 1995).

Roberts, F. *Dealing with Dictators: The Destruction and Revival of Europe 1930–1970*, (Weidenfeld and Nicolson, 1991).

Ruffner K. C. (ed.) *Corona: America's First Satellite* (Washington DC: CIA Center for the Study of Intelligence, 1995).

Rusk, D. *As I Saw It* (New York, W. W. Norton, 1990).

Russell, B. *Unarmed Victory* (Penguin, 1963).

Sagan, S. D. *Moving Targets: Nuclear Strategy and National Security* (Princeton, New Jersey: Princeton University Press, 1989).

—— *The Limits of Safety – Organisations, Accidents, and Nuclear Weapons* (Princeton, New Jersey: Princeton University Press, 1993).

Sagan S. D. and Waltz K. N. *The Spread of Nuclear Weapons: A Debate* (W. W. Norton, 1995).

Schecter, J. L. and Deriabin, P. S. *The Spy Who Saved the World: How a Soviet Colonel Changed the Course of the Cold War* (New York: Charles Scribner's Sons, 1992).

Schell, J. *The Fate of the Earth* (Picador, 1982).

—— *The Abolition* (Picador, 1984).

Schlesinger, A. *A Thousand Days – John F. Kennedy in the White House* (Andre Deutsch, 1965).

—— *Robert Kennedy and His Times* (Boston: Houghton, Mifflin, 1978).

Schneider, S. H. *Encyclopaedia of Weather and Climate, Volume 2* (New York: Oxford University Press, 1996).

Schwartz, D. N. *NATO's Nuclear Dilemmas* (Washington DC: The Brookings Institution, 1983).

Scott, L. V. *Macmillan, Kennedy and the Cuban Missile Crisis: Political, Military and Intelligence Aspects* (Basingstoke: Macmillan, 1999).

Seaborg, G. T. *Kennedy, Khrushchev and the Test Ban* (Chapel Hill: University of California Press, 1981).

Senate Report No. 94-465 20: Interim Report: Alleged Assassination Plots Involving Foreign Leaders, 94th congress 1st session (Washington: US Government Printing Office, 1975).

Skierka, V. *Fidel Castro: A Biography* (Cambridge: Polity, 2004).

Snyder, G. *Deterrence and Defense* (Princeton, New Jersey: Princeton University Press, 1961).

Sorensen, T. C. *Kennedy* (Hodder and Stoughton, 1965).

Stein, P. and Feaver, P. *Assuring Control of Nuclear Weapons: The Evolution of Permissive Action Links* (Cambridge, Mass: CSIA, University Press of America, 1987).

Stern, S. M. *Averting 'The Final Failure': John F. Kennedy and the Secret Cuban Missile Crisis Meetings* (Stanford: Stanford University Press, 2003).

—— *The Week the World Stood Still: Inside the Secret Cuban Missile Crisis* (Stanford: Stanford University Press, 2005).

Stromseth, J. E. *The Origins of Flexible Response: NATO's Debate Over Strategy in the 1960s* (Macmillan, 1988).

Talbott, S. *Deadly Gambits: The Reagan Administration and the Stalemate in Nuclear Arms Control* (Pan, 1985).

—— *The Master of the Game: Paul Nitze and the Nuclear Peace* (New York: Alfred A. Knopf, 1988).

Taubman, W. *Khrushchev: The Man, His Era* (New York: Free Press, 2005).

Taubman, W., Khrushchev, S. and Gleason, A. (eds) *Nikita Khrushchev* (New Haven: Yale University Press, 2000).

Tetlock, P. E. and Belkin, B. *Counterfactual Thought Experiments in World Politics: Logical, Methodological and Psychological Perspectives* (Princeton, New Jersey: Princeton University Press, 1996).

Tetlock, P. E., Lebow, R. N. and Parker, G. (eds) *Unmaking the West: 'What-If' Scenarios That Rewrite World History* (Michigan: University of Michigan Press, 2006).

Thomas, H. *Cuba or the Pursuit of Freedom* (Eyre and Spottiswoode, 1971).

Thompson, E. P. [*et al*], *Exterminism and Cold War* (Verso, 1982).

Thompson, R. S. *The Missiles of October – The Declassified Story of John F. Kennedy and the Cuban Missile Crisis* (New York: Simon and Schuster, 1992).

Trachtenberg, M. *History and Strategy* (Princeton, New Jersey: Princeton University Press, 1991).

—— *A Constructed Peace: The Making of the European Settlement, 1945–1963* (Princeton, New Jersey: Princeton University Press, 1999).

Twigge, S. and Scott, L. *Planning Armageddon: Britain, United States and the Command of Nuclear Forces, 1946–1964* (Amsterdam: Routledge, 2000).

Vaisse, M. (ed.) *L'Europe et la Crise de Cuba* (Paris: Armand Colin, 1993).

Volkogonov, D. *The Rise and Fall of the Soviet Empire: Political Leaders from Lenin to Gorbachev* (HarperCollins, 1998).

Weldes, J. *Constructing National Interests: the United States and the Cuban Missile Crisis* (Minnesota: University of Minnesota Press, 1999).

White, M. J. *The Cuban Missile Crisis* (Basingstoke: Macmillan, 1996).

—— *Missiles in Cuba: Kennedy, Khrushchev, Castro and the 1962 Crisis* (Chicago: Ivan R. Dee, 1997).

Wicker, B. (ed.) *Britain's Bomb: What Next?* (SCM Press, 2006).

Wills, G. *The Kennedy Imprisonment: A Meditation on Power* (Little, Brown and Company, 1981).

Wohlstetter, A. and Wohlstetter, R. *Controlling the Risks in Cuba* Adelphi Paper No. 17 (Institute for Strategic Studies, 1965).

Wynn, H. *The RAF's Strategic Deterrent Forces: their origins, roles and deployment 1946–1969* (HMSO, 1994).

Zaloga, S. *The Kremlin's Nuclear Sword: The Rise and Fall of Russia's Strategic Nuclear Forces 1945–2000* (Washington DC: Smithsonian Institution Press, 2002).

Zelikow, P. and May, E. (eds) *The Presidential Recordings, John F. Kennedy, The Great Crises, Volume Three, October 22–28, 1962* (W. W. Norton, 2001).

Zubok, V. and Pleshakov, C. *Inside the Kremlin's Cold War* (Cambridge MA: Harvard University Press, 1996).

Articles

Allyn, B. J., Blight, J. G. and Welch, D. A. 'Essence of Revision: Moscow, Havana and the Cuban Missile Crisis', *International Security* 14/3 (Winter 1989/90).

Baylis, J. 'British Nuclear Doctrine: The "Moscow Criterion" and the Polaris Improvement Programme', *Contemporary British History* 19/1 (Spring 2005).

Baylis, J. and Stoddart, K. 'Britain and the Chevaline Project: The Hidden Nuclear Programme, 1967–82', *Journal of Strategic Studies* 26/4 (December 2003), pp. 124–55.

Bernstein, B. J. 'The Cuban Missile Crisis: Trading the Jupiters in Turkey?', *Political Science Quarterly* 95/1 (Spring 1980).

—— 'Understanding Decisionmaking, US Foreign Policy and the Cuban Missile Crisis: A Review Essay', *International Security* 25/1 (Summer 2000).

Betts, R. K. 'A Golden Nuclear Age? The Balance Before Parity', *International Security* 11/3 (Winter 1986–87).

Blight, J. G., Nye, J. S. and Welch, D. A. 'The Cuban Missile Crisis Revisited', *Foreign Affairs* 66/1 (Fall 1987).

Blight, J. G., Allyn, B. J. and Welch, D. 'Kramer Vs. Kramer, Or How Can You Have Revisionism in the Absence of Orthodoxy?', *Cold War International History Project Bulletin* Issue 3 (Fall 1993).

Blight, J. G. and Welch, D. A. 'Risking "The Destruction of Nations": Lessons of the Cuban Missile Crisis for New and Aspiring Nuclear States', *Security Studies* 4/4 (Summer 1995).

Boyle, P. G. 'The British Government's View of the Cuban Missile Crisis', *Contemporary Record* 10/3 (Autumn 1996).

Brenner, P. 'Cuba and the Missile Crisis', *Journal of Latin American Studies* 22/1 (February 1990).

—— 'Turning History on its Head', National Security Archive, undated http://www.gwu.edu/~nsarchiv/nsa/cuba_mis_cri/brenner.htm

Burr, W. National Security Archive Electronic Briefing Book No. 130, 'The Creation of SIOP-62: More Evidence on the Origins of Overkill', posted 13 July 2004, http://www.gwu.edu/~nsarchiv/NSAEBB/NSAEBB130/index.htm.

—— 'The Nixon Administration, the "Horror Strategy", and the Search for Limited Nuclear Options, 1969–1972, Prelude to the Schlesinger Doctrine', *Journal of Cold War Studies* 7/3 (Summer 2005).

Burr, W. and Richelson, J. 'Whether to "Strangle the Baby in the Cradle": The United States and the Chinese Nuclear Program, 1960–64', *International Security* 25/3 (Winter 2000/1).

Caldwell, D. 'A Research Note on the Quarantine of Cuba, October, 1962', *International Studies Quarterly* 22/4 (December 1978).

Cline, R. S. 'Commentary: The Cuban Missile Crisis', *Foreign Affairs* 68/4 (Fall 1989).

Coleman, D. 'Camelot's Nuclear Conscience', *Bulletin of the Atomic Scientists* 62/3 (May/June 2006).

Costigliola, F. 'Kennedy, the European Allies, and the Failure to Consult', *Political Science Quarterly* 110/1 (Spring 1995).

Criss, N. B. 'Strategic Nuclear Missiles in Turkey: The Jupiter Affair, 1959–1963', *Journal of Strategic Studies* 20/3 (September 1997).

Desch, M. '"That Deep Mud in Cuba", The Strategic Threat and US Planning for a Conventional Response During the Missile Crisis', *Security Studies* 1/2 (Winter 1991).

Dominguez, J. I. 'The @#$%& Missile Crisis: (Or What Was "Cuban" about U.S. Decisions during the Cuban Missile Crisis?)', *Diplomatic History* 24/2 (Spring 2000).

Fischer, B. 'The Soviet–American War Scare of the 1980s', *International Journal of Intelligence and CounterIntelligence* 19/3 (Fall 2006).

Fursenko, A. and Naftali, T. 'Using KGB Documents: The Scali–Feklisov Channel in the Cuban Missile Crisis', *Cold War International History Project Bulletin* Issue 5 (Spring 1995).

—— 'The Pitsunda Decision: Khrushchev and Nuclear Weapons', *Cold War International History Project Bulletin* Issue 10 (March 1998).

Garthoff, R. L. 'Handling the Cienfuegos Crisis', *International Security* 8/1 (Summer 1983).

—— 'Cuban Missile Crisis: The Soviet Story', *Foreign Policy* 72 (Fall 1988).

—— 'Some Observations on Using the Soviet Archives', *Diplomatic History* (Spring 1997).

—— 'Some Reflections on the History of the Cold War', *The Society for Historians of American Foreign Relations Newsletter* 26/3 (September 1995).

—— 'US Intelligence in the Cuban Missile Crisis', *Intelligence and National Security* 13/3 (Autumn 1998).

—— 'New Evidence on the Cuban Missile Crisis: Khrushchev, Nuclear Weapons, and the Cuban Missile Crisis', *Cold War International History Project Bulletin* Issue 11 (Winter 1998).

Gleijeses, P. 'Ships in the Night: The CIA, the White House and the Bay of Pigs', *Journal of Latin American Studies* 27 (1995).

Healey, D. 'The Bomb That Didn't Go Off', *Encounter*, 1964.

Hershberg, J. 'Before "The Missiles of October": Did Kennedy Plan a Military Strike Against Cuba?', *Diplomatic History* 14/2 (Spring 1990).

—— 'Anatomy of a Controversy: Anatoly Dobrynin's Meeting with Robert Kennedy, Saturday 27 October 1962', *Cold War International History Project Bulletin* Issue 5 (Spring 1995).

Holland, M. 'A Luce Connection: Senator Keating, William Pawley, and the Cuban Missile Crisis', *Journal of Cold War Studies* 1/3 (Fall 1999).

Horelick, A. L. 'The Cuban Missile Crisis: An Analysis of Soviet Calculations and Behavior', *World Politics* 16/3 (April 1964).

Howard, M. 'Nuclear Danger and Nuclear History', *International Security* 14/1 (Summer 1989).

Husain, A. 'Covert Action and US Cold War Strategy in Cuba, 1961–62', *Cold War History* 5/1 (February 2005).

Kaplan, F. 'JFK's First Strike Plan', *Atlantic Monthly* (October 2001).

Kent, S. 'The Cuban Missile Crisis of 1962: Presenting the Photographic Evidence Abroad', *Studies in Intelligence* 10/2 (Spring 1972).

Kohn, R. H. and Harahan, J. P. 'U.S. Strategic Air Power, 1948–1962: Excerpts from an Interview with Generals Curtis Le May, Leon W. Johnson, David A. Burchinal, and Jack J. Catton', *International Security* 12/4 (Spring 1988).

Kramer, M. 'Tactical nuclear weapons, Soviet command authority, and the Cuban missile crisis', *Cold War International History Project Bulletin* Issue 3 (Fall 1993).

—— 'The Lessons of the Cuban Missile Crisis for Warsaw Pact Nuclear Operations', *Cold War International History Project Bulletin*, Issue 5 (Spring 1995).

—— 'The Cuban Missile Crisis and Nuclear Proliferation', *Security Studies* 5/1 (Autumn 1995).

Kramer, M., Allyn, B. J., Blight, J. G. and Welch, D. A. 'Correspondence: Remembering the Cuban Missile Crisis: Should We Swallow Oral History?', *International Security* 15/1 (Summer 1990).

Lebow, R. N. 'The Cuban Missile Crisis: Reading the Lessons Correctly', *Political Science Quarterly* 98/3 (Fall 1983).

—— 'Domestic Politics and the Cuban Missile Crisis: The Traditional and Revisionist Interpretations Reevaluated', *Diplomatic History* 14/4 (Fall 1990).

Leiber, K. A. and Press, D. G. 'The Rise of Nuclear Primacy', *Foreign Affairs* 85/2 (March/April 2006).

—— 'The End of Mad? The Nuclear Dimension of US Primacy', *International Security* 30/4 (Spring 2006).

Lewis, J. 'Disarmament v. peace in the twenty-first century', *International Affairs* 82/4 (July 2006).

Lindley, D. 'What I Learned since I Stopped Worrying and Studied the Movie: A Teaching Guide to Stanley Kubricks's "Dr Strangelove"', *Political Science and Politics* 34/3 (September 2001).

McNamara, R. S. 'The Military Role of Nuclear Weapons: Perceptions and Misperceptions', *Foreign Affairs* 62/1 (October 1983).

McNamara, R., Bundy, M., Rush, D., Sorensen, T., Gilpatrik, R. and Ball, G. 'The Lessons of the Cuban Missile Crisis', *Time* (27 September 1982).

Maloney, S. M. 'Berlin Contingency Planning: Prelude to Flexible Response, 1958–63', *Journal of Strategic Studies* 25/1 (March 2002).

May, E. R. 'Thirteen Days in 145 Minutes', *National Forum* 81/2 (Spring 2001).

Nathan, J. 'The Heyday of the New Strategy: The Cuban Missile Crisis and the Confirmation of Coercive Diplomacy', *Diplomacy and Statecraft* 3/2 (July 1992).

Norris, R. S. 'Where They Were', *Bulletin of the Atomic Scientists* 55/6 (November/December 1999).

Oppenheimer, J. R. 'Atomic Weapons and American Policy', *Foreign Affairs* 31/4 (July 1953).

Paterson, T. G. and Brophy, W. J. 'October Missiles and November Elections:

The Cuban Missile Crisis and American Politics, 1962', *The Journal of American History* 73/1 (June 1986).

Rawnsley, G. D. 'How Special is Special? The Anglo-American Alliance During the Cuban Missile Crisis', *Contemporary Record* 9/3 (Winter 1995).

Rosenberg, D. A. 'The Origins of Overkill: Nuclear Weapons and American Strategy, 1945–1960', *International Security* 7/4 (Spring 1983).

Sagan, C. 'Nuclear War and Climatic Catastrophe: Some Policy Implications', *Foreign Affairs* (Winter 1983/4).

Sagan, S. D. 'Nuclear Alerts and Crisis Management', *International Security* 9/4 (Spring 1985).

—— 'SIOP-62: The Nuclear War Plan Briefing to President Kennedy', *International Security* 12/1 (Summer 1987).

—— 'The Perils of Proliferation: Organization Theory, Deterrence Theory and the Spread of Nuclear Weapons', *International Security* 18/4 (Spring 1994).

Sagan, S. D. and Suri, J. 'The Madman Nuclear Alert: Secrecy, Signaling and Safety in October 1969', *International Security* 27/4 (Spring 2003).

Savranskaya, S. V. 'Tactical Nuclear Weapons in Cuba: New Evidence', *Cold War International History Project Bulletin* Issue 14/15 (Winter 2003/Spring 2004).

—— 'Soviet Submarines in the Cuban Missile Crisis', *Journal of Strategic Studies* 28/2 (April 2005).

Scott, L. 'Espionage and the Cold War: Oleg Penkovsky and the Cuban Missile Crisis', *Intelligence and National Security* 14/3 (Autumn 1999).

Scott, L. and Smith, S. 'Lessons of October: historians, political scientists, policy-makers and the Cuban missile crisis', *International Affairs* 70/4 (October 1994).

Tannenwald, N. 'Stigmatizing the Bomb: Origins of the Nuclear Taboo', *International Security* 29/4 (Spring 2005).

Thorson, S. J. and Sylvan, D. A. 'Counterfactuals and the Cuban Missile Crisis', *International Studies Quarterly* 26/4 (December 1982).

Trachtenberg, M. 'The Influence of Nuclear Weapons in the Cuban Missile Crisis', *International Security* 10/1 (Summer 1985).

—— 'Commentary: New Light on the Cuban Missile Crisis', *Diplomatic History* 14/2 (Spring 1990).

Turco, R. P., Toon, O. B., Ackerman, T. P., Pollack, J. B. and Sagan, C. 'Climate and Smoke: An Appraisal of Nuclear Winter', *Science* 222 (1983).

Uhl, M. and Ivkin, V.I. '"Operation Atom": The Soviet Union's Stationing of Nuclear Missiles in the German Democratic Republic, 1959', *Cold War International History Project Bulletin* 12/13 (Fall/Winter 2001).

Welch, D. 'Intelligence Assessment in the Cuban Missile Crisis', *Queen's Quarterly* 100/2 (Summer 1993).

White, M. J. 'Belligerent Beginnings: John F. Kennedy on the Opening Day of the Cuba Missile Crisis', *Journal of Strategic Studies* 15/1 (March 1992).

—— 'Dean Rusk's Revelation: New British Evidence on the Cordier Ploy', *The Society for Historians of American Foreign Relations Newsletter* 25/3 (September 1994).

Wohlstetter, R. 'Cuba and Pearl Harbor: Hindsight and Foresight', *Foreign Affairs* 43/4 (July 1965).

Wolske, J. A. 'Jack, Judy, Sam, Bobby, Johnny, Frank . . . : An Investigation into the Alternate History of the CIA–Mafia Collaboration to Assassinate Fidel Castro, 1960–1997', *Intelligence and National Security* 15/4 (Winter 2000).

Yost, D. S. 'France's New Nuclear Doctrine', *International Affairs* 82/4 (July 2006).

Young, J. W. 'Great Britain's Latin American Dilemma: The Foreign Office and the Overthrow of "Communist" Guatemala, June 1954', *The International History Review* VIII/4 (November 1986).

Zelikow, P. 'American Policy and Cuba, 1961–1963', *Diplomatic History* 24/2 (Spring 2000).

Films

Dr Strangelove or How I Learned to Stop Worrying and Love the Bomb (Columbia Pictures, Director: Stanley Kubrick, 1964).

Fail Safe (Columbia Pictures, Director: Sidney Lumet, 1964).

Thirteen Days (New Line, Director: Roger Donaldson, 2000).

K-19: The Widowmaker (Paramount Pictures, Director: Kathryn Bigelow, 2002).

Unpublished PhD Theses

Byrd, M. 'Political Firepower: Nuclear Weapons and the US Army 1945–1973' (University of Wales, Aberystwyth, 1999).

Grant, M. 'Civil Defence Policy in Cold War Britain, 1945–68' (University of London, 2006).

Thomas, G. 'Trade and Shipping to Cuba 1961–1963: An Irritant in Anglo-American Relations' (University of Wales, Aberystwyth, 2001).

Index

215